The Natural
Habitat Garden

THE
NATURAL
HABITAT
GARDEN

KEN DRUSE

with MARGARET ROACH

PHOTOGRAPHS BY KEN DRUSE
DESIGN BY BARBARA PECK

Timber Press
Portland · Cambridge

To *America's nature writers, nature lovers, and all*
the native-plant nursery owners and garden designers
who, against great odds, have held fast to finally
see the day when their efforts are recognized.
These people have devoted their careers to
propagating and planting wildflowers—
never collecting them—so, although the homes
of native plants vanish, they will live on
in habitat gardens.

FIRST PAGE: *Anise hyssop,* Agastache foeniculum.
TITLE PAGE: *Northern California native flowers.*
RIGHT: *Taughannock Falls, near Ithaca, New York.*
OPPOSITE: Clematis ochroleuca, *leather flower.*
OVERLEAF: *A well-balanced pond in New England.*

Paperback edition published in 2004 by

Timber Press, Inc.   Timber Press
The Haseltine Building   2 Station Road
133 S.W. Second Avenue, Suite 450   Swavesey
Portland, Oregon 97204-3527 U.S.A.   Cambridge CB4 5QJ, U.K.

Printed in Hong Kong

Library of Congress Cataloging-in-Publication Data
Druse, Kenneth
   The natural habitat garden / Ken Druse ; photographs by Ken Druse ;
   design by Barbara Peck.
     p. cm.
   Originally published: New York : Clarkson Potter, ©1994.
   Includes bibliographical references (p.).
   ISBN 0-88192-632-9 (pbk.)
   1. Natural gardens. 2. Natural landscaping. 3. Habitat (Ecology) I. Title.

SB439.D66 2004
635.9'51—dc22

                                    2003063438
A Catalogue record for this book is also available from the British Library.

ACKNOWLEDGMENTS

ENVIRONMENTALISTS WANT TO PRESERVE THE earth—natural habitat gardeners also want to replenish it.

The Natural Garden, published in 1989, presented an unpretentious approach to landscape design. *The Natural Shade Garden,* in 1992, relied a bit more on natives to help plantings reach self-sufficiency. The first book was for sun, the second for shade. *The Natural Habitat Garden,* on the other hand, is for the twenty-first century; and it may be controversial. Although it is a warning against uncontrolled consumption, it is not an indictment of conventional gardening—just a plea to give back to our environment some of the beauty and pleasure it has given us. This book will help to create niches, however small, that considered together can expand the realm of the indigenous plants and animals. I think the nature writer Joseph Wood Krutch's telling pun sums it up best, "A bird in the bush is worth two in the hand."

There are many people to thank for helping to promote this ideal and who contributed to bringing this book to light. At Clarkson Potter, I must thank my editor, friend, and promoter, Lauren Shakely; and Carol Southern, who was the first person to embrace this concept for publication; Art Director Howard Klein and this book's designer, Barbara Peck, whose contributions to the Natural Garden series are evident to everyone who shares these works. I'm proud to recognize others at Clarkson Potter: Andrea Connolly, Joan DeMayo, Jo Fagan, Phyllis Fleiss, Bruce Harris, Nancy Maloney, Barbara Marks, Mark McCauslin, Teresa Nicholas, Gail Shanks, Michelle Sidrane, Laurie Stark, Robin Strashun, Jane Treuhaft, Alberto Vitale, and Tina Zabriskie-Constable.

I'm proud to be associated with Helen Pratt, the agent for this work. Somehow she manages to remain true and sane throughout turbulent quests for common ground.

I would like to acknowledge horticultural and environmental advocates: Neil Diboll, Judith Stark, David Mahler, Judy Walther, Ken Moore and the organizers of the Cullowhee Native Plant Conference, Tovah Martin, Patti and Schellie Hagan, Charles Cresson, Suzanne Frutig Bales, Barbara Pryor and the staff and members of the New England Wildflower Society, Bob Zeleniak, John Trexler, Judy Zuk, Marco Polo Stufano, and Kim and Bruce Hawks. Helpful supporters: Marilyn Ratner, Patrick Smith, Miranda Genova, and Kristin Frederickson. Caring friends: George Waffle, Tom Dolle, Jim and Conni Cross.

I hope this new book will be as much of a source of pride to my parents, Helen and Harold Druse, as my first.

I would also like to thank Louis Bauer who is not only a devoted naturalist and a talented and tireless gardener but also an artist who has inspired me and helped me to improve every aspect of my work and life.

The contribution made by Margaret Roach to this book cannot be overstated—it can barely be expressed. She not only helped to write the text but also provided the discipline I needed to keep me on track when my train-of-thought derailed. (She would probably thank Taco Bell for her locomotion.) She is a brilliant environmentalist and writer and the greatest friend.

CONTENTS

PREFACE

WHEN I WROTE THE NATURAL GARDEN IN THE mid-1980s, I proposed that nature be the source of design. Now instead of just making gardens that resemble the earth, I want to enlarge the earth's diminished domain by growing native-plant gardens modeled on nature's original communities. I still believe that we need to go back to nature, but farther back—to the land as it was before development.

My previous book, *The Natural Shade Garden,* explored this strategy, emulating the woodland to create homes for shade-loving plants. But assembling plants from all corners of the world does not create a self-sufficient, ecologically appropriate community.

Evolution has produced a harmony that contrived gardens defy. Too often, man-made gardens counter the natural order of things. In the twenty-first century, the availability of water will have the greatest influence on gardening. The best way to garden without supplemental water is to welcome back indigenous vegetation.

As yet, I haven't ripped out my hostas and other collector plants. But the path I have taken since I began this book has certainly changed the way I look at them and has led me to pay attention to their place in the bigger ecological picture. I have also set out to find ways to apply my evolving views to gardening.

When people asked what I was working on during the last couple of years, I sometimes jokingly answered, "The Super-Natural Garden." What I meant was that the gardens I was seeing, the ones represented in this book, were more than just naturalistic. They attempt to simulate natural habitats. Each and every gardener whose work is included here discovered that once indigenous plants were brought back to the site, native birds, animals, and insects followed. It's no longer good enough to simply make it pretty, they have come to understand; it has to work, too.

I have always felt that the rhythm of the earth was my divinity, and researching *The Natural Habitat Garden* has certainly been a religious experience. With my colleague and friend Margaret Roach, I have traveled around the country, seeking instruction not just from nature's aesthetic side, but from the actual workings of the nation's dwindling reserve of wild places. We also sought out gardeners and gardens that were similarly inspired by the same functional models, America's habitats.

What we found, sometimes in very unlikely spots, was that a grass-roots movement—well, a grass-roots movement whose lawn has been dug up and replaced with natives—was quietly sweeping across the United States, one garden at a time.

An insightful landscape designer in Texas said it is reminiscent of the way the women's movement grew, and, although the comparison may seem grandiose, I think he's exactly right. It's happening all over the country, but not because of any central edict handed down from on high. It's happening simply because all these separate people sense, as I do, that habitat gardens are essential to the planet's future.

"Someday, they'll all come together to form a new order as influential as the Liberation movement," David Mahler, the visionary Texan, said.

I like to think of this book as the first public meeting place for many of these disconnected, but like-minded, advocate factions.

"A thing is right when it tends to preserve the integrity, stability and beauty of the biotic community," Aldo Leopold, father of the conservation movement, wrote in *A Sand County Almanac* in 1949.

Today, a garden is right when it does the very same thing. As a significant bonus, growing a natural habitat garden is also one of the most important things each of us can do to help restore a little order to a disordered world. Powerful stuff—and beautiful stuff, too.

KEN DRUSE
NEW YORK

"NATURE HAS NO HUMAN INHABITANT WHO AP-preciates her," Henry David Thoreau wrote from his cabin at Walden Pond, Massachusetts, nearly 150 years ago. Imagine if he had lived to see what man-kind hath wrought lately, particularly since the postwar building boom that created suburbia's anti-natural landscape.

Today, we hear almost daily about the shrinking tropical rain forest, but somewhat frighteningly Americans seldom mention the deforesting of the Pacific Northwest, home of our very own rain forest

INTRODUCTION

and a repository of incredible biodiversity whose full extent has only been guessed.

Who in the course of a week gives even a minute to lamenting how little of the great American prairie still exists, or to the fact that 700,000 acres of this nation have been converted into parking lots in the short time since man, and his cars, have landed upon it? Meanwhile, the human population multiplies at a staggering rate: The current 5.4 billion tally is ex-pected to reach 8.2 billion by the year 2020 and level off at 10 billion by the mid-twenty-first century. Forty percent of the world's population is now ur-banized, triple the number since the 1950s, and de-velopment continues full-tilt.

A quarter of the earth's organisms may become extinct in the next thirty years—all gone in the mo-ment of a single human generation—and many will vanish without a trace. Only 1.4 million plant and animal species have been recorded so far by scientists, who estimate that there are 10 million to 100 million out there. Not since the time of the dinosaurs, 65 million years ago, has there been such a mass ex-tinction as the one a single species—humankind—

Walden Pond, RIGHT, *still remains an inspiration to countless environmentalists who revere the works of Henry David Thoreau. He wrote from his cabin,*

ABOVE, *re-created on the site. Only now, nearly 150 years after Thoreau preached respect for nature, are people beginning to pay attention and act to preserve the little bit that's left.*

has wreaked in the name of progress, convenience, and prosperity.

Gardening is indeed part of this scheme—or can be. If even a fraction of America's 38-million gardeners turned a quarter of their landscape into a re-wilded spot that recalls, at least roughly, its presettlement state, there would be a measurable impact. If every gardener gave just one tenth of an acre back, the instant net gain would be 3.8 million acres of native plants.

Even an imprecisely restored habitat has vastly more plant and animal diversity than America's ubiquitous turfgrass lawn (particularly a chemically treated one). The simplest wildflower meadow is more complex, more botanically varied, than a grass lawn, offering a long season of pollens, nectars, and finally seeds, along with nesting sites and shelter for all those creatures that used to live somewhere before we arrived.

Perhaps most important of all, a habitat-style garden of native plants welcomes the whole food chain —not just flowers, birds, and butterflies, but also a magnificent decaying tree stump teeming with life, ringed by otherworldly fluted layers of fungi. Rather than carting away decaying wood or mopping up puddles here, the natural habitat gardener rejoices at such happenings and the creatures who come in to bathe, drink, feed, or breed because of them. In the habitat garden, such "imperfections" are reasons for celebration—not a bout of obsessive tidying up. These spots are where the action is, and more effective than the most elegant birdbath or feeder money could buy. Never have the words *don't fight the site* held so much meaning. It is the habitat gardener's guiding principle.

Once nature's wrinkles come to be seen as opportunities, instead of problems to eliminate, a whole new flora and fauna can begin to unfold. And as the

TOP: *The northern cardinal, a familiar suburban resident, also frequents the desert when native vegetation is allowed to flourish.* ABOVE: *The tallgrass prairie is all but extinct, and although our Pacific Northwest rain forest,* OPPOSITE, *may not receive the media attention afforded the tropical jungles, its future is similarly imperiled.*

gardener gets the message about native plants—the effect they can have in making this all happen—things really start to take off.

Wonder of wonders, it happens on the very same territory that used to be near-monoculture—that lawn, that rose garden—a place that was barely hospitable to any but the "trash" birds, as opportunists like cowbirds, starlings, and the like are known. (Many animals feed on specific plants and accept no substitutes.) And with a little luck, the gardener himself will be drawn in by the small miracle unfolding in the yard, and increase the share of the property planted in this style. Before long, the next link in the chain is connected: Spurred to action by the new-found convictions, the habitat gardener begins to voice concern that local highways, parks, school-yards, and businesses start doing likewise, and even more potential habitat moves back into the pool.

More habitat, more biodiversity—the greater number of distinct species that can coexist.

"When you increase the area of a habitat ten-fold," says Edward O. Wilson, the noted Harvard biologist, "you double the number of species that can live there."

So as we enter what Dr. Wilson calls the critical bottleneck of the next fifty years, a time of exploding human population and shrinking biodiversity, we had each better think about our actions. We must act to save every species—from bacteria on up, scientists say, since even the little-studied, unseen world of microbial soil life-forms may prove to possess the key to global survival.

We must eliminate the use of potentially hazardous chemicals from all phases of our life, from house-cleaning to pest control in the garden. The toxic effects of herbicides, pesticides, and fungicides have been well documented in recent years, but chemical nitrogen fertilizers, too, greatly reduce the inhabita-bility of the soil and water they touch. Increasing soil life, not killing it, has to take top priority in our agendas, since the soil is the source of much life on earth.

Reduce, reuse, recycle—this time with a vengeance—and be particularly careful to conserve when water or energy is at stake. Compost, indoors with the help of earthworms, outdoors in a more traditional heap.

Grow a garden, but not just turfgrass lawn and hybrid tea roses. Create instead a natural habitat garden based on indigenous plant species that are appropriate to the precise site conditions and geographic location, not just to how cold or hot the area gets in an average year. In evaluating your site, take into consideration what would have been there and nearby presettlements working from researched models (in regional and local guides, old topographical maps, museums, and arboretums, for example) —before the bulldozers pulled in and put up a parking lot—not just what exists today.

This kind of leap forward in landscaping styles and plant selection can actually help offset the losses of habitat elsewhere on the planet. Plants and animals being forced out of their native range may find refuge in these little, privately created safety zones. Though the plight of global preservation efforts in the world's hotspots—zones targeted by scientists as being particularly diverse, and therefore urgently in need of protection—will continue to be more critical with every passing day, here is something else every gardener can do, in addition to supporting green organizations with donations.

Standing dead trees are homes for birds. Fallen logs support hosts of insects, mammals, mosses, ferns, tree seedlings, and perhaps a colony of fluted agatelike fungi, OPPOSITE, ABOVE. Every bit of captured water is useful, and every bit of matter used. A rock crevice makes a convenient watering stop for birds, BELOW.

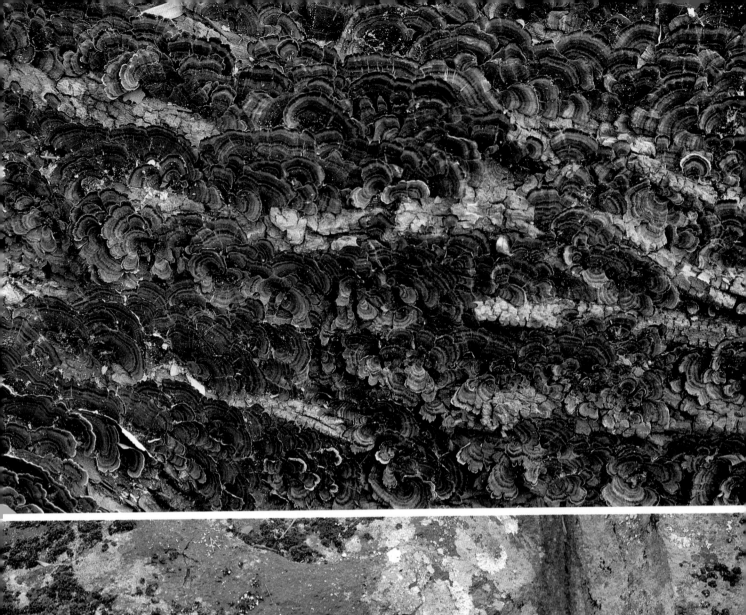

Never bring an invasive plant into the landscape. In 1935 the federal government planted 73 million seedlings of kudzu, BELOW *(swallowing a tree)*, to control erosion along road cuts. This monster has covered and choked trees and fields, and has virtually swallowed the Southeast. Although it is somewhat controlled by harsh winters, it has been spotted in New York State. Japanese honeysuckle, Oriental bittersweet, multiflora rose, crown vetch, and autumn olive are devastating counterparts in the North, yet all of these plants are still sold as "quick problem-solvers" by less conscientious nurseries. Purple loosestrife, banned in a few states, causes millions of dollars in damage to crops and wildlife. In its native European habitat, it is controlled by indigenous insects. Allegedly "sterile" hybrids, able to contribute viable pollen, are still sold. These plants, along with countless diseases and pests, have been introduced intentionally or accidentally over the centuries.

Less is more in the home landscape of Ken Moore, assistant director of the University of North Carolina Botanical Garden at Chapel Hill, TOP RIGHT. He gardens by a process of elimination, editing out the plants he doesn't want. Often he hand-weeds or simply mows down some of the plants he wants to discourage. With an artful eye, and a great sense of humor, Moore, who is one of the founders of the Cullowhee (North Carolina) Native Plant Conference, arranged colorful gazing balls down an allée of grasses and forbs in November. RIGHT CENTER: Sources for native plants were rare; now places such as Native Texas Nurseries, which features silver cenizo (Leucophyllum candidum), are proliferating. Some of the native-plant seed sources for supplying the nurseries and home landscapes have come from unexpected areas—spared from development. One example was the rough of an old golf course; another the railroad easements of the Midwest, BOTTOM RIGHT.

IT'S NOT A JUNGLE
OUT THERE

Few of us are willing to just let our property over-grow and go wild, and it's not the most sensible course in any case. Without intervention, the already-disturbed habitats we live in would simply head down the path to decline, with aggressive, opportunistic exotics increasing their domain over natives, and diversity succumbing to various versions of the "kudzu phenomenon," where an exotic plant overtakes whole regions of its new homeland.

"While nature herself is variable, disturbance is typically simplistic," Andropogon Associates, the Philadelphia-based ecological planning and design firm, wrote in a proposal on restoring the woodlands of New York's Central Park. "When disturbance is uncontrolled, deterioration usually accelerates and a once-rich site steadily diminishes in diversity, value, and interest. . . . Once disturbance is controlled," the report added, "the landscape will be far more able to control itself."

Although there is disagreement on how to manage and restore land, I believe the same hand that moved to hurt it can now help it to heal.

Instead of just letting things go, the habitat gardener may selectively handweed or mow each year at the appropriate time. Sometimes controlled burning can scarify hard-to-germinate seeds, remove layers of built-up debris that are hampering the growth of desirables, and otherwise get things moving (more on the powerful, natural tool of fire in the section on grasslands). Though you might guess it would be to the contrary, land grazed by herds of livestock on a sensible schedule may actually fare better over time in retaining some of its original diverse character than similar tracts that are fenced off—supposedly "protected"—and allowed to overgrow.

Friendly interventions like these help rekindle a dormant plant community whose seeds and other vestiges may still be hidden in the soil. Or in the worst cases, where nothing remains, not even the original topsoil, the habitat gardener can replant at least a symbolic version of the scene long vanished.

In the long run, a habitat-style garden will be easier to maintain once established than its more conventionally designed counterparts, but in the beginning, this approach is not low-maintenance. As landscape architect Gary Smith of the University of Delaware, a proponent of native landscapes, reminds us, a garden is a relationship between two living things, garden and gardener. "And how many no-maintenance relationships have you had in your life?" he quips.

Likewise, you need not cast out hostas, or alpines, or your favorite collector plants, so long as they do not have invasive, aggressive habits or impact negatively on the environment.

"Nature has a place for the wild clematis as well as for the cabbage," Thoreau wrote in his famous essay "Walking," though today, with things so far off-balance, he would probably reverse the emphasis between the indigenous plant and the introduced. "The matrix needs to be native to support the biodiversity we need to survive," Gary Smith concurs. Natural habitat garden design has a much bigger picture in mind than the confines of a bed or border.

Most homeowners, even those with just weekend homes, have at least a patch of lawn that would serve the planet and the place better as a prairie, or a wet sump that could begin to support wetland plant species if cultivated as such. Instead of struggling against nature in the arid American Southwest in order to install a lawn or herbaceous border, the natural habitat gardener can surrender aboveground sprinklers that waste money and water and create a home landscape that revels in the beauty of the desert.

Making the commitment to garden in the habitat style is enriching, both for the gardener's life and for the future of the planet. One recent study in the Southwest, for example, showed that vegetation is the single most important factor in attracting birds, and that the greater the presence of native vegetation, the larger the population of native birds.

In some cases, these relationships are so strong that one cannot exist without the other. Survival of monarch butterflies depends on their being unpalatable to birds because of the toxins they ingest from certain milkweeds. Now that *Asclepias sylvaniaii* is disappearing, butterflies munch other, more available milkweed species, thus getting less predation protection per mouthful, increasing their risk of extinction.

Traditionally, butterfly bush (*Buddleia* spp., from China) and fuchsias (Central and South America and New Zealand) have been planted to attract butterflies to the garden. Yet native North American flora such as butterfly weed (*Asclepias* spp.), columbine, coneflowers, and penstemons are only a few of many enticing candidates that might make the difference in whether a species endures, at least in the immediate locale. In the natural habitat garden, spring is marked not by the emergence of crocuses (natives of Asia and Europe) but by skunk cabbages and shooting star (*Dodecatheon* spp.).

Hundreds of years ago, the New World's flora

were first imported to Europe and treated as the finest garden treasures. Now we are finally discovering them ourselves, learning from this new landscape an awareness of our surroundings—dare I say roots?—as we can from no other garden. It teaches lessons of interdependence of species, wisdom man has lost living in his high-tech ivory tower. Americans spend only 5 percent of their time outdoors.

As I mentioned, the home habitat garden is also a place to grow and preserve plants that are threatened in the native ranges, though this good-doing does not condone the collection of plant specimens from the wild for use in the home landscape. Only nursery-propagated plants, or those acquired from a native-plant society or plant-rescue operation undertaken by a legitimate environmental group, are fair game. To plunder another habitat in the name of growing your own is unthinkable.

LETTING GO

"What unthinking people call design in nature is simply the reflection of our inevitable anthropomorphism," America's greatest nature writer, John Burroughs, wrote in 1920. "Whatever they can use, they think was designed for that purpose—the air to breathe, the water to drink, the soil to plant. It is as if they thought that notch in the mountains was made for the road to pass over. . . ."

Certainly such a voracious, me-first approach as the one man has taken in "developing" the land cannot continue, not even on the level of a single suburban lot. The challenge is to imagine the home landscape of the future.

"I'm not sure what the New American Garden is," says Darrel G. Morrison, dean of the School of Environmental Design at the University of Georgia, Athens, and a leading force in the native-plant move-

PRECEDING PAGES, LEFT: In the Southwest, a spiny teddy-bear cholla (Opuntia bigelovii) makes a fortified nesting site for a cactus wren whose tough feet aren't bothered by the needles. RIGHT: The red admiral butterfly, found throughout the United States, sips nectar from one of its favorite plants, purple coneflower (Echinacea purpurea). OPPOSITE: Evelyn Adams has nurtured a glade garden of Trillium grandiflorum for fifty years. She hasn't intentionally practiced conservation through propagation; this is just the way "God gardens."

ment. "But I am at least sure that it should be made of American plants." Gary Smith of the University of Delaware says the New American Garden is about letting the land speak its mind to you, about you listening. "You can't stamp [a style] on the place," he says. "You let the mystery reveal itself." For me, the New American Garden is one that respects the original archetype of the site and surrounding region, and continues to evolve over time. A living organism, it can't be trucked in and installed in time for tomorrow's tea party.

As soon as I started photographing gardens created in the habitat style—the ones I discovered in the process of producing this book—I began looking at every garden differently.

The works-in-progress contained in this book now form my new point of reference, the knowledge that I draw upon when thinking about how to design a sensible contemporary landscape in my next garden, or helping someone else to plan theirs. I call them works-in-progress because creating any garden takes

time, and this is even more relevant when you are working at more than a single border.

The gardeners behind the gardens—Neil Diboll burning his lawn to coax a prairie into life in Wisconsin; Evelyn Adams nurturing a glade of trilliums over a lifetime in Massachusetts; Dick Lighty selecting dwarf asters and goldenrods or shrub dogwoods with striking variegation on the Delaware-Pennsylvania border, and helping get them into the nursery trade, and all the rest—they are my new teachers, and my new heroes, pioneers of the new American landscape. I think as you turn the coming pages, they will become your inspirations, too.

IN THE BEGINNING

In *The Natural Garden,* I suggested thinking of the average home landscape as different areas that addressed the needs of the people who used the place. The natural habitat encompasses not just the needs of human beings but of plants and animals.

We have to devise new ways
to get into the landscape:
mowed paths, OPPOSITE;
viewing platforms, ABOVE;
boardwalks, RIGHT, *for
instance one at Tower Hill
Botanic Garden; and even
treehouses, TOP, such as
Carter and Suzanne Bales's
elaborate retreat.*

The inner area of the homesite is still the high-traffic area with easy access to the house, a place for entertaining, for example, usually covered in a hard surface for utility. The outer area remains the zone with the lowest-maintenance, longest-lasting plants and also serves as a screen from the surrounding properties, if desired. The in-between area continues to house whatever suits the gardener's interests, but because the habitat gardener's focus has evolved, this area has undergone substantial change.

Now, the pavement of the inner area (a place for a dining set or a chaise, for instance) is chosen for environmental soundness, not looks alone. I have always recommended that it appear appropriate—that is, granite sets for a rocky area of New England, for example—but now it must really work, too, for the good of the site. Soil beneath a slab of concrete or asphalt just doesn't support much in the way of life, whereas individual stones or bricks actually form a favorite hiding place for soil-dwellers, and many plants like to tuck their roots underneath into the trapped pockets of moisture and grow mightily out of the cracks. In any paved area, water must be able to percolate downward, meaning that mortared joints are less desirable than sand or soil.

Raised decking makes a good choice for the hardscape of the inner area, both because it leaves the soil below unstressed and because it gives humans a lift—up high, where they can really look out into the habitat beyond, and enjoy the sights. If the in-between area is to be in meadow, for instance, or wetland, or some other hard-to-traverse planting, a boardwalk extending from the deck through it invites participation without trampling. Viewing towers, boardwalks, platforms—these are all important additions to the habitat garden. At the very least, a mown path wide enough to accommodate two people side by side should be figured into the plan, though its precise course can vary from year to year.

The outer area should be as wild as possible. Give special thought to creating cover for birds, who on windy winter days will particularly appreciate an evergreen perching place (*Juniperus virginiana,* red cedar, is a favorite in many regions of the country).

Brushy edge areas offer protection from predators as well as nesting sites for many species; plan to make them edible as well as secure. Native plants like raspberry relatives (*Rubus* spp.), elderberry (*Sambucus* spp.), holly (*Ilex* spp.), native roses (including *Rosa palustris, R. virginiana, R. carolina, R. setigera*), black cherry (*Prunus serotina*), hawthorn (*Crataegus* spp.), cranberrybush (*Viburnum* spp.), blueberries (*Vaccinium* spp.), dogwood (*Cornus* spp.), spicebush (*Lindera benzoin*), red chokeberry (*Aronia arbutifolia*), non-invasive honeysuckle, such as *Lonicera sempervirens,*

Many plants are for the birds. ABOVE, LEFT TO RIGHT: *Swamp rose* (Rosa palustris) *will have nutritious hips. Eastern baccharis* (Baccharis halimifolia), *a wild seaside shrub, bears fuzzy white puffs called achenes attached to dry fruits containing a single seed. Elderberry* (Sambucus canadensis) *grows in waste places.*

sumac (*Rhus* spp.), baccharis (*Baccharis halimifolia*), cactus (*Opuntia* and *Ferocactus,* among others), ceanothus (*Ceanothus* spp.), and manzanita (*Arctostaphylos* spp.) are just a sampling of the many indigenous possibilities to tangle together.

Use your imagination to design blends of plants that weave into what I call biohedges—intermediate-height mixed plantings that serve multiple purposes to encourage, protect, and feed wildlife.

In this outer area, let a dead tree stand—remember, this is not a loss, but a cause for celebration, an offering from nature—unless it endangers people or property. In such cases, remove unwieldy limbs and top the tree if its uppermost portion is badly decayed, but leave as much of the trunk standing as possible—it's still a good place to raise a family. Leave removed portions of the trunk on the ground to decay in place, and use discarded twigs and branches to form a brush pile, a favorite home for numerous animal species.

The outer area doesn't have to be thought of as existing along the back, or fringe, of the property, either. It could be developed along the front and sides, too, so that the house is enclosed in its own cozy little sanctuary. If noise is a problem, a berm of soil developed as a mediating element between the home and the street is a possibility. It needn't be the landscapers' pile of dirt—dotted with spots of juniper. The berm itself can be another whole habitat, since its soil composition and terrain may differ from the rest of the property.

The in-between area, which in the past might have contained a mix of lawn and ornamental islands or borders of exotic perennials, for instance, is now the principal area of interactive habitat—where you and the other garden residents, both plants and animals, will come into closest contact. Ideally, the lawn is gone or reduced even further in favor of some more diverse planting, specifically natives, as in the outer area. In the best of scenarios, plant collections (like that perennial garden) may be modified to reflect the gardener's increased awareness of native plants.

Collections are probably afforded less space than before, in favor of plantings that give more to the big picture ecologically. Where vegetable or "collection gardens" remain, though, they need to be corralled by a fence or stone wall, or some other feature that sets them apart from the looser native landscape. A water element, which in the natural garden may have been simply a small garden pool, may receive greater emphasis in the habitat garden, where 15 percent of the total landscape should be planned as some kind of wetland—pond, bog, wet meadow, stream, or at the very least a significant garden pool. Even in the desert, where 15 percent would be too much, some consistently available source of water is welcome.

ABOVE, LEFT TO RIGHT: *American cranberry bush* (Viburnum trilobum), *one of the birds' favorites; the spikenard* (Aralia racemosa); *many cacti have fleshy fruits, such as prickly pear* (Opuntia rufida). *Caution: Do not eat any plant with which you are not familiar!*

Picture for a moment a suburban lot, one hundred feet along the front and one hundred feet deep, planted in a conventional style. The house is centered on the land with a garage on one side; the straight twenty-five-foot driveway leads from the street to the garage doors. Maintenance of this "picture-perfect" setting requires more than labor—chemical fertilizers and insecticides that pollute the water through runoff, gas-guzzling mowers that pollute the air (and drive the neighbors crazy with noise), water wasted to irrigate during dry spells, and so on. There is a foundation planting of yews and azaleas, and the remainder of the property is planted in lawn—hours of mowing every Saturday morning.

In the habitat garden, the lawn has been reduced, probably by 50 percent or more, to the least amount necessary for recreation. This not only saves on gasoline but also on petrochemical-based products associated with traditional lawn-care regimens, like fertilizers, and in turn on expense: Americans spend more than $1.5 billion a year on fertilizers alone.

Precious water resources will no longer be wasted on thirsty grass (the home landscape today consumes a ridiculous 50 percent of our resources, much of it for lawns) and the habitat style of gardening forbids wasteful watering systems or practices of any kind. No sprinklers spray into the air on a preset timer; the latest drip irrigation setups with in-line emitters will be used instead, and sparingly, since habitat principles do not condone heroic artificial life-supports.

Where there is mown grass lawn, it will be from endophyte-enhanced seed—resistant to aboveground chewing pests—and will green up without too much help, grow slowly to reduce mowing, and thrive with little supplemental moisture. As it moves toward the wild outer area, it might blend into a meadow or prairie, creating a more natural transition than lawn right up against trees.

Even better than this turfgrass compromise are the low-growing native grasses and sedges, or a blend of native ground covers, many of which also offer wildlife food and cover. Turfgrass might be home for beetle grubs, but a wild cover made of a mix of plants closely resembling a local plant community model would support much more. Native plants, by varying estimates, support ten to fifty times more local animal species as exotics.

Particular attention must be paid throughout the new landscape to nectar plants, host plants, and others that are preferred nesting and shelter sites. The goal is to provide year-round support for potential members of the community.

The nonliving features of the homesite have to be adapted, too. In some builders' textbook it must be written that the shortest distance between two points is a driveway. A short, straight run is easiest to plow in snow country, but it will never blend into a naturalistic landscape. A winding access creates more potential "edge," the transition zone between the driveway and what's beyond it. The driveway can work as part of the habitat when its edges are a mix of berry-bearing shrubs or grasses and nongrass flowering plants called forbs that provide seeds for winter nibbling by birds.

If there is a choice, situate the garage on the north or northwest side of the house, to insulate from winter winds. Where suitable to the habitat, evergreens planted on the north will also increase protection; deciduous trees are important for their summertime sun-blocking effect to the south and west.

OPPOSITE: *The three areas of the landscape are the high-traffic inner area,* FAR RIGHT, *where collections of exotics may be contained; the wildlike outer area; and the in-between area,* RIGHT, *where lawn may meet meadow. In one outer area,* TOP, *Lorrie Otto and her native-plant group The Wild Ones built a large berm of mounded soil to buffer traffic noise outside the home of a compatriot who was terminally ill.*

The plantings around the house can do more than visually anchor it to the ground. Instead of plants that will soon outgrow their spots and require perpetual pruning, there are others that can participate in a landscape repertory company, playing more than one role at a time. Gray dogwood, for instance, is a highly ornamental but little-used shrub whose beautiful fruit birds adore; American viburnum species provide showy blooms plus wildlife food. Oregon holly grape (*Mahonia aquifolium*) is an evergreen with desirable fruits. Besides fruit, blueberries and deciduous hollies boast great fall foliage color. Many more species specific to particular habitats are mentioned in the chapters following.

IDENTIFYING YOUR HABITAT

GRASSLANDS are areas dominated by herbaceous plants like grasses and forbs; a prairie is a grassland, and so are plains and meadows and even many old fields.

WOODLANDS are those where woody plants, particularly trees, have the upper hand, which means that shade must be contended with all or part of the year.

WETLANDS are literally wet at least part of the time. Water controls what lives in this environment.

Absence of water is what makes DRYLANDS what they are. In these areas of low precipitation, and frequently high heat as well, all life-forms learn to make every drop of water count.

In each of these general habitats there is overlap—meadow-style plantings can be found in both wetlands and grasslands, for instance, since some prairie and meadow plants prefer wet soils and some do not.

A habitat does not obey the arbitrary man-made county lines or boundaries between your neighbor's home and your own. Habitats are living systems

Consider parts of your homesite in terms of general habitats, OPPOSITE, TOP TO BOTTOM: *grassland; woodland; wetland; and dryland. There are tiny subsystems called niches within these habitats. For instance, a shaded rock at Jennings Preserve in western Pennsylvania,* RIGHT, *is home to mosses, ferns, and* Clintonia umbellulata *(in flower).*

with many subsystems called niches—a pocket of rock outcropping within a woodland, for instance, is a niche. Habitats blend into one another regularly, and their boundaries also ebb and flow according to vagaries like weather. The tallgrass prairie recedes in times of prolonged drought, and the intermediate-height mixed-grass prairie steps into its place.

Start identifying your habitat by paging through this book to see what looks familiar, and by reading locally appropriate field guides. Since most of us in America live and garden in disturbed habitats, areas whose original character has long since given way to man's physical domination, the process may take some detective work. Armed with your notes, identify the oldest trees near your property, particularly native ones as clues to its presettlement character.

In the absence of such telltale landmarks, examine written records, such as county maps at the hall of records that indicate presettlement vegetation. If a group like The Nature Conservancy (see the "Source Guide" for addresses of native-plant societies and organizations) has protected some land nearby, it may provide clues to what used to grow where only your lawn does today.

Sometimes, the clues to what habitat is most appropriate come serendipitously, the way they did when P. Clifford Miller, a landscape designer in Lake Forest, Illinois, saw a dead fox squirrel in the road near a client's home. Miller knew that the fox squirrel was indigenous to savannas, an all-but-eliminated American grassland with sparse trees. Miller uses such animal indicators, along with other tools, such as the plants that grow along the nearby railroad

Within the habitat categories are smaller divisions called plant communities. An example lies among huge marble outcroppings at Bartholomew's Cobble, OPPOSITE, *in the Massachusetts Berkshires. This specific woodland is dominated by Canadian hemlock* (Tsuga canadensis) *over mosses, ferns, and pure white stone,* ABOVE.

easements, to help solve the puzzle of what plant communities and habitat styles would be most appropriate for the site. Animal-indicator tips are included in the best field guides, so don't overlook the opportunity they may provide.

A NEW WAY OF SEEING

It takes a sophisticated eye combined with a developed consciousness to find the beauty in the golden brown grasses of fall, or to accept that sometimes the stereotypical, brilliant succession of color we have always thought of as a "garden" simply isn't going to happen all the time. This new kind of garden requires an enduring sense of stewardship, so that the "huns"—as landscape restoration specialists Andropogon Associates, of Philadelphia, call those hungry exotics waiting to take over if permitted—never get their opportunity. Habitat gardeners think long-term —like forever. They start to think that way because evolution over time is the natural order of things. The natural habitat gardener can pass on the legacy by asking estate executors to use life insurance proceeds to remove potentially invasive plants and maintain the property with thoughtfulness toward the environment.

In nature, there is no truly independent action without impact.

NATIVE OR INDIGENOUS?

What is a locally appropriate plant? Purists suggest that we must seek out not just native plants from our region, but locally specific, or indigenous, species to help preserve the genetic integrity of the immediate local plant community. Grow species native to within fifty miles of your site, they recommend. If this sounds right to you, then subscribe to their fundamentalist ethic; you will be in good company among some prominent botanists and environmentalists.

Other scientists and native-plant experts, including David K. Northington, director of the National Wildflower Research Center, say such a tight interpretation of "native" is just too restrictive. Neil Diboll, an ecologist and owner of Prairie Nursery in Wisconsin, stresses, as does Northington, the sometimes-overlooked fact that it is normal for plants to undergo large-scale migrations over time. "People are biased toward animals migrating, but against plants doing so," says Diboll.

It is well documented geologically that plant communities migrate according to climatic conditions as minor as an extended drought or as dramatic as an ice age. Other natural forces including wind, birds, and other animals are also responsible for moving plants, usually in the form of seed, beyond their "normal" boundaries.

Here's what might happen if you order seeds or plants from one region to grow in another, says Northington: Seeds of a Georgia strain of rudbeckia (black-eyed Susan) for instance, accustomed to early springs in the warm South, might start to grow too early if planted by a gardener in Wisconsin. The reverse—trying a Wisconsin-grown species in Georgia—probably wouldn't be as difficult, and in either case you might succeed. So what's so awful, so dangerous about that? Probably nothing in the rudbeckia example, but a worse scenario, he explains, is that in some cases the local species and the imported species might cross and create a hybrid with greater vigor than either parent. This new generation might eventually outperform each parent until it disappears, forcing an extirpation (when a species vanishes from a particular area), or even an extinction —possible but rare.

Since most native-plant gardens don't even put their roots down into native soil, thanks to the bulldozers that carted it all away and sold it, I think we can be a little more flexible than the fifty-mile rule, too. Adhere to wider regional models, and patronize native-plant nurseries as close to home as possible that specialize in the plants of your region.

Many reference books call plants in wild places "wildflowers." But are these plants truly indigenous or are they naturalized—aliens that spread? The nearby fields of natives that explode with color are the inspirations for The National Wildflower Research Center, founded by Lady Bird Johnson in Austin, Texas.

ALL IN A NAME

A "genus" is a group of related species, i.e., the first word in a Latin name. A "species" (abbreviated "spp.") includes like individuals that can breed with each other. A "subspecies" is a division of plants that differ in small ways from the species and are usually found in specific populations and places. In horticulture, a "variety" is a group within a species that has small differences from the rest of the members. A plant known only in cultivation that may have been selected from a naturally occurring variety and propagated for garden use is a cultivated variety or "cultivar." A "hybrid" results from the cross-fertilization of two species, subspecies, or varieties.

Some of the more disease- and insect-resistant, more or less compact, or interesting plants for future habitat gardens are cultivars. For instance, in the genus *Echinacea,* there are a few versions of the species *purpurea,* the purple coneflower. These have white flowers: *E.p.* 'Alba' and *E.p.* 'White Swan'—white purple coneflowers. Another example occurred around the turn of the last century. A spectacular version of the rather unassuming native shrub *Hydrangea arborescens* was discovered in a garden by two women in Union County and transplanted to Anna, Illinois, in 1910. Unlike its single-flowered predecessor, this sturdy one had voluptuous double flowers. In 1960, it was introduced to gardeners. Now it is known as the familiar cultivar 'Annabelle'.

WILDFLOWER OR WEED?

The country roadside in many regions in summertime is positively captivating: waves of Queen Anne's lace (*Daucus carota*) and blue chicory (*Cichorium intybus*), or embankments sweet with the perfume of thousands of tiny white roses (*Rosa multiflora*). Wildflowers, right? Not so, at least not by the standards of the National Wildflower Research Center.

NWRC would like gardeners to regard all native plants—whether trillium or little bluestem grass or a dogwood tree—as wildflowers, and to use naturalized plants to refer to roadside aliens like chicory and Queen Anne's lace.

Some foreign plants just settle into American soil for a time, then fade away; others spread slowly in their new land; and a third class really gets going—the kudzu types, or purple loosestrifes. As even a short visit by a nonnative can upset the balance of the community enough to cause extirpation or even extinction of a native plant, all of these invasions are undesirable.

NWRC wants gardeners to understand the concept of environmental weeds, like the multiflora rose, that have a deleterious impact on the environment. The mockingbirds may love the rose, but the birds who enjoyed its predecessors, the native raspberry (*Rubus* spp.) and seed-producing herbaceous plants, have disappeared. Put simply, two plants can't share the very same spot. That, in a sentence, is perhaps the most compelling case of all for natives.

ABOVE: *"Naturalized" wildings, or "weeds," daylilies, the common buttercup, and Queen Anne's lace.*
CLOCKWISE FROM BELOW: *A propagated selection of* Hydrangea arborescens *called 'Annabelle'; the cultivar of purple coneflower* (Echinacea purpurea) *'White Swan'; a floriferous form of New England aster* (Aster novae-angliae).

To become a new American landscaper, whether professional or hobbyist, the gardener needs to stretch beyond the current suburban models for inspiration and to stop mimicking the intricate imposing borders of English garden books.

We must start gardening and landscaping according to habitat. This book is organized into general habitat categories called grasslands, drylands, wetlands, and woodlands. If you live in a desert, you probably know it; in fact, you may have moved to your current home because it was in an arid zone and you wanted to enjoy its dry climate. Woodlands are identifiable too, particularly if you're in the middle of one. But some of America's habitats are a lot less obvious, and even among what we loosely call deserts there is great variability: high deserts and low ones, for instance, with considerable differences of temperature extremes and annual precipitation that alter the plant palette.

More important, when you look beyond the habitat level, the differences really begin to stand out. Scientists have identified more than one hundred plant communities in America, named according to the dominant species and inhabited by plants similarly adapted to the local climate, soil type, and other factors, including their ability to grow successfully together as a group. A sedge meadow is an example of a plant community; so is a pine-oak woodland, or a tallgrass prairie.

Botanists, conservationists, and experts in landscape restoration frequently think in terms of these

It may take a more sophisticated sensibility to find beauty in the amber waves of grasses in late summer, LEFT. OPPOSITE: *No plant is an island. Plants grow in societal groups called plant communities, such as these dryland citizens: a brushy agave surrounded by tall ocotillo* (Fouquieria splendens) *and opuntia cacti.*

communities. Once you start growing a natural habitat garden, such plant associations will quickly become more apparent, and will also become the reference point for designing successful plantings.

Get to know the habitats and corresponding plant communities appropriate to your locale and begin to garden with this information in mind. Even in a subdivision where all traces of the past have been bulldozed into oblivion, residents can learn from nearby undisturbed sites or from books about what habitat is most natural for their sites.

Every gardener should have in his or her home library several local field guides for wildflowers, butterflies, birds, and trees, as well as one geared to the ecology of the area and its principal habitats. These will be invaluable in plant selection, in siting plants successfully, and in caring for them in the way they have evolved to expect in their native ranges. A plant may have evolved to expect an annual drought period, for instance, a precise soil acidity or alkalinity, or even a dependence on the cleansing effects of periodic fires. *The Natural Habitat Garden* will not replace such guides, but will help you translate their information into real garden possibilities.

Sometimes, particularly for the gardener with a small lot, this translation simply means scaling down. A ten-by-twenty-foot patch of prairie plants does not a prairie make, and fifteen trees are not a woodland. But even such small, symbolic plantings as those two hundred square feet can be done in the habitat style, giving back at least a little bit to nature.

First, grow native—and grow it in a native style, recalling the nation's great habitats. You will find more inspiration, more hints to extract and boil down to garden size, in Muir Woods, or the New England forest around Walden Pond, or the relict and restored prairie in Madison, Wisconsin, or Arizona's Saguaro National Monument—these are far more

fitting and more pleasing muses for today than the "hot" border at Hidcote.

Aldo Leopold, one of the great naturalists of all time, began his career working for the then newly formed United States Forest Service in 1909. At first, he proposed the elimination of predacious animals to protect herds of cattle and sheep, and also to keep natural areas well stocked with desirable game for the enjoyment of hunters. It did not take too long for him to realize that the land is a single, complex organism, and that every element—not just some priority list designed according to man's whims and intellect—must be afforded equal protection.

Conservationists know this. They realize that if any link in the chain of interdependent species is disturbed, a ripple may begin that only ends when the final domino falls on you, the human being (who all too often began the chain reaction).

I try not to think of this when I swat a mosquito. Even this tiny annoyance is a part of the ecosystem, after all. In its larval stage, it is food for numerous other species, and as an adult it is fed upon by amphibians, reptiles, fish, birds, and even carnivorous plants. This insect feeds on us, of course, but people tend to think of themselves as the highest form of life on earth, not mere mosquito fast food.

I, for one, haven't given up hope about halting those falling dominoes. I concentrate on hopeful, beautiful images in this book and on the simple message contained in the translation of the Latin word for goldenrod, *Solidago*. It means making whole. With solidago and other natives, I think that we can make the earth whole, or at least a little closer.

The plant that might be considered a symbol for the regeneration of the earth could be the familiar goldenrod (Solidago spp.). Not only do some of the nearly one hundred species of this plant grow throughout North America but also its generic name carries a simple message —translated from the Latin, it means "making whole."

What a wealth we would have if our prairie roads could

be lined with this rich carpet of colors, miles of flowers

reflecting their colors in the sky above, or millions of sungods

(sunflowers) in the strong prairie breeze nodding their

heads to the sun that had given them their golden hue.

But perhaps that is too much to hope for,

as man seems unappreciative of these gifts.

~ JENS JENSEN

THE AFTERNOON HAD A SENSE OF DISCOVERY about it, as if we were witnessing something no one had ever seen before—hardly the case, but definitely the feeling. Walking through the three-thousand-year-old prairie at the University of Wisconsin–Madison was not unlike coming face-to-face with a woolly mammoth or some other creature thought to be extinct, a compelling organism sadly lost forever —or nearly lost, in the prairie's case.

The three-thousand-year-old prairie at the University of Wisconsin–Madison, RIGHT, *hosts tall prairie dock (Silphium terebinthinaceum) and the white spikes of Culver's root (Veronicastrum virginicum).* ABOVE: *A goldfinch gleans tasty seeds.*

LEFT, TOP TO BOTTOM:
*Prairie plants include willow-
leaf sunflower* (Helianthus
salicifolius), *bergamot*
(Monarda fistulosa),
and yellow coneflower
(Ratibida pinnata).

ABOVE: *Once prairie-dog
towns stretched across the
plains and into the deserts.
Estimates of former
populations range between
forty-eight million and
several billion.*

Although not as colorful as the rest of the university's extensive layout of restored and re-created prairies, this ecological elder was the one we had traveled to see. While other visitors on the same hot, cloudless August afternoon were unable to take their eyes off the mass of lavender bergamot (*Monarda fistulosa*) and yellow coneflower (*Ratibida pinnata*) in adjacent, man-made plantings by the parking lot, Margaret and I, like a pair of pilgrims at an ancient shrine, headed for the relict area—the "persistent remnant of an otherwise extinct flora or fauna or kind of organism," as the dictionary explains the term.

It was a far cry from today's trendy wildflower meadow plantings, but what this rugged survivor before us lacked in flash appeal it more than made up for in soul.

With each footstep along its trails and firelanes (bare strips that serve to control the burning performed in spring to stimulate new growth and check invasion by woody species), we knew we were treading on soil fertile enough to have produced several millennia of plant life. In turn, the prairie flora before us had given life, in the form of pollen, nectar, seed, and, of course, those nutrient-rich grass blades and leaves, to countless generations of animal creatures whose presence could almost be felt.

We also knew that the same deep, rich soil underfoot has proved to be the prairie's undoing.

Once, America's grasslands counted half a million Native Americans, 25 million bison, and 48 million prairie dogs (other estimates range upward to several billion prairie dogs) among the life-forms they supported. Today, many of these indigenous citizens are nearly extinct, and the habitat-turned-heartland instead feeds one in every twelve of the planet's human inhabitants. Where once three hundred or more predominantly herbaceous native species of plants coexisted, digging down their soil-improving roots into the ever-richening earth, there are giant tracts of monoculture: corn, wheat, soybeans. Three tons of soil—soil it took millennia and geologic events on a grand scale to build—is now squandered for every ton of food produced.

Wisconsin, the first state to ban DDT, is a good starting point for our education about American grasslands, and specifically prairies, because in Wisconsin "new" garden ideas such as replacing your lawn with wildflowers or going native are anything but new. This is largely because of the trickle-down effects of the work at the University of Wisconsin–Madison, where the sixty-acre Curtis Prairie, adjacent to the ancient relict area and long used as cropland and pasture, was brought back to its original state starting in the late 1930s by workers from the Civilian Conservation Corps. The United States has other restorations, both at Madison and elsewhere, but Curtis is the world's oldest, and largest, restored tallgrass prairie, for more than half a century a working laboratory of the prairie's ecology and its plants.

No wonder, then, that people in those parts seem to know their wildflowers, or that in suburban Wisconsin neighborhoods a noticeable number of homeowners have been defying the norm for a decade or two by plowing under their lawns in favor of something wilder. (There are enough such homes in the Milwaukee area alone that an annual prairie-garden tour has been conducted for busloads of interested visitors for more than fifteen years.) Not just local botanists and graduate students found themselves influenced by the prairie restoration movement. Gardeners did, too.

Lorrie Otto started tearing up her lawn north of Milwaukee more than twenty-five years ago. Actually, refraining from mowing was the least of it; Otto went so far as to raze nine eighty-year-old non-native spruces to let the sun shine in on her would-be prairie garden. "That was a very gutsy thing to do," she says now, pointing to where the trees once stood. "It's not much to stop mowing your lawn, but to cut down eighty-year-old trees . . ." But Otto was determined to make room for wildflowers like downy sunflower, *Helianthus mollis,* with its fuzzy stems and leaves, her favorite from among the thirteen sunflower species that grow in the state.

Twenty-five years ago—or even ten years ago, for that matter—Otto couldn't just drive down to the local garden center and buy three quart pots of this native and seven of that one to place in her ex-lawn. Then, wildflowers were just that—wild.

"I used to stop and ask the farmers for a little bit of what was growing in their fencerows," she recalls of her early plant-acquisition method.

Translating the gestalt of the prairie into garden-sized terms has been just one contribution of this queen of the prairie. By organizing early wildflower conferences, fighting against outdated practices and laws like those that mandate mowing (and therefore forbid front yards full of prairie plants), Otto quickly evolved past gardener to environmentalist, activist, and pure inspiration.

Wild Ones—Natural Landscapers, Ltd., a group she formed, now lists 1,200 professionals and hobbyists among those who subscribe to its newsletter, "The Outside Story," and satellite groups have been created elsewhere in Wisconsin and in other states, using the original group as role model.

Voicing an acquired wisdom heard among long-time native-plant people we visited in all the nation's habitats, Otto says she was more open to nonnatives in her plantings twenty-five years ago. A romantic grapevine-covered arbor is a vestige of the earlier garden. "Just as long as it wasn't lawn," she says of her former viewpoint. "Today, though, I'm more particular about natives-only."

What the prairies at Madison and the Wild One's prairie gardens show so convincingly is that American gardeners' knowledge of grasslands began years ago, in our own backyards. We incorporate black-eyed Susan, blazing star, and asters—prairie plants all—into our perfectly tame flower borders.

Though some form of grassland occurs on every continent except Antarctica, making up more than 35 percent of the earth's land surface, the prairie is unique to America. Grasslands are usually on flat or gently rolling land, and wind continually buffets these wide-open spaces. There is no shade here, or very little, so high light intensity is another fact of life that plants must endure. Rainfall helps dictate that an area will be grassland, too; generally speaking, grasslands have more water than deserts, but not so much as woodlands.

America has other grass-dominated communities. The Great Plains, for instance, have short- and mixed-grass communities stretching from the tall-grass midwestern prairies to the Rocky Mountain range. There are also less stable transitional areas like fields and meadows. But it is the legendary prairie that once stretched six hundred miles across the continent's interior from the Appalachians to the Rockies, covering 250 million acres. In addition, pockets of prairie existed as far east as Long Island, where sixty thousand acres once stood on the place called Hempstead Plain. Today, not even 1 percent of that original eastern tract remains, that bit saved from development as the rough of an old golf course.

So irresistible was this sea of flat, prime land to the

OPPOSITE, ABOVE: *A rare plant community called a savanna includes clusters of trees.* RIGHT: *Lorrie Otto began her unorthodox front yard twenty-five years ago with natives such as purple coneflower.* FAR RIGHT: *Many neighbors now subscribe to her philosophy.*

pioneers that in a mere half century some 150 years ago they turned a great and diverse ecosystem into farmland, farmland, and more farmland. Once, a whole train of covered wagons could be lost from view, swallowed up in the amber waves of (native) grain. Now, prairie enthusiasts must travel far to find a remnant big enough in which to lose even themselves for a single afternoon.

The great American tallgrass prairie is nearly extinct. A prairie, from the French word for meadow, is actually not a meadow at all, but a midwestern phenomenon, a plant community of species adapted to higher temperatures, extended drought, and less rainfall than in the East in any given year. Meadows, which tend to proliferate in the East, comprise plants that enjoy the five to fifteen inches more annual rainfall that that area receives compared with the Midwest. About thirty to thirty-five inches a year fall in the tallgrass prairie region; in the East, the total is more like forty-five to fifty inches.

Meadows are also spared the incidence of summer fires common in the prairie region, because meadows occur in places that are typically humid in the summer. Some meadows will be addressed in this chapter, others in "Wetlands."

There are three basic kinds of prairie communities in nature, categorized by available soil moisture: tallgrass (big bluestem and switchgrass, for example, want more soil moisture than shorter grasses); mixed grass (a blend of short and tall species); and shortgrass (little bluestem, prairie dropseed, and sideoats grama, to name a few). Historically, in times of prolonged drought, the community boundaries ebb and flow, only to retreat or advance again when the weather returns to "normal" and gives the former occupant the edge again over the temporary opportunist. Savannas are areas where trees become established and remain to tough it out through dry years. Meadows

conjure up images of cool-season grasses, like fescues. This is a general expression of the differences between the communities; prairie grasses also grow in the East, and cool-season grasses in the Midwest.

A prairie—and by this I mean a natural prairie like the one in Madison, not a man-made garden of prairie plants—is basically a tree-free community, and will remain so. Given time and neglect, a meadow happily becomes a woodland.

Prairies stay basically treeless because of several influences, including, historically, regular burning (started by Native Americans or lightning) and grazing (by bison, pronghorn, and elk, for instance), as well as climate factors such as regular periods of drought that discourage trees. To grow a successful prairie or prairie-style garden, these essential management tools must be simulated, through properly timed mowing and raking and/or burning where possible. A prairie also stays grassland simply because of the difficulty that seeds have getting into the soil through all the built-up remains of grass, and the hard time trees have establishing themselves among all those powerful roots.

"The power of the prairie is vested in its roots," says Neil Diboll, a botanist-turned-nurseryman in Wisconsin, whose Prairie Nursery is helping make it possible for gardeners and restorationists alike to grow Culver's root (*Veronicastrum virginicum*), compass plant (*Silphium laciniatum*), cup plant (*Silphium perfoliatum*), rattlesnake master (*Eryngium yuccifolium*) and big bluestem (*Andropogon gerardii*), and dozens of other prairie stars. If Lorrie Otto is queen of the prairie, then Neil Diboll is its current crown prince.

OPPOSITE, TOP TO BOTTOM: *Culver's root* (Veronicastrum virginicum), *rattlesnake master* (Eryngium yuccifolium), *and two important soil-enriching legumes, wild senna* (Cassia hebecarpa) *and prairie clover* (Petalostemum purpureum). FAR RIGHT: *Cup plant* (Silphium perfoliatum).

What Diboll calls the "root-to-shoot ratio" is two to one among prairie plants, meaning that two thirds of the plants' biomass is below ground—"a real storehouse," Diboll says—reaching down into the earth to access moisture and meanwhile redistributing nutrients, aerating the soil, and performing other important functions. Even young plants that show only an inch of growth aboveground may already have produced a foot or more of downward life.

Just because prairies never evolve into forests does not mean that they are either static or homogeneous. Prairies, and even small prairie gardens, are ever-changing organisms—plants that dominate this season may recede into the background next year, so wise prairie gardeners never become too attached to a picture-perfect image.

"We must learn to appreciate the innate wisdom of nature's chaos," says Diboll.

Besides grasses, prairies are typically made up of a large number of composites (daisy- or sunflowerlike flowers in the *Compositae* family) and also a high percentage of legumes, such as purple prairie clover (*Petalostemum purpureum*), milk vetch (*Astragalus agrestis*), and leadplant (*Amorpha canescens,* one of the few woody prairie plants). By fixing nitrogen into the soil, the legumes help boost productivity of the grasses; conversely, the grasses also seem to have a beneficial effect on the legumes, which produce more seed when grown in tandem than when grown alone.

Composites across the country. OPPOSITE, FROM LEFT TO RIGHT, TOP ROW TO BOTTOM ROW: *Black-eyed Susan* (Rudbeckia hirta); *boltonia* (Boltonia asteroides); *cup plant* (Silphium perfoliatum); *sneezeweed* (Helenium autumnale); *hardy ageratum, or mist flower* (Eupatorium coelestinum); *garden coreopsis* (Coreopsis tinctoria); *calico aster* (Aster lateriflorus); *Maximilian daisy* (Helianthus maximiliani); *and* Rudbeckia 'Goldsturm', *the famous European cultivar of our native* R. fulgida. RIGHT: *Prairie blazing star* (Liatris pycnostachya).

Understanding what grows well with what will result in more sustainable, easier-to-manage plantings.

We were quick to learn that prairies, like people, show their age. The relict prairie at Madison has little in common, appearance-wise, with man-made "baby prairies," as relatively new installations are fondly called by the naturalists and others who plant and manage them. Over time, the grasses win out over the nongrass, or broadleaf, wildflowers (technically known as forbs), unless a firm human hand manipulates the results by planting few, and less-zealous, grasses at the outset and/or by caring for the planting in a way that favors flowers.

Though the classic makeup of a prairie has been repeatedly expressed as eighty to twenty grasses to forbs, that doesn't mean that gardeners must observe that precise proportion when planting.

In fact, says Diboll, in most home applications a mix with "strong curbside appeal" is desirable, perhaps as much as 50 percent forbs blended with shorter bunchgrasses like little bluestem, prairie dropseed, and sideoats grama.

"When you make a prairie you stack the deck," Diboll says. The way the cards fall is up to you—lots of spring color, or late-summer color only, or more flowers than grasses—or at least it's your call to a point. "Mother Nature plays the last card," he adds. "She's the boss."

There are plants to see in the prairie in spring while the familiar cold-season grasses and forbs emerge. One of the most beautiful is shooting star (Dodecatheon meadia), OPPOSITE. *Others to look for include Canada anemone* (Anemone canadensis), *columbine* (Aquilegia canadensis), *blue false indigo* (Baptisia australis), *white false indigo* (Baptisia leucantha), *prairie larkspur* (Delphinium virescens), *prairie smoke* (Geum triflorum), *lupine* (Lupinus perennis), *bird-foot violet* (Viola pedata), *downy phlox* (Phlox pilosa), *pasqueflower* (Anemone patens), *and wild geranium* (Geranium maculatum).

To make a prairie it takes a clover and one bee,
One clover and a bee
and revery.
The revery alone will do
If bees are few.

~EMILY DICKINSON,
"TO MAKE A PRAIRIE"

The questions that face the beginning prairie gardener are more complicated than they might at first appear: whether to mow or not, whether to plug young transplants of desired wildflowers into what's already growing or to kill off the existing vegetation and start from scratch.

There is no one right way to get started, though each expert consulted offered a preferred technique, from nontoxic methods like repeated cultivation or soil solarization under plastic to the use of chemical herbicides. (Space constraints prevent outlining every detail here, so what follows are some of the basics to consider when planting a prairie or meadow of your own. Be sure to consult the "Source Guide" for further references; native-plant and seed catalogs often have the best hands-on information of all.)

At one extreme, Neil Diboll recommends the take-no-prisoners approach to site preparation—killing off all existing vegetation by repeatedly applying an herbicide containing glyphosate, or by repeatedly tilling or a combination of the two, thereby making it possible to start with a blank canvas. Organic gardeners may be uncomfortable with using even a less-toxic herbicide like glyphosate; each gardener must decide the chemical question for him- or herself.

Both methods take a full growing season, meaning no planting can be done for another year—a lot to ask of the impatient gardener, but the results are worth it, Diboll says. To use herbicides, start by mowing in early spring, then spray in midspring, midsummer, and early fall.

To remove unwanted vegetation without chemicals, cultivate every two weeks from early spring through fall, to a depth of four to five inches. Wait no longer than two weeks between cultivation sessions or the plants will begin to reestablish.

In each case, prepare the soil so it is smooth and free of clods, then wait until spring to plant—and only after a final weed-killing treatment is performed. With herbicides, apply when spring weeds are two to three inches high, then cultivate shallowly (just an inch) and plant right away. Only cultivation can be used at this time, too, to a depth of an inch timed a week after the first spring rain occurs, Diboll recommends. Again, plant immediately after treatment.

Lorrie Otto agrees that all existing undesirables must be eliminated.

"You simply must get every last perennial weed out before starting planting," she says, drawing on more than twenty-five years of hands-on experience.

Sometimes, particularly when working with small areas, undesirables can be simply dug out—as when you lift and discard (to the compost pile, please) a section of turfgrass before preparing any garden. Soil solarization—covering the area to be planted with black plastic for most or all of a growing season so that the undesirable plants are cooked and suffocated —is an easy method in small areas, and can even be translated to a large-scale landscape.

Certain soil-building styles may smother existing weeds, too. When Otto wanted to grow prairie plants adapted to sandy soils on her clayey site, she first laid a thick layer of newspaper over the ground, then piled on a very thick layer of leaves, then "great piles of sand," and then repeated the leaves and sand,

"to simulate a sand prairie." Many existing weeds would necessarily be thwarted this way, though it would be impractical for a large-scale planting.

On the topic of soil-improvement, be realistic. Although landscapers typically force grass to grow on a mere three inches of topsoil, deep-rooted prairie plants need much more. While they don't require a double-dug bed full of peat moss and rotted manure (in fact, it is best to avoid manure since it may contain a great number of weed seeds), examine the conditions the plants want in nature and try to approximate them. Two examples: Sand, rotted leaves, and compost can help break up clayey soils, for instance, and organic materials such as the leaves and compost also improve overall soil life that is dangerously low in very acid soils. Follow the instructions provided by your supplier of seeds or plants for best results.

PICKING THE PLANTS

Any prairie garden is necessarily going to be interpretive, since it is man's hand, not nature's, that is doing the designing and planting. To grow a loosely designed meadow is perhaps the easiest way to start using prairie plants. At the New York Botanical Garden, former Native Plants Garden curator Kathryn Venezia advocates minimeadows as lawn alternatives.

"Even a loosely interpreted meadow offers much more botanical diversity than a grass lawn," she says, recommending that gardeners "start small, one hundred square feet at a time" unless helpers and a tractor are at the ready.

Venezia's meadow-making methods: If your lawn is spotty and sparse, you're in luck. You can plug in groups of wildflower transplants without removing the turf first. Simply cultivate patches of the lawn and introduce prairie plants into these prepared spots.

To establish a "new" suburban prairie of her own, ABOVE, *Lorrie Otto placed thick layers of newspaper over the ground to smother the grass. Next came heaps of leaves, great piles of sand, more leaves, and more sand to simulate the sand-prairie soil. This process naturally thwarted weeds that might have taken over, and it built the soil.* RIGHT: *In an older section of Otto's garden, a romantic vine-covered arch is reminiscent of the days before she implemented her once-controversial philosophy.*

A Palette of Prairie Plants

Though generally rugged, adaptable creatures, prairie grasses and forbs, like any other plants, do have their favorite conditions. The three lists that follow were prepared by Neil Diboll, a prairie ecologist and owner of Prairie Nursery in Wisconsin, whose work can be seen on pages 54–57.

For Dry, Sandy Soils

Amorpha canescens, leadplant
Anemone cylindrica, thimbleweed
Anemone patens, pasqueflower
Asclepias tuberosa, butterfly weed
Aster azureus, sky blue aster
Aster ericoides, heath aster
Aster laevis, smooth aster
Aster ptarmicoides, white aster
Aster sericeus, silky aster
Astragalus canadensis, Canada milk vetch
Callirhoe triangulata, poppy mallow
Campanula rotundifolia, harebell
Coreopsis palmata, stiff coreopsis
Echinacea pallida, pale purple coneflower
Epilobium angustifolium, fireweed
Euphorbia corollata, flowering spurge
Geum triflorum, prairie smoke
Helianthus laetiflorus, showy sunflower
Helianthus mollis, downy sunflower
Helianthus occidentalis, western sunflower
Helianthus strumosus, woodland sunflower
Heuchera richardsonii, alum root
Lespedeza capitata, roundheaded bush clover
Liatris aspera, rough blazing star
Liatris cylindracea, dwarf blazing star
Lithospermum caroliniense, hairy puccoon
Lupinus perennis, lupine
Monarda fistulosa, bergamot
Monarda punctata, dotted mint
Penstemon gracilis, slender beardtongue
Penstemon grandiflorus, beardtongue
Petalostemum purpureum, purple prairie clover
Ranunculus rhomboideus, prairie buttercup
Ratibida pinnata, yellow coneflower
Rudbeckia hirta, black-eyed Susan
Solidago nemoralis, gray goldenrod
Solidago rigida, stiff goldenrod
Solidago speciosa, showy goldenrod
Tradescantia ohiensis, spiderwort
Verbena stricta, hoary vervain

GRASSES
Andropogon gerardii, big bluestem
Andropogon scoparius [*Schizachyrium scoparium*], little bluestem
Bouteloua curtipendula, sideoats grama
Elymus canadensis, Canada wild rye
Koeleria cristata, Junegrass
Panicum virgatum, switchgrass
Sorghastrum nutans, Indian grass
Sporobolus heterolepis, prairie dropseed

For Medium Soils

Allium cernuum, nodding pink onion
Amorpha canescens, leadplant
Anemone cylindrica, thimbleweed
Asclepias syriaca, common milkweed
Asclepias tuberosa, butterfly weed
Aster spp.
Astragalus canadensis, Canada milk vetch
Baptisia leucantha, white false indigo
Baptisia leucophaea, cream false indigo
Cassia hebecarpa, wild senna
Ceanothus americanus, New Jersey tea

CLOCKWISE FROM TOP LEFT: *Big bluestem* (Andropogon gerardii) *dominates the tallgrass prairie; butterfly weed* (Asclepias tuberosa); *Culver's root* (Veronicastrum virginicum); *rattlesnake master* (Eryngium yuccifolium); *New England aster* (Aster novae-angliae).

Coreopsis palmata, stiff
  coreopsis
Desmodium canadense, Canada
  tick trefoil
Dodecatheon meadia, shooting
  star
Echinacea spp., purple
  coneflower
Eryngium yuccifolium,
  rattlesnake master
Euphorbia corollata, flowering
  spurge
Helianthus laetiflorus, showy
  sunflower
Helianthus occidentalis,
  western sunflower
Helianthus strumosus,
  woodland sunflower
Heliopsis helianthoides, oxeye
  sunflower
Heuchera richardsonii, alum
  root
Lespedeza capitata,
  roundheaded bush clover
Liatris aspera, rough blazing
  star
Monarda fistulosa, bergamot
Parthenium integrifolium, wild
  quinine
Penstemon digitalis, smooth
  penstemon
Petalostemum candidum, white
  prairie clover

Petalostemum purpureum,
  purple prairie clover
Ratibida pinnata, yellow
  coneflower
Rudbeckia hirta, black-eyed
  Susan
Rudbeckia subtomentosa, sweet
  black-eyed Susan
Silphium integrifolium,
  rosinweed
Silphium laciniatum, compass
  plant
Silphium terebinthinaceum,
  prairie dock
Solidago rigida, stiff
  goldenrod
Solidago speciosa, showy
  goldenrod
Tradescantia ohiensis,
  spiderwort
Veronicastrum virginicum,
  Culver's root
Zizia aptera, heartleaf golden
  Alexanders

GRASSES
Andropogon gerardii, big bluestem
Elymus canadensis, Canada
  wild rye
Panicum virgatum,
  switchgrass
Sorghastrum nutans, Indian grass
Sporobolus heterolepis, prairie
  dropseed

For Wet Soils

Anemone canadensis, Canada
  anemone
Asclepias incarnata, red
  milkweed
Aster novae-angliae, New
  England aster
Baptisia leucantha, white false
  indigo
Chelone glabra, turtlehead
Coreopsis tripteris, tall
  coreopsis
Desmodium canadense, Canada
  tick trefoil
Dodecatheon meadia, shooting
  star
Eupatorium maculatum, Joe-
  pye weed
Eupatorium perfoliatum,
  boneset
Filipendula rubra, queen-of-
  the-prairie
Gentiana andrewsii, bottle
  gentian
Heuchera richardsonii, alum
  root
Iris shrevei, wild iris
Liatris pycnostachya, prairie
  blazing star
Lilium superbum, Turk's-cap
  lily

Lobelia cardinalis, cardinal
  flower
Lobelia siphilitica, great blue
  lobelia
Monarda fistulosa, bergamot
Ratibida pinnata, yellow
  coneflower
Rudbeckia subtomentosa, sweet
  black-eyed Susan
Silphium integrifolium,
  rosinweed
Silphium perfoliatum, cup
  plant
Silphium terebinthinaceum,
  prairie dock
Solidago rigida, stiff
  goldenrod
Vernonia fasciculata, ironweed
Veronicastrum virginicum,
  Culver's root

GRASSES
Andropogon gerardii, big
  bluestem
Calamagrostis canadensis,
  bluejoint grass
Elymus canadensis, Canada
  wild rye
Spartina pectinata, prairie
  cordgrass

CLOCKWISE FROM TOP
LEFT: *Planting for medium
soil includes pink nodding
onion (Allium cernuum);
detail; moist-soil plants such
as white boneset (Eupatorium
perfoliatum); cup plant
(Silphium perfoliatum); blue
false indigo (Baptisia
australis).*

If the lawn is thick and healthy, the turf is probably best lifted before replanting. Either way, selective hand-weeding is a critical part of follow-up maintenance, and an annual mowing in spring, followed by thorough raking up (and composting) of debris.

Know your aesthetic goal before you order a single plant or seed. If a month-long show is all you want, classic prairie plants and grasses will oblige with their main event from July into August (the grasses then look good as they mellow come fall, and even all winter long once your eye is adjusted to their subtle beauty). An added spring show can be achieved by including in your design a few low-growing "ephemerals," early-season flowers that bloom and fade quickly to make space for main-season plants. Shooting star, downy phlox, and prairie smoke, all springtime bloomers, will happily share the same turf as asters, goldenrods, and sunflowers, for instance.

Whatever your goal, from loose meadow to more traditional grass-dominated prairie, be sure to select a plant list from among those best adapted to your existing (or intended) soil type. A chart of plants for various soil types appears on pages 46–47. Plants well-matched to the site conditions will always win out over those that don't belong, so don't waste money or time on the latter.

SEED OR TRANSPLANTS?

Which raw material—seeds or transplants—would be best for your purposes? Each has its merits, not the least of which is price. At an average of one plant per square foot, a mere one-acre prairie (meaning 43,560 plants, since there are that many square feet per acre) would cost a literal fortune, plus labor, which is roughly figured at twice the plant materials cost. High-quality seed for the same area would cost

between approximately four hundred dollars (grasses only) and fifteen hundred dollars (grasses and forbs), not including sowing, which would bring the total to about two thousand dollars an acre. (Remember, neither total includes soil preparation.)

Even the two-thousand-dollar seed-method price may sound high, but think of it this way: If the area under consideration is now in lawn, and you pay even fifty dollars to mow it once a week, by the end of a six-month growing season you have spent more than twelve hundred dollars just for mowing.

Another plus: A seed-grown prairie planting will have more genetic diversity than if you begin with young plants—it will be more like a natural community.

"With transplants, you're growing a garden, not a plant community," says Diboll, his ecologist's orientation surfacing. The reason, he explains, is basically this: It is extremely difficult to replicate the relationships between plants—to site your 43,560 baby plants in a way that they would assemble themselves. And one plant per square foot is a mere fraction of the forty to sixty seeds Diboll typically sows per foot, expecting ten to germinate and four to six to survive. With a seeded planting, you simply start with more individual plants, perhaps six times as many. More plants, more genetic information— more diversity.

Transplants, however, are frequently more reliable —in an unfavorable weather year, certain seeds may never germinate in a nonirrigated seeded planting at all, whereas transplants may have a better chance. Transplants also get off to a faster start since they are already at least a year old, sometimes two, when you buy them. By their second, and certainly third, year in your ground, they will be quite showy and full. Seeded plantings take more like five years to fill in

GRASSLAND TIPS

Prairies started from seed are often sown with "nurse crops," TOP, *such as annual rye, annual flax, or oats to suppress weed growth as desirables become established.*
ABOVE: *Once bison were an integral part of the prairie's success, along with fire and management by native American people. Occasional grazing encourages sturdy plant growth.*

Sun is a must. Don't try to grow prairie plants in the shade.

Don't fertilize. More often than not, fertilizer will just encourage unwanted weeds that lurk in the soil or that blow in from elsewhere.

Match the plants to the site carefully (see the list of plants for various soil types on pages 46–47). If your site is dry, stick to shorter species like little bluestem, sideoats grama, needlegrass, or Junegrass. Giants like big bluestem and Indian grass demand more soil moisture.

Be prepared to wait, especially when starting from seed. Many prairie plants spend their first couple of years developing roots, not flowers.

If you're thinking of introducing transplants into an existing sod, a caveat: It's one thing for baby plants to successfully compete if set into patches carved out among clump-forming bunchgrasses, another for them to make a stand against rhizomatous invaders—plants like lawn grasses that make a nearly impenetrable network of horizontal, modified stems just below the soil surface. Carefully evaluate their opponents.

REKINDLING THE ELEMENT OF FIRE

Fire creates plant diversity, a fact that Native Americans knew well. Many plant communities, from prairie to the scrubby semiarid chaparrals—even Yellowstone, as we learned recently—actually depend on the presence of periodic fires, sometimes spaced years apart, to keep them healthy.

Burning has also long been recognized by farmers as an effective tool for management of fields. Today it may not be possible in some areas to get permission to burn at all. This could be a good chance to teach children about the power, danger, and necessity of fire. Obviously, their safety, and that of pets and property must be considered above all, but we've never heard of a case where a responsible burning went awry. Never start any kind of fire, however small, without checking to see if it is both safe and legal to do so in your area. In agricultural zones, gaining approval may be as simple as calling the fire tower to alert them; in more populated zones, you may have to apply for a permit and have the fire department on hand. Contact your local agricultural extension service or botanic garden for more detailed instructions. Never use any gasoline, chemical agents, or discarded tires (an

old and very hazardous farm trick) to start a fire.

The timing of a burn depends on the desired annihilation or encouragement— what are you trying to set back, and what are you trying to promote? To reduce cool-season weed grasses like bluegrass in a meadow or prairie planting, but stimulate warm-season prairie grass species, burning must be timed after the former starts growing but before the latter has put on much growth—mid- to late spring. Burning then will also set back cool-season weeds, sedges, and forbs, which may not figure into your plan.

Sometimes dormant-season (late winter or early spring) burns are better. This can only be determined by knowing the growing habits of *all* the plants in the target area.

Even if your management strategy dictates a particular time for burning, it simply may not be possible. Is there enough fuel (old dried plant material) to get a fire going? If not, wait another growing season for more fuel to build up, or mow instead.

Even the lightest rain can moisten the "fuel" sufficiently to make burning impossible. Windy days are not meant for burning.

Always burn in sections,

like a crazy quilt. Map out the sections with your mower, and mow double-wide paths between them with the blade on its lowest setting. Then moisten these firebreaks with water.

Consider burning only part of the entire planting in a single year; burning the whole thing may eliminate overwintering butterfly chrysalises and other beneficial insects, as well as bird nesting sites.

The black ash returns nutrients to the soil and absorbs heat from the sun, warming the soil faster. It will disappear soon beneath emerging plants.

In some cases, burning actually helps the opponent. Fire scarifies the seed of white sweet clover (*Melilotus alba*), for example, perhaps the number-one enemy of prairie makers (even in Brooklyn, New York). Country Wetlands Nursery recommends pulling it at the time of petal drop instead.

Don't underestimate the heat or rapid movement of even a small fire. A hose and a strong water supply are essential, as are enough people armed with metal rakes and shovels to manage each section. Start with a tiny section—ten by ten feet—to see how fire works.

If you're nervous about fire, don't try this method.

(this estimate is based on a diverse seed mix of grasses and other perennials, not one loaded with showy, flash-in-the-pan annuals).

It sounds like a mix of seeds and transplants would be the best of all, but it's not. A mix causes a management nightmare, since the seeded area must be mowed regularly the first couple of years (to about six inches) to retard weeds, and transplants would recover slowly if mown down.

An area of transplants could be used, however, to disguise a slower-growing seeded area—say a wide swath of plants at the most visible edge of your seeded planting, so that it will appear at least from a distance that things are really off to a quick start.

Seeding is often done in late spring or early summer to take advantage of warm weather, which prairie plants favor. Remember: You will be doing a final early spring preparation of the seedbed to eliminate more of the undesirable cool-season weeds, so early planting is neither possible nor useful. However, many forb seeds require a period of cool stratification —cold and moisture—to break dormancy, meaning that they may lie dormant until that need is satisfied. Some nurseries dry-stratify the seeds (put them in a refrigerator to simulate the winter that many seeds need to undergo in order to germinate) in advance of selling them to you and you need only moisten and refrigerate them for several weeks before sowing. There are other more specialized cases, too; ask your seed supplier for specific instructions.

Fire is an important tool for prairie makers, OPPOSITE, LEFT. *They burn in small sections, delineated by mowed strips,* OPPOSITE, RIGHT, *that are water-soaked for firebreaks. These edges can be made amazingly precise. The Sauk prairie restoration in Wisconsin,* LEFT, *might be a candidate for late spring burning. The burn kills the early-emerging alien weeds. The dark color of the burned ash absorbs sunlight and warms the ground, giving the late-to-sprout natives a head start while contributing nutritious ash to the plants.*

ORNAMENTAL AMERICAN GRASSES

Ornamental grasses have won favor in recent years as naturalistic additions to the landscape, but many current favorites—*Miscanthus* and *Pennisetum,* for instance—are actually invasive foreigners. They have demonstrated an inclination to self-sow around the landscape, while simultaneously doubling in girth each season. A very watchful eye must be kept on such aliens as the Mediterranean and Australian grasses being promoted in horticulture today—they are fine for the conscientious collector but perhaps not for less-attentive gardeners.

Fortunately, grasses needn't be exotic to be ornamental; many American species are at least as handsome. Improved forms are being selected out of native populations by a number of nurseries. Here are some to consider:

BIG BLUESTEM (*Andropogon gerardii*) was the primary grass of the original tallgrass prairie that ranged from Ohio to Colorado. Usually five or six feet tall, it can approach eight or even ten feet in a perfect site, where there is ample soil moisture in the warm-weather months. It has blue summertime foliage and bronze fall color. Selections have been made for southern climates, sandy soil, improved fall color, and other traits. Look for related species.

LITTLE BLUESTEM (*Schizachyrium scoparium* or *Andropogon scoparius*) is a shortgrass species usually reaching about three feet. Like its taller counterpart, little blue is a warm-season clump-former. Besides hillsides and prairies, it also inhabits open woodland areas that receive good light. Fall color can range from bronze to purple-red. Selections are being made for true blue foliage and other qualities.

INDIAN GRASS (*Sorghastrum nutans*) is another native of the tallgrass prairie, though it usually reaches only three feet. The foliage of this beautiful grass can be green, grayish green, or blue—the last being one of the favored characteristics, and a form called 'Sioux Blue' has been named to celebrate its beauty.

PRAIRIE CORDGRASS (*Spartina pectinata*) is a denizen of low-lying areas where moisture is ample, as at the water's edge. This spreading grass has graceful arching leaves that take on yellow fall color. A gold-margined variety called 'Aureomarginata' is even more ornamental.

PRAIRIE DROPSEED (*Sporobolus heterolepis*) forms two-foot hummocks of arching emerald green leaves, which are topped in August with flowerheads that have a distinct fragrance that faintly recalls buttered popcorn.

CLOCKWISE FROM TOP LEFT: *Indian grass* (Sorghastrum nutans); *and flower detail; northern (or inland) sea oats* (Chasmanthium latifolium); *little bluestem* (Schizachyrium scoparium *or* Andropogon scoparius); *golden grass* (Milium effusum 'Aureum'); *switchgrass* (Panicum virgatum).

SWITCHGRASS (*Panicum virgatum*) is versatile and much appreciated by wildlife as winter and early spring cover. Its fall color is exceptional, usually yellow. It is typically three or four feet tall. The selection 'Heavy Metal' has steel-blue summer foliage and turns bright yellow in fall; 'Hanse Herms' is orange-red to burgundy in fall.

DEERGRASS (*Muhlenbergia rigens*) is a standout for dry western gardens, where it can retain its green color despite low summertime moisture. Its foliage is about three feet tall, with long-lasting whiplike flowers borne above it in summer. It is excellent for holding coastal slopes. Other "muhlies" being promoted for landscaping include *M. lindheimeri* (Lindheimer muhly), with its clumps of blue foliage, and *M. filipes* (purple muhly), a southeastern native with purple flowerheads.

CALIFORNIA FESCUE (*Festuca californica*) is a clumping, medium-height California native for dry areas in sun or part shade, reaching about two to three feet tall. Selections with good blue color are particularly desirable, and turn purplish at frost. The selection 'Salmon Creek' is blue-gray flushed with burgundy.

RIBBON GRASS (*Phalaris arundinacea* 'Picta'), also called gardener's garters, is a showy grass variegated green and white, that is tol-

erant of part shade. It is highly ornamental, but also zealous, so keep a careful eye on its movements. Avoid the species, which is troublesome in wetlands. Good for holding banks in moist soil, which it favors.

SIDEOATS GRASS (*Bouteloua curtipendula*) is medium sized, with highly ornamental flowerheads touched with orange and purple followed by decorative oatlike seeds. Grow it in dry to medium soil.

NORTHERN SEA OATS (*Chasmanthium latifolium*) turns from green to copper in fall and then to a wheat brown. Its seedheads are among the most beautiful of any grass, drooping and shaped like tiny flattened pinecones. Northern sea oats prefers rich, moist soil and part shade, but is adaptable to other conditions.

BUFFALO GRASS (*Buchloe dactyloides*) is an outstanding native lawn substitute, using little fertilizer and water. Research at Texas A&M (which released the all-female variety 'Prairie') and the University of Nebraska (the variety '609', also female) is continuing to breed better buffalo grass— shorter, darker color and one requiring even less mowing. A native of the middle third of the country, it is now being tested as far east as New Jersey, where the wetter climate is not exactly the twelve to twenty-four inches of water per year that buffalo grass likes—yet.

RIGHT, TOP TO BOTTOM: *Meadow muhly* (Muhlenbergia rigens, *detail in winter*); *a specimen of meadow muhly; split beard bluestem* (Andropogon ternarius, *detail in winter*). *Many of the grasses become most ornamental after the autumn frost.*

NEIL DIBOLL
WESTFIELD, WISCONSIN

THERE IS THE SMELL OF BUT-
tered popcorn in the air, or is it
fresh cilantro? Neither, Neil Diboll, owner of the Prairie Nursery, assures his perplexed guests
—it's August, when the aroma
of ripening prairie dropseed
(*Sporobolus heterolepis*), one of the
most beautiful of native prairie
grasses, wafts through the fields.

Diboll's attention is quickly
turned to one clump of the dropseed among thousands growing
in orderly rows at Prairie Nursery in Westfield, Wisconsin,

PRINCE OF THE PRAIRIE

which he has owned for more
than a decade.

"I used to be an ecologist, but
they're turning me into a horti-
culturist," says Diboll, spying a
plant with distinctive yellow
stems unlike the rest of the crop.
He'll transplant the "better" one
to a special observation bed to
see if it merits a future as a named
selection.

The yellow-stemmed prairie
dropseed, or one of many glaucous selections of little bluestem
that he is propagating to name—
all of these are examples of phe-
notypic variation, natural occur-
rences within a larger population
that display measurably distinctive traits. The difference may be
purely aesthetic, like the yel-
lower or bluer stems of certain
clumps of a grass species, or
qualities like greater resistance to
disease, a longer bloom period, a
dwarfer form, and so on.

The future of native plants,
horticulturists agree, is in making selections that are just a little
better for garden use than the

*A monoculture is never encouraged
in an intentional planting except
in a nursery where harvesting specific
plants or pure seeds necessitates this*

*isolation. At Prairie Nursery,
plantings such as these of* Liatris
and Veronicastrum, RIGHT, *are
attractive to visitors, including a
monarch butterfly that lands on a
nearby purple coneflower,* ABOVE.

general population—and the scientist in Diboll concurs, if a bit grudgingly.

Diboll doesn't fancy himself a designer; most of his projects are large-scale restorations. He does, however, have some observations on design. There are basically three prevailing approaches to prairie planting, he notes: the general method ("plant 'em all and let God sort it out!"); the patchwork prairie (plant many different "subcommunities"); and the "artsy" prairie (plant drifts and masses in specific areas).

The first, usually accomplished by seeding, is likely to yield the most diverse and functional prairie, since what grows from among the many species you sow will be those best adapted to the site and other existing conditions. The patchwork method allows for the creation of several different kinds of prairies in the space: a shortgrass mix in one area, for instance, with a tallgrass area nearby—distinct habitats that appeal to different wildlife. (A tip: Keep the shortgrass to the north and west of the tall, which will otherwise seed into and overrun the little ones.)

In the artsy prairie, monotypic waves of a single plant can even be planted for drama—which,

Diboll says, will certainly catch the eye, but its value shouldn't be overrated. "When only one, or maybe two or three species of flowers are planted in an area, one doth not a community create," he warns.

At the nursery, of course, that very approach has to be taken to propagate efficiently, and whole blocks of a single species in bloom, though hardly recommended, are indeed arresting. Tasty, too, it seems. A goldfinch perches on a barely ripe seedhead of prairie blazing star (*Liatris pynostachya*), capturing Diboll's attention—and stealing a bit of next year's inventory. No matter. "It's a total bird restaurant," he says of the nursery fields in his characteristically positive style.

Despite the negative facts and figures on shrinking biodiversity that he knows all too well as a scientist, Diboll's is an upbeat, and infectious, message: that through restoring native-plant communities, we can make a difference.

"We're like adolescents becoming adults," he says of the United States. "Our mandate was to subdue the environment. . . . Now we realize that people are becoming extraneous to the environment and we have to learn to live *with* it."

TOP: *Rocky Mountain blazing star* (Liatris ligulistylis).
CENTER: *Queen-of-the-prairie* (Filipendula rubra).
LEFT: *Cardinal flower* (Lobelia cardinalis).
OPPOSITE, ABOVE: *One species, oxeye sunflower* (Heliopsis helianthoides), *is grown on its own, not just to be pretty but to facilitate the harvest of pure seed.*
BELOW: *Prairie dropseed* (Sporobolus heterolepis) *in the nursery rows.*

DICK AND MARSHA
KRUEGER
MEQUON, WISCONSIN

MORE THAN A DECADE HAS passed since Dick and Marsha Krueger's Kentucky bluegrass lawn gave way to something more accurately Wisconsin: a miniature prairie, backed by a shrubby edge composed principally of highbush blueberries (*Vaccinium corymbosum*).

Both front and backyard were begun simultaneously, but using different methods. Because of serious drainage problems and construction relating to an easement, the front of the property required extensive regrading, so

A LAWN LONG GONE

it was scraped to bare clay, then seeded with a mixture of native grasses and forbs including baptisia, silphiums, bee balm, and coneflowers.

Behind the house, the Kruegers simply stopped mowing the bluegrass and plugged in transplants of desirable prairie species, which over time have come to dominate the former lawn-grass monoculture. Between the front and back miniprairies, a portion of the place is still closely mown, providing a stark contrast to the shaggy native portions and also serving as a reminder—a shrinking reminder, since every year the remaining lawn gives way to a few more wildflowers—of how dull and lifeless the yard used to be.

Today, each area continues to develop and evolve mainly by the emergence of self-sown seedlings—those left behind by the birds, that is—but the Kruegers regularly add a few plants, too, and Dick gives the prairie a little help by collecting the seeds himself and scratching them in.

He does an annual mowing in spring, followed by a thorough raking to simulate the effects of burning. Regular hand-weeding reduces pesky invaders like Queen Anne's lace, ragweed, white sweet clover, and curly dock—remnants of the old field that covered the whole street before the houses were built, whose seeds still lurk in the soil. Krueger describes his maintenance routine as a simple one, and it is clearly one performed with love.

"He is the custodial parent," says Marsha, who brings the prairie inside with bouquets of fresh flowers. "I was just a birthmother."

CHICAGO BOTANIC
GARDEN
GLENCOE, ILLINOIS

NO ONE EVER TOLD CURA-tor Kristin Perry that powdery mildew, rodents, and sunflowers would prove her most stubborn opponents in the job as curator of the Chicago Botanic Garden's quarter-acre demonstration prairie garden. To expect the unexpected is the byword of habitat-style gardening, and since she took the job in 1985, Perry has learned as much as she can from

A NEW PRAIRIE PRIMER

the surprises of the trail-blazing garden.

A strip of brick delineates mown from unmown areas in the demo garden, and stockade fencing further lends a sense of home, as if someone has turned a backyard into a miniprairie. Though charming, the fence has proved somewhat of a hindrance, since it restricts air circulation and thereby encourages powdery mildew, particularly on the grasses. Little and big blue-stem and prairie dropseed are troubled by the mildew, says Perry; panic grass (*Panicum virgatum*) doesn't seem to succumb.

Besides the grasses, bergamot (*Monarda fistulosa*), rattlesnake master (*Eryngium yuccifolium*), purple coneflower (*Echinacea purpurea*), Culver's root (*Veronicastrum virginicum*), nodding onion (*Allium cernuum*), obedient plant (*Physostegia virginiana*), butterfly weed (*Asclepias tuberosa*), compass plant and prairie dock (*Silphium* spp.), red milkweed (*Asclepias incarnata*), and senna (*Cassia hebecarpa*) comingle in the planting. Woody members of the

The quarter-acre demonstration prairie garden at the Chicago Botanic Garden exhibits a planting scheme for local home owners. This controlled space utilizes

mown grass paths to make the plantings accessible, RIGHT, *and brick mowing strips make their maintenance easy—no edging is necessary, the mower wheels just drive along the brick border. Plants such as red milkweed* (Asclepias incarnata), ABOVE, *can be viewed as visitors walk along the paths.*

community include two sumacs (*Rhus typhina* and *R. glabra*) and a native rose, *Rosa carolina,* which Perry recommends for its red stems in winter and colorful hips.

Deadheading has proven effective for minimizing invasion by certain aggressive seeders, says Perry, who cuts off some flowerheads of such overeager plants as sweet black-eyed Susan (*Rudbeckia subtomentosa*). Oxeye sunflower (*Heliopsis helianthoides*) had also managed to insinuate itself in one spot, calling for an even stronger counterattack: digging out unwanted plants.

When the bergamot consistently grew to four feet instead of the two and a half typical in Chicago Botanic's fifteen-acre restored prairie nearby, the staff attributed it to greater available moisture in the demonstration area. "Now we think it's lack of root competition because there

are not so many grasses," says Perry. "As a result, the forbs are getting taller."

For the first several years, the planting was cut down by hand at winter's end and the debris raked off. Recently, Perry has been burning it.

"To me, the basic difference is the amount of labor involved," she says. "Something I didn't even think of until we tried it. It saves a lot of time that I can use for other work. Burning also puts nutrients back into the soil rather than hauling them all away, and the plants seem to come up sooner in spring."

To prepare to burn, Perry knocks down everything so all the "fuel" is concentrated on the ground, then rakes brush away from trees, shrubs, and fencing, and also off the brick edging so that it isn't discolored by fire. For better control she divides the

plot into three convenient sections and, on a windless day, burns them one at a time. The results have been so positive that she has begun burning some patches of ornamental grasses elsewhere on the grounds.

Burning has been done just before spring "because we like the ornamental look all winter," but Perry thinks the time has come for a fall burn. Her rationale: organic rodent control.

Burning early would eliminate an overwintering habitat for the remarkably large population of voles, mice, and rabbits who have made the quarter acre their home—and the crowns of grasses and other plants their cafeteria. Their presence may testify to the success of habitat gardening, but in a public garden meant to inspire homeowners, mounds of stubble are no replacement for prairie plants.

OPPOSITE: *The Demonstration Garden exhibits prairie plants and shrubs next to the visitors' building (right).* TOP AND RIGHT: *The garden in August is a perfectly balanced tallgrass prairie.* LEFT: *A selection of native shrubs, including sumac (Rhus typhina).* ABOVE: *The path blends human needs with grasses and forbs.*

TOWER HILL
BOTANIC GARDEN
BOYLSTON,
MASSACHUSETTS

THERE IS A TIME AND A place to garden, and a time and a place simply to let things be. Discerning one from the other is the lesson in the rolling fields at Tower Hill Botanic Garden in Boylston, Massachusetts, where the community of grasses and forbs is particularly handsome from midsummer through fall.

But how to accomplish such understated beauty, particularly on a large and unevenly graded site such as this? By doing very little at all—far less, even, than

FIELDS OF DREAMS

The field at Tower Hill Botanic Garden, RIGHT, *is a managed grassland. Mowing takes the place of burning or grazing for the*

purpose of maintaining the dominance of the grasses and forbs. Without mowing, the field would become woodland. ABOVE: *Swallows and bluebirds are attracted to the boxes dotted throughout the fields.*

if the same area were managed as lawn, and with lower cost and more rewarding results.

"A field is supposed to be simple and pleasurable, not complicated," says John Trexler, director of Tower Hill, and his prescribed regimen bears out that philosophy.

A single mowing, timed after the first killing frost (late October or early November, in a typical year) is the mainstay of the field-management program at Tower Hill, headquarters of the Worcester County Horticultural Society, one of the nation's oldest horticultural organizations. The fallen material is left right where the tractor blades put it, and from it many seeds will serve as food for wildlife, or sprout over time, with the remaining debris gradually returning to the soil—all that isn't carried off by birds the next spring for nesting material, that is.

A system of paths is mown into the fields; again, says Trexler, keep it simple.

"Paths come about because you want to get from Point A to Point B. Follow the contours of the land and make the route as comfortable as you can—truly the path of least resistance." (If you have a dog, watch where it walks. It will define a path for you.)

Because there are almost no "problem" plants in the natural makeup of this field dominated by little bluestem (*Schizachyrium scoparium*), other maintenance chores are minimal. Poison ivy (*Toxicodendron radicans*) did move in, seeded around by birds when the fields were in pre–botanic-garden years. Now, after the bobolinks and other grass-nesters have finished their reproductive cycle (about August), gardeners attack patches by spot spraying with herbicide. (Poison ivy can also be cut down and dug out. Never burn the remains; the smoke is toxic.)

"Fields make ideal antechambers between one studied garden area and another," says Trexler, "a calming, uncomplicated habitat."

ABOVE: *Paths are mowed through the field to keep them open for visitors all summer.* RIGHT: *In fall, fading grasses and goldenrod enhance the foliage colors of the trees.*

THE TRIANGLE GARDEN
BROOKLYN, NEW YORK

NOW, HERE'S A STORY ABOUT those worst-case scenarios I referred to earlier. Even without a bucketful of the original topsoil or one living native plant within a twenty-mile radius, there is hope. I am especially familiar with disastrous sites, having gardened on a rooftop in Manhattan's SoHo district, and more recently in ground-level urban sites in Brooklyn.

On my old roof, many prairie plants proved especially well-suited to exposure to baking sun, wind, and the drought-simulat-

THE WORST OF TIMES

In a highly visible community garden, OPPOSITE, ABOVE, *quick color was a priority, so annuals and biennials were sown the first season. Plants used*

included, LEFT TO RIGHT FROM ABOVE, *the variable form of black-eyed Susan* (Rudbeckia hirta) *'Gloriosa' daisy; California poppy* (Eschscholzia californica); *another 'Gloriosa' daisy; and garden coreopsis* (Coreopsis tinctoria).

ing conditions of life in containers. The knowledge I gained there was helpful recently, when I was asked to develop a design for a triangular (one-hundred-by-eighty-by-sixty-foot) rubble-filled vacant lot near my city home that people wanted to turn into a park. Some local factions wanted a traditional community garden with vegetable plots, others a formal park, and so on, but when we discovered that the budget for the whole project was a hundred dollars, we agreed seeds were all we could afford. After trucking in clean fill of practically pure sand, provided by a local community-garden agency, some peat moss, and rotted leaf compost that we obtained free from a nearby municipal site, I bought a hundred dollars' worth of seeds of prairie-type plants that had thrived on my city rooftop. After all, I reasoned, this place was like a prairie—hot and dry in summer, freezing in winter.

The blend of seeds used wasn't what I would recommend in most cases, since it included such showy annuals as cosmos and sunflowers. However, with the whole community looking on, I figured we'd better have a colorful show the very first year.

The cosmos did prove to be a mistake, since they self-sow prodigiously in the following year, but they have faded for the most part as the garden has given way to American perennials like coreopsis and black-eyed Susan. In the third year, when the perennials took over, the garden was its best ever, and we hardly needed to water. Though our garden isn't a true prairie of grasses and forbs, I can assure you that whatever local wildlife had survived decades of asphalt confinement were happy to see even these familiar, if insufficiently diverse, floral faces.

Meadow-style plantings like the one at the Triangle Garden are probably the most popularized form of native-plant garden to date, and seeds and nursery plants for some of them have been available for a number of years. Growing more complete habitat gardens like most of the ones in this book, made up almost exclusively of locally appropriate native-plant species, has been a challenge until very recently. Today there is no excuse for a "meadow in a can" or a woodland underplanted in Asian astilbe species when reputable native-plant nurseries have become so widespread that there are outstanding vendors to buy from in every region.

P. CLIFFORD MILLER
LAKE FOREST, ILLINOIS

COMPARED TO MANY OF HIS clients' properties, landscape designer P. Clifford Miller's double city lot in Lake Forest, Illinois— a mere 50 wide by 270 feet deep—is confining indeed. But Miller, a proponent of the plant-community–based approach to landscaping, has managed to pack bits of several locally appropriate habitats into his environment nonetheless.

Beyond the house and garage is a patio, and then a bit of lawn —just enough to suit the recreational needs of Miller's small

LEARNING TO LET GO

Despite the confining scale of his small town lot, landscape designer P. Clifford Miller manages to have just enough backyard lawn for his

kids, surrounded by a miniprairie, OPPOSITE, TOP, *in which common milkweed* (Asclepias syriaca, ABOVE) *flourishes. He also has a touch of woods (with cimicifuga and ferns),* OPPOSITE, FAR RIGHT, *and even a small wetland in the form of a tiny pond, planted with blue-flowered pickerelweed* (Pontederia cordata) *and arrow arum* (Peltandra virginica), RIGHT.

children, no more. The turf is surrounded by a swath of miniprairie, and an electric fence; a group of pines and hemlocks forms a scaled-down north woods. He has a touch of savanna, a little ravine, and even a wetland, in the form of a small pond, with arrow arum (*Peltandra virginica*) and pickerelweed (*Pontederia cordata*)—truly a case of mixed ecological use in a small space.

Miller could develop any one of these miniature systems into a larger theme, he knows, but some plants are taking up too much room. "My problem is that like a lot of plantsmen I haven't let go of some plants," he says. "I have too many rhododendrons. I'm still attached to my Japanese maple and Kousa dogwood. I get more and more toward the natural every year, but I'm not there yet."

One thing that will help, Miller says, is when better forms of more native plants become available in the nursery trade. Although a growing number of nurseries are devoted to enlarging the native repertoire, production of natives still lags far behind that of "standard" landscape fare. "We've put billions into development of roses and carnations," he says, "but hardly a nickel into a *Viburnum lentago* that resists mildew."

**PRIVATE RESIDENCE
LAKE FOREST, ILLINOIS**

2.5 ACRES, PARK VIEW

This landscape's inner area, OPPOSITE, *at the front of the house includes a small lawn and a "collection" area of more traditional perennials such as Sedum 'Autumn Joy', with columbine, prairie dropseed, and other native wildflowers mixed in. In the field beyond,* ABOVE, *part of a park preserve established by the Lake Forest Open Lands group when the neighborhood was formed around it, yellow coneflower dominates the scene in summertime.*

SAFEGUARDING OPEN SPACES and building homes seem two pursuits in opposition, but that did not prove the case when the Lake Forest Open Lands group wanted to make a park on thirty acres of Illinois cornfield.

The creative solution: Instead of developing the whole parcel, the nonprofit organization coordinated the project, selling homesites on just half the land, with the proceeds establishing the rest as West Skokie Nature Preserve.

The owners were attracted by the possibility of building on a site adjacent to land that would remain open, and designer P. Clifford Miller, who also consulted on the park, helped them make their two and a half acres into a three-part landscape.

The property, a former bur

oak savanna, had become more "a jungle," Miller recalls, "with lots of invasive aliens." A portion is now modeled after savanna, and another section is an oak woodland.

The fact that such forward-thinking developments continue to be built is encouraging, stirring the hope that more and more people will eventually come to understand the ethic and aesthetic of habitat-style landscaping, where the homeowner is just one small part, instead of master of it all.

Closest to the house is a mix of popular herbaceous nonnatives like *Sedum* 'Autumn Joy'—the collection area. Even within these confines, prairie-region natives are represented. Echoing the parkland are prairie dropseed (*Sporobolus heterolepis*) and columbine (*Aquilegia canadensis*).

"They help carry the feel of the prairie right up to the front door," says Miller.

PRIVATE RESIDENCE
LAKE BLUFF, ILLINOIS

"A GOOD, ESTABLISHED PRAI-rie requires not much more expense than a matchstick once a year," natural landscape designer P. Clifford Miller is fond of saying, and then proving, to his incredulous clients.

At this private residence in Lake Bluff, Illinois, that statement proved particularly relevant, since the owners were thinking of installing lawn on the thirty-acre cornfield running down to the shore of Lake Michigan that became their yard. Or they were, at least, until Miller made them look at all the

WHAT PRICE, PRAIRIE?

The owners were going to sow seed for a lawn on the thirty-acre former cornfield that became their yard.

Instead, they planted a prairie with flowers such as goldenrod, ABOVE, *which now stretches to Lake Michigan,* TOP RIGHT, *to a lone giant oak,* ABOVE RIGHT, *the remaining trace of a onetime savanna. Wide pathways,* OPPOSITE, TOP, *provide access to the house,* OPPOSITE, BOTTOM.

possibilities and also the costs.

It would have been difficult or impossible to mow the steep slope leading down to the lake, and Miller also knew that the prairie plants could tolerate the strong breezes off the water and that he could count on their deep roots to hold the soil and prevent erosion.

"I explained that a prairie could go in for a lot less than it would cost to maintain that large a lawn each year," says Miller, who designed a meadow mix of prairie plants instead for the site, which was subsequently drill-seeded into the old fields. Goldenrods (*Solidago* spp.), prairie coneflower (*Ratibida columnifera*), big bluestem (*Andropogon gerardii*), gaillardia (*Gaillardia* spp.), and purple coneflowers (*Echinacea purpurea*) are just a few of the colorful members of the meadow.

At one corner of the largest

prairie where they are planted, a giant single oak tree is now a monument to the Wisconsin savanna, and a lone bench below it has become a place to contemplate the now-rare habitat.

Today, the owners do not listen to the weekly sound of mowers, or pay a lawn-maintenance bill. Nor do they have to buy and apply fertilizer and herbicides and other lawn-care supplies. Their landscape is now a healthier environment, not only for wild visitors but for domestic pets such as the family dog, too.

The meadow is basically on its own—all except for a match, to start the annual springtime burn.

PRIVATE RESIDENCE
AUSTIN, TEXAS

AUSTIN LIES BETWEEN THE two Texases, the richer woodland soils and the drier, hilly parts of the state. This private residence codesigned by Kay Wagenknecht-Harte and Environmental Survey Consulting had to take into account that blend of disparate elements, despite its tiny, half-acre scale. In all, 150 species of plants are represented.

Hints of prairie, savanna, and woodland came into play in what David Mahler of Environmental Survey calls "a combined land-

SUBURBAN SAVANNA

Under a natural canopy of native oaks and cedar elms, TOP RIGHT, *shade-tolerant shrubs, forbs, and grasses were planted,* RIGHT, SECOND FROM TOP. *Bold stonework helped to create*

workable areas from this hilly half-acre lot, BOTTOM RIGHT, *and even made a level for a bench,* ABOVE. *Shrubby cenizo* (Leucophyllum candidum), *with its silvery leaves and purple flowers, likes the sunnier spots,* RIGHT, THIRD FROM TOP. OPPOSITE: *The grass meadow muhly* (Muhlenbergia rigens) *and rich pink salvia* (Salvia greggii) *are featured accent plants.*

scape/habitat restoration." Existing large trees included Texas oak, shin oak, and cedar elm, and they were underplanted with shade-tolerant shrubs and forbs like Turk's-cap mallow (*Malvaviscus arboreus*) and grasses like northern, or inland, sea oats (*Chasmanthium latifolium*), whose seedheads are particularly ornamental.

Other principal grasses used among the more than twenty on the property include big muhly (*Muhlenbergia lindheimeri*), which makes a bold statement as a specimen or en masse, and little bluestem (*Andropogon scoparius* or *Schizachyrium scoparium*). Silvery-foliaged cenizo, a shrubby plant with lavender flowers, is striking against the bold stonework, and more color is created in the sunnier areas with bursts of liatris (*Liatris mucronata*), plateau goldeneye (*Viguiera dentata*), Texas bluebells (*Eustoma grandiflorum*), penstemon (*Penstemon co-*

baea), and wine cup (*Callirhoe digitata*). What Mahler calls "an active maintenance program" of selective hand-weeding helps them stay artfully clustered for maximum impact. Thinning, regular cutting back during dormant phases, and shaping are also done to enhance the visual appeal, he says.

"It would be too ragged for an in-town look otherwise," Mahler says.

The plant palette on the small front yard includes 150 species. CLOCKWISE FROM OPPOSITE PAGE, TOP: *Magenta berries of beautyberry (Callicarpa americana); Helenium amarum; northern or inland sea oats (Chasmanthium latifolium); long-blooming Salvia greggii; and the beautyberry shrub from a distance.*

OWEN CONSERVATION
PARK
MADISON, WISCONSIN

A PRAIRIE SHOWS ITS AGE—
to those who can read its wrinkles. Owen Conservation Park of the City of Madison, Wisconsin, is a living chronology of the early stages in succession of prairie plantings. Every couple of years since 1980, the park has added five acres to its prairie landscape. The thirty-five or so acres completed thus far form a timeline—from a mass of indistinguishable infant plants, to baby prairie full of medium-height flowers like rudbeckia and echinacea, to adolescents where

LIVES OF A PRAIRIE

The former caretaker's house, BELOW, *is the only trace of the farm that is now Owen Conservation Park. Today the land supports young prairies in*

various stages of succession. In summer, yellow coneflower (Ratibida pinnata) *and other sun-colored composites bask in the light,* NEAR RIGHT. *The older plantings,* OPPOSITE, FAR RIGHT, *have become more of a democratic planting of grasses and forbs.*

taller grasses and forbs have begun to arrive, to nearly adult prairies, with grasses like big bluestem dominating as the forbs wane.

Owen Conservation Park was prairie before the first settlers reached the area, naturalists speculate, but for more than a century, at least, it had been otherwise. The park is named for a former professor at the nearby University of Wisconsin, who in the 1890s bought the land as a summer retreat, raising pigs and other barnyard animals in a farmlike setting. The land was purchased by the City of Madison in 1972, and eight years later, once old fencerows of small trees (principally buckthorn, black locust, and Norway maple) were removed and prairie seeds were sown, the old fields of alien chicory, Queen Anne's lace, and daisies slowly gave way to prairie. Although the area had been grazed, and the smaller understory trees diminished, a nice

example of savanna, one of Wisconsin's rarest plant communities, exists on the property, and it is being rekindled.

Today, it is not barnyard animals but birds that inhabit the place, notably bluebirds, sedge wrens, yellowthroats, and, in spring and fall, woodcock and meadowlark. The prairies are managed principally by springtime burning, but seeds are harvested in fall and shared with other conservation parks undertaking the same kind of work. Care is taken to exempt a portion of the prairie from burning each time to protect a share of overwintering butterfly chrysalises.

On almost any summertime day you will see adult butterflies in abundance, and during their migration there is a special treat: hordes of monarchs roosting on the big oaks in the savanna near eveningtime, waiting until morning when the sun will warm them so they can continue on their journey.

A caretaker's house still stands on the site, but Owen's original home is long gone. Traces of him remain, though, in the form of vegetation: A lover of landscaping, he left behind many exotic plants, including a legacy of periwinkle in the surrounding woodlands.

SARA STEIN
POUND RIDGE, NEW YORK

AUTHOR SARA STEIN ISN'T
just a gardener, but a naturalist as
well. So when it came time to
begin landscaping the property
that she and her husband, Marty,
had bought in the late 1970s, one
of her inclinations was just to let
the lawn grow.

The results were beautiful. In
the first year countless "wildflowers" bloomed, and the second year was good, too. But
then Stein realized that something wasn't working. By the
third year, what had looked like
dainty flowers—oxeye daisy and

INTERPRETING THE LAND

*On a tiny man-made island in her
pond,* BELOW, *Sara Stein
plugged in prairie dropseed*
(Sporobolus heterolepis), *making
planting holes with a bulb planter, then*

*tossing in a little topsoil and a
young plant. Elsewhere, Stein is
hard at work turning old fields,*
TOP RIGHT, *into prairie-style
plantings,* OPPOSITE.
*Crabapples with small fruits to
attract birds are planted in a walled
garden,* CENTER RIGHT. *Among
her many successful birdhouses is a
cluster of hollow gourds,*
BOTTOM RIGHT.

Queen Anne's lace, for instance
—had joined forces with choking
thugs such as horse nettle, mug-
wort, Canada thistle, and bind-
weed to make a full-scale mess.
This was no way to create a
meadow, she realized; it had become a jungle of alien field
weeds. Only one native plant
was even represented, little
bluestem (*Schizachyrium scoparium*), a grass that her father called
"poverty grass" because it would
grow anywhere, even on the
poorest soil.

She decided to take the first
step toward making a real
meadow, the beginning of an experiment with native plants that
continues today.

Stein started by carefully preparing the site, eliminating all existing vegetation, then sowed
seeds that required some watering at first to become established.
Along the shore of a pond at the
rear of the property, plugs
(young nursery plants) were used

to speed erosion control. Swamp
milkweed (*Asclepias incarnata*),
Joe-pye weed (*Eupatorium maculatum*), New York ironweed
(*Vernonia noveboracensis*), and
sweet black-eyed Susan (*Rudbeckia subtomentosa*) were installed. Then, when the pond
was rehabilitated, the last bit of

clay dredged from the bottom was used to make an island.

"This is blue clay," says Stein, "devoid of anything organic. It turns to concrete when it dries." The Steins used a bulb planter on the island and made five hundred holes like clay flowerpots, into which they put prairie dropseed plants and store-bought bagged topsoil. "It worked—all of the prairie dropseed plants took and have grown into the hard clay."

The easiest kind of meadow to make is a monoculture of grass, like prairie dropseed or switchgrass, but that isn't the best kind, says Stein, who works instead with a variety of prairie grasses and forbs. Culver's root (*Veronicastrum virginicum*), rudbeckia, and liatris are just a few showy species she has sown. Since her Pound Ridge, New York, property has more rain and generally moister summers than true prairie country, this is more meadow than prairie, but she chooses those plants that will be as at home here as in Kansas.

To prevent succession to woodland from occurring in her meadows, Stein burns each section every third year (rotating this way spares two thirds of the butterflies and other overwintering desirables). It would take a day to burn the whole thing, she figures, meaning that all the work required to maintain these established sites is a day every three years.

Burning permits from the local health department are required, and Stein prepared her application carefully. Her explanation that she was growing protected plants helped sell the authorities and get her the permit.

The black gold left behind from the burn absorbs sunlight and warms the soil faster, waking the sleeping prairie plants as if by magic.

Sara Stein created a little woodland of native river birch (Betula nigra 'Heritage'), OPPOSITE, TOP ROW; *two European clump birch were delivered by mistake— without spraying, these two languished and died. Butterflies are drawn to asclepias, both the red (Asclepias incarnata),* ABOVE, *and orange (A. tuberosa),* LEFT. *There is much for the birds, too, including nesting boxes,* FAR LEFT.

NATIONAL WILDFLOWER
RESEARCH CENTER
AUSTIN, TEXAS

TEXAS BLUEBONNETS HAVE always had special status with flower lovers, and through the work of former First Lady and wildflower lover Lady Bird Johnson, fields of *Lupinus texensis* have become world-famous. The vast expanses of bluebonnets that burst into bloom each spring inspired her to initiate programs to beautify America and save such natural resources, work that culminated in 1982 in the formation of the National Wildflower Research Center in Austin, Texas, a nonprofit research and educa-

GRASS-ROOTS SUPPORT

There is more to the Texas growing season than spring bluebonnets; there are swaths of blanket flower (Gaillardia pulchella), ABOVE RIGHT.

Others, BELOW RIGHT, FROM LEFT, *include wine cups* (Callirhoe involucrata); *Indian paintbrush* (Castilleja coccinea); *and wands of* Liatris micronata *with yellow snakeweed* (Xanthocephalum dracuncerloides). *Cattle egrets,* ABOVE, *frequent nearby fields.*

tional organization and national clearinghouse of information on the preservation and reestablishment of native plants.

Bluebonnets do not a plant community or a season make; there is much more than that single April highlight to Texas's credit. Rare wine cup (*Callirhoe digitata*), Indian paintbrush (*Castilleja indivisa*), evening primrose (*Oenothera speciosa*), wild bergamot (*Monarda fistulosa*), snow-on-the-mountain (*Euphorbia bicolor*), Mexican hat (*Ratibida columnaris*), Maximilian sunflower (*Helianthus maximiliani*), Indian blanket (*Gaillardia pulchella*), purple coneflower (*Echinacea sanguinea*), prickly poppy (*Argemone* spp.), Mexican poppy (*Eschscholzia mexicana*), and standing cypress (*Ipomopsis rubra*) are just some of the other noteworthy sights.

The season in central Texas, including Austin, where the NWRC is headquartered, is a

long one, and unusual. After winter, there is a spring season of wonderful growth, then as the weather heats up to extreme intensity in June, many plants enter a period of semidormancy. Some have produced basal growth, as northern plants might in fall, so when things begin to cool in August, they send up flower spikes. This second wave may not be as showy as in spring, but is nonetheless a boon to gardeners who know how to use it.

A tour of nearby wildflower meadows yielded confirmation of the case for informed management of land. Land that was grazed continually had little or no floral show, save a blossom of thorny Texas bull nettle (*Cnidoscolus texanus*); areas that were fenced off and "protected" in the name of conservation also had little going on, and had moved a step or two along the path of succession to a shrubby tangle. Land that was lightly grazed was the most diverse of all—a strong point in favor of appropriate management methods. Land has never been unused or untouched —whether by bison, native people, or simply by nature, in the form of fire.

Teaching gardeners and others in the care of the land to simulate such natural-management strategies of American plants is a priority on the center's agenda. Through its journal, newsletter, fact sheets, and other publications, including a state-by-state list of recommended wildflowers for cultivation, NWRC helps its growing membership make a contribution to what it hopes will be an ever-larger native American landscape.

OPPOSITE: *The flower stalks of a variant of* Ipomopsis rubra, *the standing cypress, at the demonstration garden at The National Wildflower Research Center.* THIS PAGE, CLOCKWISE FROM BOTTOM: *Also displayed there are prickly poppy* (Argemone albiflora); *prairie verbena* (Verbena bipinnatifida); *purple coneflower* (Echinacea purpurea); *black Sampson* (Echinacea angustifolia); *Mexican hat* (Ratibida columnaris *or* R. columnifera); *and Texas bluebonnets* (Lupinus texensis).

JOE AND CAROLYN
OSBORN
AUSTIN, TEXAS

THERE IS NO LANDSCAPE plant more popular than turf-grass—lawn—despite all we now know about its wasteful, polluting habits. And we are as hooked on it as it is on water and chemicals. Without a lawn, the common lament goes, how do you make a landscape—and how do you make a lawn without mowable exotic grasses that guzzle resources?

Joe and Carolyn Osborn of Austin, Texas, are among a new breed of Americans who are having it both ways: They have their

A NEW AMERICAN LAWN

The Osborns have it both ways: the look of a traditional lawn, but one made of native buffalo grass (Buchloe dactyloides, *detail* BELOW) *that requires less*

mowing, watering, or fertilizing and remains green much of the growing season. The use of local stonework, TOP RIGHT AND OPPOSITE, BELOW, *adds to the natural character of the property. A trellis-covered walkway leads from the garage to the house (*RIGHT AND OPPOSITE, ABOVE*).*

traditional-looking lawn, but it is made up of native grasses that demand less water, fertilizer, and mowing—lawns that fit the profile of a natural habitat garden. Landscape architect Steve Domigan developed the plan for their yard, and Environmental Survey Consulting installed large-scale local rock to further enhance the natural character of the design.

The Osborns' lawn is buffalo grass (*Buchloe dactyloides*), a native plant whose range extends throughout the Great Plains states—roughly the middle third of the country and extending north to Canada and south into Mexico. It grows in alkaline, heavy clay, and other conditions.

The Osborns' buffalo grass lawn was installed as sod, which must be cut very thick to accommodate enough of the root system, making this an expensive but nearly instant method of coverage. Buffalo grass can also be installed as plugs, spaced about eight inches apart, or

seeded. However, some of the best varieties are not available as seed since they are vegetatively propagated to ensure consistency, such as all-female strains that create a denser appearance.

Now established, their buffalo grass is fertilized half the recommended amount in fall with an all-natural organic formula, and watered only as much as needed to keep it green (a twenty-minute soak two or three times a summer). If left unwatered, it will not die but will brown down to a dormant state. Although the Osborns still prefer to mow once or twice a season to keep the grass about six inches high, it can be left to grow to a somewhat shaggy foot and a half.

SALLY TAPPEN
LITTLE COMPTON,
RHODE ISLAND

THE LARGEST WETLANDS ON earth are the oceans, and yet, the land that lies along the coast is more like grassland or even dryland. Desiccating winds scrape across the shoreline, especially in winter. And scorching sun, reflected off the water, toasts unprotected plants. Sally Tappen is an accomplished and a fearless gardener, whose main passion is played out in a rock garden filled with a collection of plants arranged in a Japanese style. The rock garden is off to one side of the house—a bit protected from

LITTLE PRAIRIE ON THE HOUSE

When Sally Tappen needed to enlarge her family's summer home, she built down instead of up, BELOW, NEAR RIGHT. *But not to disturb the view, she created a version of a sod roof: a prairie*

planting with grasses and even blue lupines, ABOVE, ABOVE RIGHT, *and* OPPOSITE, FAR RIGHT—*perfect for the windy oceanside site. Imagine rooms hidden beneath the prairie,* BELOW, FAR RIGHT.

the harshest winds of this island off the coast of Rhode Island.

The house she lives in had been a summer and occasional weekend retreat for her family for years. When it was time for her husband, David, to retire, they decided to leave New York City and live here year-round. But the house was too small. Building up above the little cottage didn't seem right. And adding wings, left or right, would have eaten up the areas where she gardens.

The solution came to her as she was reading a building magazine. "I saw a house with a sod roof, and I called the architect immediately," she recalls. "I could have my house and save the view as well. I could even make it better." They decided to build down, right into the hillside on which the cottage stands.

The view stayed the same from the windows that look out on the ocean. However, when

you walk toward the sea and gaze back at the house, you can also see a series of rooms with huge windows that face the water. Instead of sod, Tappen guessed that a kind of prairie planting of low grasses and forbs would be the right choice. In this way, she could have a handsome foreground with color through spring to fall and golden grasses that blend into the horizon in wintertime.

Drought-tolerant and wind-resistant plants such as indigo lupines and tons of butter yellow coreopsis star in the little prairie on the house. This is a planting for eye-appeal, so red clover and daisies were permitted in the mix. The plants are naturally short, but the exposure to relentless winds dwarfs them as well. Sod or, more precisely, lawn would have been impossible to maintain in what actually is a rooftop container garden. But these plants need no feeding or watering, and best of all, only a once-yearly mowing in spring.

A bit of house was ultimately added on the level of the original building. It's a living room with a tall clerestory window.

"It just seemed right to have even more chances to enjoy the unending view of the water," says Tappen. And of the colorful flowers that introduce it.

DRY

The deserts are not worthless wastes. . . .

They are the breathing spaces of the West

and should be preserved forever.

~ JOHN C. VAN DYKE, 1901

COMPARED WITH A DESERT, OTHER DRYLAND communities may seem drenched. But anyone who has lived in, or more to the point gardened in, a California chaparral, or tried to coax life out of pockets in rocky cliffsides, knows that they are just as defined by their lack of water. Both of these, not just the desert, are examples of drylands, places that get twenty inches or less of rainfall a year. Deserts have to get by with less than ten.

The very word *desert* conjures up images of a vintage-film scene in which soldiers of the Foreign

The desert is far from a desolate place—on the contrary it teems with animal and plant life, RIGHT. *A cactus wren,* ABOVE, *the largest North American member of its family, surveys its domain from the flower spike of an agave and fills the air with its cacophonous chug chug chug chug.*

LANDS

Legion crawl toward a pool of water only to find it a cruel mirage.

In reality, a desert is hardly a wasteland, but a complex (if initially somewhat difficult to interpret) community of plants and animals. All but the harshest of our deserts teem with life: loud-mouthed cactus wrens perching on an agave flower spike, iridescent hummingbirds darting from hot-colored chuparosa to brilliant red penstemon, lizards scuttling across the griddle-hot earth without apparent discomfort, and denizens that protect themselves from the environment by appearing only at night, or not at all. America's deserts rarely conform to the Saharan cliché of pure sand and unrelenting sun. The Sonoran Desert in Arizona and Mexico, for example, has one of the world's greatest amphibian populations—a class of cold-blooded invertebrates usually associated with wetlands.

Eight percent of the nation or 300,000 square miles qualifies as true desert. North America's four major desert zones, stretching north as far as eastern Oregon and touching parts of Idaho, Wyoming, Utah, Colorado, all of Nevada, parts of California, Arizona, New Mexico, and right into southwest Texas, hardly make up a homogeneous landscape, however.

Evaporation rates also influence how dry a desert will be; dryness is influenced by temperature, wind, and other variables such as whether the sun appears on the days rainfall occurs. Elevation, too, plays a large role in dictating what grows in each of the various arid zones. For example, though rainfall is similar and both have hot summers, winter temperatures in Albuquerque can get twenty degrees colder than in Phoenix. A desert is not a desert is not a desert.

Dry places are also subject to another harsh reality: regular periods of drought—either seasonal, or longer. Months pass without any precipitation; even

a five-year span is possible. Los Angeles's last drought began in 1988–89 with only 4.56 inches of rain.

In each of our home landscapes, there may be dry spots, or niches, that are much tougher on plants than almost every other place. Learning to cultivate them as such with appropriate native flora is much more sensible than insisting on planting a thirsty variety and then constantly irrigating it, wasting our own labor and the earth's resources.

The need to conserve water will increase rather than decrease as time goes on. Scientists report that much of the nation, and the planet, is facing or will be facing the realities of drought and/or a shortage of clean, fresh water in the not-so-distant future—and not just typically dry places. In Florida, where the average annual rainfall is a generous fifty-five inches, some areas are already experiencing problems with saltwater infiltrating the water supply, because of a too-great human demand.

It is heartening to see the gradual emergence of the landscape philosophy known as Xeriscaping, a system of water conservation through creative landscaping developed in 1981 by the Denver Water Department. The name was later trademarked and given to the nonprofit National Xeriscape Council of Roswell, Georgia, which serves to promote the practice. In Xeriscaping, plants are chosen not just for regional suitability, but for use in the specific microclimate being landscaped. Turf areas are planted with species adapted to the local precipitation; irrigation is provided by the most efficient method possible, or in some cases even eliminated. (Antiturf ordinances have been proposed in the desert, but have yet to succeed.) There is great wisdom in the Xeriscape approach, but in one aspect it falls short. Native plants that have evolved under local rainfall patterns are best adapted for Xeriscaping but are not always preferred. In California, in particular, gardeners concerned

An iridescent hummingbird, TOP LEFT, *can always be found darting among tubular red flowers, while lizards skip across the hot desert floor,* TOP RIGHT. *Although the desert might be the first dryland that comes to mind, arid places exist all over the country. California coastal cliffs,* LEFT, *encounter desiccating winds and have little soil, resulting in equally parched conditions. The desert itself presents various environments—elevation plays a role. The low desert may have forests of tall saguaro,* BELOW FAR LEFT, *while the higher desert has a different vegetation due to its climate,* BELOW LEFT.

Kate Wyckoff of Beach Plum Gardens in Sag Harbor, New York, points out that seaside sites compound sandy soil with high winds to create arid conditions even in regions with adequate rainfall, such as coastal Long Island, RIGHT. Stabilizing the dunes is a difficult task. Often native dune grasses can be planted in the sand to fight erosion, ABOVE. Post oak (Quercus stellata) and eastern red cedar (Juniperus virginiana) are the dominant trees in this windswept site, BELOW.

about water consumption tend to work with Mediterranean plants—although as far back as 1920 researchers warned against these incredibly successful interlopers, with their massive seedbanks and choking growth habits, which make them successful "weeds." In California's lower elevations, where most of the principal cities lie, the nonnative percentage soars as high as 75 percent. Today, Australian and South American plants are also being touted as well suited to the dry regions of North America.

In Phoenix, the situation is even more critical. In this, the largest city in the United States situated in a desert, 80 percent of the residents are from elsewhere, and too many of them brought their stereotypes of alien landscapes along with their golf clubs. Lawn sprinklers pour gallons of water onto hot pavement areas, beyond the confines of the grass, where it quickly enters the air like steam from an iron. Popular Mediterranean natives and heat-radiating still lifes of rock and gravel punctuated by a token cactus or two are not appropriate desertscapes, any more than are manicured lawns.

Residents might take note of the gardening conversion experience of Dr. Robert Breunig, director of the Desert Botanical Garden in Phoenix, who decided to remove the nonnative vegetation from his typical homesite and grow desert wildflowers instead.

"I took out the lawn and the nonnative trees," says Breunig, "and at first it looked like a lot of weeds. But when the wildflowers really started coming in, the poppies and penstemons and campanulas and so on, my neighbors said, 'What are these?'

Dryland diversity, RIGHT, TOP TO BOTTOM: *thistle sage* (Salvia carduacea); *creosote* (Larrea tridentata); *prairie verbena* (Verbena bipinnatifida). FAR RIGHT: *The low-maintenance alternative to water-wasting lawn is a Phoenix wildflower "meadow," but it will need to have aliens weeded out.*

OPPOSITE: *Cacti may be known for their needles, but they all flower, and many, such as prickly pear, are beautiful. To conserve moisture, they evolved swollen stems and an absence of leaves.* ABOVE, LEFT TO RIGHT: *brittlebush* (Encelia farinosa); *saffron buckwheat* (Eriogonum crocatum); *desert marigold* (Baileya multiradiata).

"All were native Sonoran Desert plants, but not one of my neighbors recognized them. I realized at that moment the estrangement these people felt from the desert around them. I had to bring these native plants back into the city so that they could finally see them."

MODELS OF ADAPTATION

"Living in a desert isn't a sacrifice; it's adaptation," says botanist and water conservation specialist Kent Newland, who works for the City of Phoenix helping promote xeric landscape practices. And adaptation is what the botany, and biology, of the desert is about.

From the cracks of an urban sidewalk, where life couldn't be much hotter or drier, to a tiny pocket of soil on a sunbaked rock cliff, or a vast stretch of true desert, the plants that thrive in extreme conditions have much in common. Brittlebush (*Encelia farinosa*), desert marigold (*Baileya multiradiata*), and desert mallow (*Sphaeralcea ambigua*) are just a few of the plants that first come to mind as typical desert plants. All have gray foliage—a common sight in sunny, dry places, and hardly a coincidence. Light-colored fo-liage helps the plants reflect some of the sun's rays. Another telling quality about the leaves of these plants is that they tend to be tiny or even nonexistent. The most obvious example is the cacti, which have evolved with a modified stem instead of leaves. They conduct photosynthesis in this green "skin." Likewise, the bark of palo verde trees (*Cercidium* spp.) is a brilliant green.

Less leaf surface means less transpiration of water, and leaves made up of tiny separate leaflets, as is characteristic of many leguminous plants, is a good defense against an uneven climate. Large leaves are more vulnerable to water loss through evaporation; also a plant with leaflets can shed some in response to drought and heat—reducing leaf surface, but retaining enough to survive. Shrubs like *Calliandra eriophylla* and *C. californica,* fairy dusters, and the *Dalea* species fit this description. One, *Dalea greggii,* the trailing smokebush, makes an outstanding ground cover with its blue-gray leaves and purple flowers.

The arid zone landscape is generally of much shorter stature than other places we have looked at, another adaptation to winds and limited water. Acacias (*Acacia* spp.), mesquites (*Prosopis* spp.), desert willows (*Chilopsis* spp.), and palo verdes and leadtree

or golden ball (*Leucaena retusa*)—none of these trees gets very big. In the Sonoran Desert, for instance, the tallest native trees are in the twenty-to-thirty-foot range, meaning that the largest cacti like the saguaros (sah-WAH-ros) get tree status, at least visually. Ocotillo (*Fouquieria splendens*) provides another sharply vertical accent, but generally little grows much above eye-level.

Drought-resistant and drought-tolerant plants are commonly known to gardeners around the country, but the desert has an even cleverer category of plants: drought-avoiders. Over time, they have developed mechanisms for not being there, or not being vulnerable, when the driest days roll around. Plants that drop their leaves in hard times and go dormant—a trait called drought-deciduous—include ocotillo and palo verde. Within five days of a rainstorm, an ocotillo that looked dead can be leafed out and green again, as if by a miracle. In another example of adaptation, many springtime wildflowers simply time themselves to bloom and fade before the dry season thwarts their procreative energy.

Some plants have devised protective coatings like powder, down, wax, or hairs on their leaves to reflect the sun and to conserve moisture. The hairy foliage of Texas silverleaf (*Leucophyllum frutescens*) comes to mind—the selection 'Texas Ranger', developed by the breeding program at Texas A&M University in Dallas, is prized for its consistent appearance. Another favorite: *Eriogonum crocatum*'s chartreuse flowers are positively breathtaking against its tiny silver leaves. Chuparosa (*Beloperone californica* or *Justicia californica*) has tiny, finely hairy gray-green

CLOCKWISE FROM TOP, LEFT: *Leguminous woody plants include shrubby fairy duster (*Calliandra californica); *and trees such as honey mesquite (*Prosopis glandulosa); *mimosa (*Acacia berlandieri); *palo verde* (Cercidium microphyllum); *golden-ball lead tree* (Leucaena retusa); *desert willow (*Chilopsis linearis).

leaves and a brilliant display of red flowers that is irresistible to hummingbirds, hence the common name that is Spanish for the tiny, highly active birds.

Part of dealing with dry times is knowing how to take best advantage of wet times, which are often not just rainstorms but deluges. The giant saguaro cactus (*Cereus giganteus* or *Carnegiea gigantea*) of the Sonoran Desert can double its weight during a rainstorm. An intricate network of spongelike roots soaks up water before it rushes away in dry steambeds called washes, or arroyos, worn into the earth by years of runoff. Although they stand thirty or forty feet tall, saguaro roots extend only a foot or less below the soil surface.

Even on the steep hillsides of the Saguaro National Monument, where runoff must be almost instantaneous, these giants stand watch between rainfalls. They can live three hundred years, it was revealed when one called "Granddaddy" died in 1992. At over forty feet tall, it had more than fifty arms. Most saguaros don't put out their first arm till they are sixty years old, and some never branch at all. At five years old, a saguaro may be only half an inch tall; by twenty, barely a foot. At thirty, it finally flowers, only at night—welcoming nectar-feeding bats who pollinate the white blooms. Fruit soon follows, attracting the many birds who appreciate its red flesh. If that were not enough, the saguaro does even more to earn its keep as part of the complex desert environment: birds like Harris's hawks nest in cavities carved up high in its trunk. A model citizen, the saguaro is a symbol of what habitat-style gardening is about.

OPPOSITE: *During rainstorms, water runs off hillsides into the arroyos, or desert washes, becoming turbulent rushing streams that disappear almost as quickly as they form. The banks are often rich with plant life because of the additional moisture. Steve Martino, one of the leading landscape architects using native plants, says, "The wash is my favorite part of the desert; it's where the action is."*
RIGHT: *A several-hundred-year-old saguaro (*Carnegiea gigantea *or* Cereus giganteus*).*

A Desert Palette

When Desert Botanical Garden was founded in 1937, the 150-acre site was dedicated to the development of a natural garden of plants representing the deserts of the world. More than half the world's cactus species and succulents from almost every arid region are represented in the vast collection, which serves as both research and the inspiration and education of desert gardeners.

The philosophy of the Phoenix public garden has from the start allowed for certain nonnative plants. But when they are recommended for landscape use outside the living archive, the criteria become much stricter to prevent possible invasion by disruptive aliens.

Potential landscape subjects must "fit the visual ecology of the area," says Robert Breunig, director of the garden. "It's a very subjective, emotional type of thing."

Aesthetics aside, though, there is one hard-and-fast rule. "We always do a lot of soul-searching before introducing anything nonnative that could be a pest," says Breunig. "You always have to be very careful."

Plants Recommended for Desert Landscapes by the Desert Botanical Garden

Trees

Acacia schaffneri, twisted acacia
Acacia smallii, sweet acacia
Acacia willardiana, palo blanco
Celtis pallida, desert hackberry
Cercidium floridum, blue palo verde
Cercidium microphyllum, little-leaf palo verde
Cercidium praecox, palo brea

Chilopsis linearis, desert willow
Lysiloma thornberi, fern-of-the-desert
Olneya tesota, ironwood
Parkinsonia aculeata, Mexican palo verde
Pithecellobium flexicaule, Texas ebony
Prosopis veluntina, honey mesquite
Sophora secundiflora, Texas mountain laurel

Perennial Wildflowers

Baileya multiradiata, desert marigold
Melampodium leucanthum, blackfoot daisy
Oenothera spp., evening primrose

Penstemon parryi, beardtongue
Penstemon eatonii, beardtongue
Sphaeralcea ambigua, globe mallow

CLOCKWISE FROM TOP LEFT: *Golden barrel cactus* (Echinocactus grusonii); *ocotillo* (Fouquieria splendens); Agave vilmoriniana; *littleleaf cordia* (Cordia parvifolia); *a hummingbird at the Desert Botanical Garden.*

Shrubs

Atriplex lentiformis, quailbush
Baccharis sarothroides, desert broom
Caesalpinia gilliesii, yellow bird of paradise
Caesalpinia pulcherrima, red bird of paradise
Calliandra californica, Baja fairy duster
Calliandra eriophylla, fairy duster
Cassia spp., senna
Cordia parvifolia, little-leaf cordia
Dodonaea viscosa, hopbush
Encelia farinosa, brittlebush
Fouquieria splendens, ocotillo
Justicia californica, chuparosa
Justicia spicigera, hummingbird bush
Larrea tridentata, creosote
Leucophyllum frutescens, Texas ranger
Leucophyllum laevigatum, cenizo
Salvia greggii, autumn sage
Tecoma stans, Arizona yellowbell
Vauquelinia californica, Arizona rosewood

Ground Covers

Dalea greggii, trailing smokebush
Lantana montevidensis, trailing lantana
Verbena peruviana, Peruvian verbena
Verbena pulchella, verbena

Vines

Antigonon leptopus, queen's wreath
Mascagnia macroptera, yellow orchid vine
Merremia aurea, yellow morning glory vine

Succulents

Agave americana, century plant
Agave murpheyi, agave
Carnegiea gigantea, saguaro
Dasylirion wheeleri, desert spoon
Echinocereus engelmannii, hedgehog cactus
Ferocactus spp., barrel cactus
Hesperaloe parviflora, red yucca
Nolina microcarpa, beargrass
Opuntia basilaris, beavertail prickly pear
Opuntia engelmannii, prickly pear
Opuntia ficus-indica, Indian fig prickly pear
Opuntia violacea (*O. santa-rita*), purple prickly pear
Portulacaria afra, elephant bush
Yucca baccata, banana yucca
Yucca elata, soaptree
Yucca rigida, blue yucca

CLOCKWISE FROM TOP RIGHT: *Trailing smokebush* (Dalea greggii); *the garden's demonstration area;* Agave americana *and* Cercidium *spp.; bladderpod* (Cleome isomeris); *mature plantings at the garden.*

There has been some conjecture as to whether the oil-rich, alien eucalyptus tree leaves contributed to the severity of the 1991 fire in Oakland, California. According to eyewitnesses, "trees were exploding all over the place." Some slow-growing natives, on the other hand, are not strangers to fire. In fact, fire exposure is necessary for the germination of giant sequoia seeds. Xeriscaping is the rage in dryland areas, RIGHT, inspired by sites such as at the University of California, Berkeley Botanical Garden; "firescaping" is just beginning to catch on, ABOVE. Several native plants are fire-resistant or even fire-retardant, such as dwarf coyote brush (Baccharis pilularis *var.* pilularis). In general, keep dead wood and brush cleared away at all times, and select low-growing natives that remain green during seasons of greatest fire hazard, such as bearberry or kinnikinick (Arctostaphylos uva-ursi), BELOW. OPPOSITE: *Colorful annuals growing with spiny agave in a Xeriscape planting.*

DRYLAND TIPS

For aesthetics as well as the possibilities of shade, capitalize on bright light conditions by creating shadow pictures on the ground or on walls. Position particularly architectural plants like ocotillo, agave, and yucca so that the afternoon sun hits them most dramatically. Use the shade to expand the plant repertoire.

"Microclimate is very important in the arid environment," says landscape architect Carol Shuler of Arizona. "For example, shade pockets in the landscape can support very different plants than other spots, and what grows on the north and south side of a berm will be very different."

Sometimes, dryland landscapes need supplemental water to thrive, but it should be applied in the most efficient way possible and also at the right time. Shuler advises her clients to water well in early June, and then around midmonth, to help plants be prepared for the hottest, driest part of the season and avoid desiccation.

Professional horticulture of the desert is very young; new varieties are being released all the time. Native-plant demonstration gardens are one of the best sources for up-to-date information on the selections best suited to your region and where to obtain them.

CAROL SHULER AND
KENT NEWLAND
CAVE CREEK, ARIZONA

WHEN LANDSCAPE ARCHI-
tect Carol Shuler and botanist
Kent Newland married, it was
the beginning of a great cactus
empire: Their cherished collections merged to become one, and
now the plants share the spot-
light in the couple's outdoor
environment.

At the back of the house, the
cactus collection is like a living
sculpture garden. The bizarre,
spiny forms of the hundreds of
specimens mimic the greater
desert around them.

Sometimes, large specimens

GIFTS TO THE GARDEN

*A palo verde tree
underplanted with penstemon,*
BELOW, *grows outside the
walled entry garden, as does
the aloe hybrids collection,*
OPPOSITE. *Inside the walled*

*area at sunset, the petals of
birdcage evening primrose*
(Oenothera deltoides),
ABOVE RIGHT, *unfurl in a
matter of minutes. Kent
Newland's "collection
garden,"* TOP RIGHT,
grows in pots behind the house.

outgrow their pots and are integrated into the landscape, particularly shrubby types of prickly
pear (*Opuntia* spp.) that grow to
three to five feet tall. "Their
round pads make a nice contrast
with the other desert plants,"
says Shuler, "and they have big,
colorful flowers."

In true scientific style, Newland groups the potted cacti by
genus—all the mammillarias together, for example—on the
deck area behind the house.
When a particular plant or group
is in its flowering season, he
shifts it to a better viewing point
on the raised, stepped platform.

The cacti are as much part of
the couple's landscape plan as
their enclosed front courtyard
garden of butterfly plants, where
each evening from March to
May a family ritual centers on
the unfurling birdcage evening
primrose flowers (*Oenothera deltoides*).

Landscaping of the 1.25-acre

property with flora of the Sonoran and other nearby deserts is a
year-round family endeavor—
even at Christmastime. Each
year, a live desert tree—a screw-
bean mesquite, a sweet acacia, a
palo verde—has first acted as the
Christmas tree, and then settles
into the outdoor landscape, underplanted with muhlenbergias
and other native grasses.

Some have found their way to
prominent status in what Shuler
calls their "mesquite bosque," a
little homemade forest of *Prosopis*
species that promises to fill in
with Christmases to come.

CINDY AND STEVE
LESHIN
PARADISE VALLEY,
ARIZONA

WHY CINDY AND STEVE
Leshin's Paradise Valley home is
set so far back into its one-acre
lot is not immediately clear, especially not to one new at desert
ecology. But it is the lay of the
land—of the washes, specifically,
those dry streambeds through
which water rushes in wet times
—that is the law here. An existing wash, which cannot be altered even to build a house,
determined the siting.

A few foothills palo verdes
(*Cercidium microphyllum*) and old

AWASH IN COLOR

The staghorn cholla (Opuntia
acanthocarpa) *has a handsome
habit,* TOP RIGHT;
translucent spines, SECOND
FROM TOP; *and beautiful
flowers,* THIRD FROM TOP.

Plantings, BOTTOM RIGHT
AND ABOVE, *have been
arranged to frame views.*
OPPOSITE: *The entrance to the
property with red chuparosa*
(Justicia californica),
*yellow brittlebush and
desert marigold, and
violet* Verbena rigida.

saguaros were all there was to
work with when the Leshins
hired designer Carol Shuler to
landscape their property more
than ten years ago. Mesquites
and acacias were among the trees
she added to the design, in which
she carefully protected a startling
view of the nearby Camelback
Mountain, framing it with well-
placed boulders and plantings.

To contend with the awkward
setback, Shuler flanked the am-
bling driveway with a mix of
shrubs and herbaceous plants,
which at its farthest edges becomes somewhat thicketlike—
creating ideal cover for birds,
which the Leshins had indicated
was one of their top priorities.
Creosote (*Larrea tridentata*), a
common sight in the American
desert with its olive foliage and
yellow flowers, and various
sculptural cacti are among the
components of the area. *Atriplex
lentiformis* (quailbush) brought in
the quails; orioles are drawn by
the aloes figured into the plan.

Today, a wildflower display of pink, coral, rust, and red desert mallows (*Sphaeralcea ambigua*), purple-flowered *Verbena rigida*, red penstemons, and fiery chuparosa (*Justicia californica*) makes the drive's edges lively spots for hummingbirds and butterflies.

Even rabbits and bees are especially appreciative of several nonliving elements: what Cindy Leshin calls "bird waterers," simply large glazed terra-cotta pot saucers sunk into the soil, leaving the lip above the surface. They are hooked into an irrigation line for replenishment, reliable oases in an unpredictable habitat.

OPPOSITE: *A young mesquite tree frames a view of the colorful plantings. Pink evening primrose* (Oenothera speciosa), LEFT, *is planted under flowering yuccas.*

ABOVE: *A wonderful trellis covers the front of the house. Landscape designer Carol Shuler sheltered the house with plantings for a sense of privacy in a setting of wide-open spaces.*

CLIFF AND MARILYN
DOUGLAS
MESA, ARIZONA

GUARDIANS IN RESIDENCE

RIGHT: *Few home landscapes are as site-sensitive as this desert oasis. Many specimens were carefully preserved on the property, and many others were brought in*

to create this place in which people and plants have equal rights. Some are as familiar as creosote bush (Larrea tridentata). Others are extraordinary, such as Opuntia violacea, *with colorful pads,* ABOVE.

IT IS AS IF A HOUSE, PATIO, pool, and guest cottage had been parachuted in, dropped gently into a patch of pristine desert without stirring up even a puff of dust.

That the end product should look like the five undisturbed acres they purchased in 1982 was the precise intention of Cliff and Marilyn Douglas, but it was not accomplished by any such simple —or aerial—means, rather by simple hard labor. Aided by landscape architect Steve Martino, who helped create an out-door scene to suit the home designed by John Douglas, the owners' son, the Douglases set out to save every plant in situ.

They shepherded through the construction process every cacti, creosote (*Larrea tridentata*), bur sage (*Ambrosia deltoidea*), ocotillo (*Fouquieria splendens*), chuparosa (*Justicia californica*), wolfberry (*Lycium fremontii*), and other natives that could be saved in place, and relocated countless others.

Today, ten acres have been added to the spectacular parcel of land in central Arizona, along with more than a few plants— some seventy-five trees, numerous specimens of fifteen species of prickly pear (*Opuntia* spp.), many of them indigenous to the Sonoran Desert, others native to other similar deserts of the world. A favorite, autumn sage (*Salvia greggii*), is from the nearby Chihuahuan Desert; its tubular red blooms brighten the landscape much of the year, delighting hummingbirds—when

they are not feeding in the branches of the desert willow (*Chilopsis linearis*) or Arizona yellowbells (*Tecoma stans*). With only seven inches of rainfall, the Douglases' garden is nevertheless a paradise.

Plants were neither saved nor added to the site for their visual effect alone, but for their enjoyment by wildlife. Seeds of mesquite trees (*Prosopis* spp.), for instance, are favored by squirrels and by peccaries (a wild nocturnal mammal related to the pig). Perhaps most unforgettable are a number of centuries-old saguaro cacti (*Carnegiea gigantea* or *Cereus giganteus*) that stand guard over the place, at thirty feet or more

at once sentinels and combination birdhouses-feeders.

Less evident are the baby saguaros. Cliff Douglas gestures to a visitor to come closer and share the secret, bending down to poke around under a bur sage. There, in the protective custody of the shrub, is a tiny saguaro.

"I've been watching this one for five years," says Douglas.

LEFT: *Tinted stucco walls offer a colorful foil for sunlight and foliage.* ABOVE: *A curved wall contains a planting and borders the walk to the front door.* OPPOSITE: *Viewed from the other direction, this destination is seen through an ocotillo.*

CULTIVATED PRESERVATION

*ABOVE: Ground covers—
silvery camphor dune
tansy (Tanacetum
camphoratum), native to San
Francisco, and sea fig
(Carpobrotus chilensis) from
Baja. OPPOSITE: Faded
fronds of the California fan
palm (Washingtonia filifera)
persist to cover trunks.*

BOTANISTS CONCERNED WITH conserving native flora often lament that California is already a lost cause. Of the nearly 3,000 plant species that are threatened or endangered in the United States, 680 are Californian, and a frightening share of the state's current flora is exotic. However, the commitment of many residents to their indigenous flora is equal to their legendary love of the great outdoors—the California Native Plant Society is probably the most active in the nation.

Rancho Santa Ana Botanic Garden was founded in 1927 by Susanna Bixby Bryant. It is primarily a botanical research and educational institution, offering a graduate degree in botany. The director, Dr. Thomas S. Elias, is one of the investigators into sources of the anticancer drug taxol, now made from the western yew and its relatives.

Conservation is another aim of the garden. Members believe that such facilities are like the best zoos of the world: repositories of endangered species as a small step toward stopping extinction. Fortunately, plant breeding in a simulated environment is usually easier than with such animals as the California condor, though not without risks.

The collection, which moved from historic Rancho Santa Ana in Orange County to Claremont in 1951, has grown to be not just a living catalog of southern California plants, but coincidentally also one of water-wise garden

plants. Nearly 40 percent of the state's precious water supply is used outdoors, in the landscape. Now, the testing, development, and promotion of natives for landscape use will become a major goal. Sophisticated seed collecting and storing, sowing, and growing techniques have yielded one hundred natives never before seen in cultivation, and nursery areas are being enlarged to support this effort; nearly sixty new ornamentals have been introduced by the garden to the nursery trade.

In the California Cultivars Garden, the rolling lawn at the entrance isn't grass at all but low-growing manzanitas (*Arctostaphylos* cultivars) selected for drought-tolerance and eye-appeal. Elsewhere, native Douglas irises, which vary in nature, have been selected for flower size and color, proving to home gardeners that

there can be as much beauty in rugged natives as in ornamental exotics. California lilacs (*Ceanothus* spp.) figure prominently because of their profuse blue flowers, but are important landscape and wildlife plants, too, producing needed cover and berries. Low-growers prevent erosion and reduce loss of soil moisture; taller ones make good screens. Fremontias (*Fremontodendron* spp.), the state shrub, and Oregon grape hollies (*Mahonia* spp.) are also cultivated and promoted.

The cacti and succulents on the eighty-six-acre grounds, usually attract the most attention—except, perhaps, for the ever-present scurrying lizards. Most plants here bloom in early spring, following late-winter rains, and quickly attract pollinators and set seed before the hot, dry season begins.

ABOVE LEFT: *Douglas iris* (Iris douglasiana) *at the lower pool.* ABOVE RIGHT: *The state flower, California poppy* (Eschscholzia californica). OPPOSITE, LEFT TO RIGHT, TOP TO BOTTOM: *California's state shrub, flannel bush* (Fremontodendron californicum); Aristolochia californica; Heuchera maxima; *California blue-eyed grass* (Sisyrinchium bellum); *coastal tidytips* (Layia platyglossa); *hedgehog cactus* (Echinocereus *spp.*).

EARTHSIDE NATURE
CENTER
PASADENA, CALIFORNIA

MANY DRYLAND PLANTS, much like the brilliant alpine meadow flora, burst into bloom at the earliest chance in spring to attract pollinators, set seeds or fruit, and quickly wrap them in tightly sealed pods—"frozen" until the next moment of moisture appears.

Kevin Connelly of Arcadia, California, has learned from the plants how to take advantage of wet times in dry places, too, and following their cues he has made wildflower gardens since 1975.

IN THE COMMUNITY SPIRIT

OPPOSITE: *One of California's many legumes, Bentham's or spider lupine* (Lupinus benthamii), *native to Los Angeles, presents a cascade of blue flowers among*

other showy natives such as deep pink owl's clover (Orthocarpus purpurascens *var.* ornatus) *on a hillside.*
ABOVE: *Sea dahlia* (Coreopsis maritima) *is a perennial native of coastal southern California.*

At Earthside Nature Center, a two-acre garden only for natives founded in 1971, Connelly and naturalist-author Elna Bakker work with more than color combinations in mind. Though the place is positively brilliant, what was first in the gardeners' minds was a desire to see plants with their natural companions.

To that end, desert bluebells (*Phacelia campanularia*), desert dandelions (*Malacothrix glabrata*), and pink lupines (*Lupinus arizonicus*) conjure up images of the Colorado desert washes they all hail from. In a section of the garden devoted to coastal species, the medley is blue-violet *Phacelia parryi,* red-violet *Lupinus hirsutissimus* and *Salvia leucophylla*— beautiful, but also true to nature.

The two-acre site is mostly flat, but at the edge of it, pathways zigzag down a dry hillside of many small plantings, some punctuated by succulents. Tidytips (*Layia platyglossa*), blue-eyed Mary (*Collinsia verna*), baby

blue-eyes (*Nemophila maculata*), and California poppies are just a few of the colors of this rainbow. Earthside has a spontaneous exuberance, but the gardener's hand is there—not just behind the plantings, but most of all in the unseen weeding, since the red bromegrass, wild oats, and white mustard must be removed the moment they sprout.

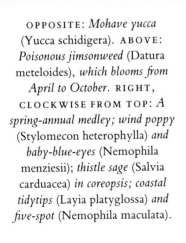

OPPOSITE: *Mohave yucca* (Yucca schidigera). ABOVE: *Poisonous jimsonweed* (Datura meteloides), *which blooms from April to October.* RIGHT, CLOCKWISE FROM TOP: *A spring-annual medley; wind poppy* (Stylomecon heterophylla) *and baby-blue-eyes* (Nemophila menziesii); *thistle sage* (Salvia carduacea) *in coreopsis; coastal tidytips* (Layia platyglossa) *and five-spot* (Nemophila maculata).

ARIZONA–SONORA
DESERT MUSEUM
TUCSON, ARIZONA

SINCE 1952, THE ARIZONA–
Sonora Desert Museum has been
teaching visitors about desert life:
how the plants (more than
twelve hundred species are represented in the collection) and
the animals (more than two hundred species) share the arid-
zone habitats re-created on the
grounds. It is a kind of outdoor
interpretive center, like the best
of contemporary zoos but for
both flora and fauna.

A demonstration home garden
area applies the lessons of the desert to a specifically human scale,

LIVING THE DRY LIFE

answering what is certainly the
principal question: how to have a
water-wise landscape, and still
make it beautiful.

There are some nonnative
plants in the demonstration area,
including ones that help fill the
midwinter gap in color common
to plants of the area, but nothing
so inconsistent with the scale of
the Sonoran Desert flora as pines
or eucalyptus is used. Care is also
taken to avoid the use of nonnative grasses, since grasses, with
their wind-dispersed seeds, are
known to be real opportunists,
and alien species would quickly
become environmental weeds,
staff botanists know.

The demonstration area, then,
is a kind of ongoing experiment
in the desert—the trying out of
new plants, new design ideas,
and new cultural tactics. In the
desert, a region developed relatively recently compared to other
parts of the country, horticulture
is a very young business, and

new plants are being tested and
promoted regularly to keep pace
with the growing interest.

At ASDM, with its roots
firmly anchored in science, it
seems that the process of ques-
tioning and learning will never
stop. Should there be walls
around a home garden, as are
common in many other suburban backyards of the nation? Or
should outdoor spaces here be
left open to the incredible views
that are the very character of the
desert? What plants fit into the
scheme, and can they be propagated successfully, and then easily grown?

The museum's mission is a lot
like a garden, which just keeps
evolving season after season but
is never quite done.

BELOW: *A pot of saffron
buckwheat* (Eriogonum
crocatum). RIGHT, TOP TO
BOTTOM: *Ideas for the home
landscape in a naturalistic*

*planting among rocks. Orange
and red flowers bloom on
cultivars of* Salvia greggii.
OPPOSITE: *Walls and
paving contain a handsome
planting in the home
demonstration garden.*

WET

What would the world be, once bereft

Of wet and wildness? Let them be left,

O let them be left, wildness and wet;

Long live the weeds and the wildness yet.

~ GERARD MANLEY HOPKINS

EVERY HABITAT IS DEFINED BY WATER. EVEN the harshest desert is described in terms of water's scarcity. Wetlands—places where water is relatively plentiful for all or part of the year—are among the earth's most productive ecosystems in terms of biological output (of both plant and animal life) for two reasons: because the sun's energy is stored by the water, and because in most wetlands, decomposition is quite efficient, so "used" materials get broken down and recycled quickly.

That wetlands rival the richest farmlands in productivity is hardly what the American government was saying when it passed down the order to "re-

In spring, swamp pink (Helonias bullata), ABOVE, shoots up a flower from a flat basal rosette. It is endangered because its habitat is vanishing. RIGHT: The vernal pool at Tower Hill Botanic Garden usually dries up by summer, but some years it's still wet through fall.

LANDS

claim" 65 million wet acres in the middle of the last century. Draining wetlands to make farmland or some other "productive" form of acreage was a misguided mandate of our emerging nation, a policy that some estimates say led to the loss of more than half the wetlands that existed when the settlers arrived in what is now the United States. A 1992 estimate, more conservative but nevertheless dismal, set the figure at 99 million acres lost from an original total of 240 million.

Despite our heightened awareness of wetlands, they remain our most imperiled habitats. In the late 1980s, various environmental groups placed the annual rate of loss at anywhere from 300,000 acres to as much as half a million (at the same time the federal government was promising, in 1988, no net loss).

Beyond the numbers, the word *swamp* is still far from summoning up images of a diverse wet woodland with exquisitely rich soil, instead of a mosquito breeding ground. Someday a prospective homeowner may gaze upon the low, damp spot in his new backyard and say "My dream bog garden come true!" but it is still more often "Bring in the bulldozer!" Incorporating water into our landscapes can serve as an object lesson for all of us, though, and will begin to make us all champions of wetlands.

"Rather than 'wastelands,' wetlands are really wonderlands," says JoAnn Gillespie, proprietor of Country Wetlands Nursery in Muskego, Wisconsin, who has been committed to the cause of these fragile and misunderstood systems for more than fifteen years. "The [wetland] plants aren't endangered," she says. "The ecosystems are."

The grassy marshlands, RIGHT, *are disappearing at an alarming rate. Wetlands, among the most threatened habitats, are prime for exploitation: They are flat, which is good for development; have great recreational possibilities; and are filled with resources such as edible species and water itself. But the tide is beginning to turn.*

Until relatively recently it was virtually open season on wetlands. Even in the "enlightened" years of regulation, it appears that still almost no one really wants one in his or her own backyard—the nursery business for wetland plants is in its infancy, far behind the rest of the nursery trade. Ed Garbisch of Environmental Concern, St. Michaels, Maryland, whose industry-leading firm has undertaken 350-plus large-scale wetlands projects, says that virtually all of them were performed because the law required that the landowner do so. "Only four of three hundred fifty projects in twenty years were voluntary restorations," he reports.

These great living systems make life possible. Some contribute to the water table, helping recharge groundwater reserves; others filter pollutants or remove sediment, mediate floods, and perform many other feats we too often fail to appreciate. That ignorance simply must change.

"We need to think of wetlands as amenities, not aggravations," says Michael Hollins, a wetlands ecologist from Envirens, Inc., in Freeland, Maryland. Indeed, too many landscapers and builders still drain wet areas or level them with fill rather than delighting in them as is.

"I do not do my gardening beside a marsh, or even have a pond," you may be saying, but no matter. This chapter is for every gardener, since each of us thinking of landscaping in the habitat style must commit to including water in his or her design. The smallest elements, mere mud puddles and water collected under a downspout, or a little homemade garden pool, can help in at least a token way to begin to reconnect the cycle of life in a place that is otherwise sadly incomplete. Even when it's accomplished in anything but a scientific manner—a brimming stock tank of waterlilies beside the barn—water works.

When a plan for a garden is begun, professionals start with what is called "the program." It is simply the needs and desires of the people who will use the landscape. Some might assign space for a swing set or a barbecue pit top priority, but for me it was a water feature. The presence of water, particularly when combined with cover and an abundance of fruiting plants, makes even my tough city lot attractive to wildlife and gives the garden a habitat character it would not otherwise possess.

TOP LEFT: *Wetlands are wonderlands, not wastelands.* CENTER: *A small waterfall in the Scanlon garden in Texas. Every bit of water brings sights, sounds, and birds. This simple ornamental cistern,* RIGHT, *at Skylands, the New Jersey State Botanical Garden in Ringwood, is a welcome stopping place for birds.*

My pool is home to my exotic fish called Koi—a kind of carp bred by the Japanese from German and Asian stock. Today, I might not recommend stocking even an isolated pool with such exotic creatures, but I think of my fish as a collection, the way another person might collect hostas.

Introducing these fish, however pretty and responsive to human attention that they are, to a wild pond or stream would be a disaster, since they root around the bottom, stirring up muck and clouding the water, which can damage the environment for other fish.

Even though my pool is anything but a natural wetland—it has a PVC liner and a pump and filter—it is the pulse of the garden. The fish gobble insects, the water is home to frogs, and a favorite place for birds—many more species and numbers than are attracted to any neighborhood bird feeder in any season. Toads, too, have found the moist, rocky edges of the pool, and eat slugs and other pests.

I have found a source for native fish, and would like to try some. In the future, I would limit the

plants around the pool to species that would be found in a wet environment in Brooklyn. There must have been plenty, the Dutch having named it "broken land" for its patchwork of wet and dry places. Already, I have some moisture-loving native Americans in my repertory, with buttonbush (*Cephalanthus occidentalis*), cardinal flower (*Lobelia cardinalis*), bog rosemary (*Andromeda glaucophylla*), jack-in-the-pulpit (*Arisaema triphyllum*), marsh marigold (*Caltha palustris*), ferns, and mosses among them. I have never had much luck with waterlilies (the carp like them, too), but there are handsome native species to be grown, including the fragrant one (*Nymphaea odorata*). (A fuller complement of water and wetland plants appears later in this section.)

For those whose gardens are larger than twenty-one by fifty feet, wetland-simulation plans can be even more ambitious. Start by analyzing all the potential water resources on the property: the rain and melted snow that run off the roof, the sump area where excess moisture is collected, even those depressions in the yard that simply never drain well after a shower. A large piece of land with a storm-water pond would make an ideal wetland garden.

Craig Tufts, director of the backyard wildlife habitat program of the National Wildlife Federation, is a

TOP LEFT: *Turtlehead* (Chelone lyonii) *is a herbaceous plant that loves the streamside.* CENTER: *Living things abound, and frequent inhabitants include amphibians, such as this toad.* RIGHT: *Stepping-stones span a pool made with a plastic liner that graces a central Texas garden.*

OPPOSITE, ABOVE: *Joe-pye weed* (Eupatorium maculatum) *is one of the best plants for moist soil and sunny places that are flooded at certain times of the year.* OPPOSITE, BELOW: *A pink cultivar of sweet*

pepperbush (Clethra alnifolia 'Rosea'). LEFT: *The swamp-loving buttonbush* (Cephalanthus occidentalis). ABOVE: *The silvery blue butterfly "mud-puddling." Most butterflies gather around standing water, and some have been observed "spitting" into dry soil, it is believed, to extract salt.*

good model for wetlands gardening. Instead of watching all the roof runoff at his suburban Virginia homesite flow wastefully across the lawn and into the curbside drains, Tufts created his own little marsh.

Someday, Tufts says, he'll live next to a real marsh. In the meantime, he's enjoying the added dimension his homemade minimarsh has brought—large numbers of butterflies "mudpuddling" on the moist soil, a wider diversity of birds, and amphibians, too, plus the potential to grow wet-loving plants like pickerel-weed (*Pontederia cordata*), sweet pepperbush (*Clethra alnifolia*), wafer ash (*Ptelea trifoliata*), and silky dogwood (*Cornus amomum*) to name just a few.

The process of creating the marsh was no more difficult than preparing for a perennial border or any other new garden area. After deciding the outline and location, Tufts lifted the sod (about 450 square feet of it) and excavated down to just over a foot deep.

To one of the downspouts from his gutter system, he connected a piece of flexible plastic pipe so that the water could be directed down and away from the house, via a ditch, into the top of the marsh basin. He had to experiment with the angle and the position of the pipe after the first few rainstorms, and he back-filled with clay to slow downward percolation, until the moisture-holding capacity of the basin and the movement of water from the pipe were what he wanted.

Then, using a tiller on the site he mixed up some "marsh soil"—lots of peat, some sand, compost, and much of the original subsoil he had excavated, and

ABOVE: *A well-tuned New England pond in autumn includes various life-forms, from tiny bacteria and microscopic animals to the cattails at the water's edge. Wetland meets woodland,* OPPOSITE. *The places where habitats meet, in this case the riparian edge, are often where the most complex communities flourish.*

lined the uneven basin with an even layer of this mix so that some areas remained deeper than others. Rainwater no longer washes across a useless lawn to become part of the sewer system; it moves slowly "downstream" toward a handsome stand of Joe-pye weed, which blooms in late summer.

Tufts chose to create a wet place by using roof runoff; for other gardeners, a good moisture supply already exists in the soil. Particularly in the East, a seasonally moist or low-lying field may become a wet meadow. Wild irises, Turk's-cap lilies, cardinal flowers, and milkweeds are just a few of the many colorful plants that would thrive under these conditions. Likewise, certain woodland environments are damp enough to support plants classified as wetland species. If water moves through your property in the form of a brook or stream, or if a pond already exists, you are among the luckiest ones. Some examples of wet meadows and wet forests will be seen later in this chapter to help you determine if such an opportunity is hidden on your property.

Even when a natural wetland exists, there may be work to be done, too—what would be called enhancement in the wetlands business, gently helping the system to achieve a better state of health. No action should be taken without prior investigation, however; always consult with a wetlands professional and read local guidelines first.

Kate Tyree of Watermill, Long Island, developed two ponds on what were unproductive low, sodden parts of her property. When the land had been developed, the disturbance created had favored a number of weed species, and she wanted to correct that at least in part. Her motivation was to create a beautiful, healthy water garden in areas that were choked with invasive exotics.

PLANTS FOR WET PLACES

Many thousands of distinct species of plants are associated with wetland systems, including a large share that adapt to wet, medium, or even dry soil. Some of my favorite shrubs are on that list, including sweet pepperbush (*Clethra alnifolia*), with fragrant white midsummer flowers and good gold fall color. The form 'Rosea' has pink flowers. Few plants can rival the autumn display of Virginia sweetspire (*Itea virginica*), with fragrant late spring flowers and then a fiery red autumn look. The selection 'Henry's Garnet' is especially brilliant.

The swamp azalea (*Rhododendron viscosum*) is another wet-soil winner, with very fragrant white springtime blooms. Inkberry (*Ilex glabra*) makes dark blue-black fruit in fall and is pleasingly evergreen. Its relative, winterberry (*Ilex verticillata*), is a deciduous holly and serves up bright red fruit. The berries of highbush blueberry (*Vaccinium corymbosum*) are followed by a red fall foliage show and finally by a glowing red cast that the new canes take on in winter. *Cephalanthus occidentalis*, buttonbush, is a delight when in flower, producing odd ball-shaped creamy blossoms about an inch in diameter. The flowers of the sweet bay magnolia (*Magnolia virginiana*) are creamy white with a citrusy fragrance, and are followed by bright red seeds in fall.

Blue flowers are among the gardener's most treasured subjects, and in moist places there are many standouts. Perhaps no genus produces more remarkably blue blossoms than the gentians (*Gentiana* spp.). These late-blooming herbaceous perennials—great season-extenders for the native garden that seem almost immune to frost—do well in moist soil.

About the most common, and easiest to grow, is the closed or bottle gentian, *Gentiana andrewsii*, with flowers that appear to be perpetually in bud. They never open, but a tiny hole at the tip permits entry by pollinators.

Great lobelia (*Lobelia siphilitica*) is the tall blue-flowered cousin of cardinal flower (*L. cardinalis*), each among the most desirable flowering perennials of wet places, including wooded riverbanks, marshes, and wet meadows.

Another choice blue-flowered plant is pickerel rush or pickerelweed (*Pontederia cordata*), a denizen of slowly moving water. Pickerelweed, which creates thick colonies of spear-shaped foliage, also does well in a pond or pool; it can be confined in a bucket or tub. The long-blooming, skyward-pointing floral spikes give a decided vertical emphasis to the water garden.

Many other water plants might be called architectural, and could be grown as much, if not more, for their foliage than for their flowers. Though each flower may last a day or two, the forceful swordlike foliage of the iris family is present throughout the growing season. Most gardeners know German iris or Siberian iris, but the northern hemisphere is rich with iris species, including many outstanding native Americans that rarely appear as horticultural subjects. Louisiana and California, in particular, have fine native species.

A familiar iris is blue flag or wild iris (*Iris versicolor*), which grows from two to three feet high in full sun in moist soil, and even adapts to partial shade along the edges where forest meets wet meadow. In the northeastern quarter of the country, its lavender, violet, blue-violet, red-violet, or (rarely) white flowers are a familiar May-to-July sight in wet meadows. A similar species, *I. prismatica*, has grasslike foliage and is a bit shorter. The red or copper iris (*I. fulva*) is found blooming in late spring from Illinois to Georgia.

Acorus, or sweet flag, a member of the arum family, also bears irislike foliage. It has an insignificant brown spadix, a fleshy floral spike containing hundreds of tiny flowers. The species has little to recommend it as an ornamental, but a variegated selection, *Acorus calamus* 'Variegata', with

ABOVE, LEFT TO RIGHT: *Closed or bottle gentian* (Gentiana andrewsii); *sweet bay* (Magnolia virginiana); *great blue lobelia* (Lobelia siphilitica). LEFT: *Fall interest from swamp rose mallow at Rock Rim Ponds in New York;* RIGHT: *Seed pod detail.*

vertical creamy yellow stripes against grass green, is striking.

Most arums have spathes (covering hoods) like a jack-in-the-pulpit (*Arisaema triphyllum*) and are happy in wet areas. There is a native calla lily, *Calla palustris* or water arum. (The tropical plants called calla lilies are in the genus *Zantedeschia*.)

The very early blooming skunk cabbage (*Symplocarpus foetidus*) has a ruddy brown hood that completely engulfs the spadix and moderates temperatures inside, though snow may still cover the ground. The interior temperatures may be as high as seventy degrees, a factor that appeals to pollinators. The skunk cabbage is better known for its large, fleshy green leaves—a true sign of the American spring. The distinctive epithet relates to the smelly nature of the leaves when crushed. Unbruised, the leaves have no malodorous drawback to dissuade gardeners. The large, waxy hood of the western skunk cabbage, *Lysichiton americanum,* recommends it as an ornamen-

tal and appears in midspring before the giant elliptical leaves unfurl.

By contrast, the golden club (*Orontium aquaticum*) has no spathe at all, just a pollen-covered spadix. In the early spring, the plant appears as a cluster of white candles dipped in bright yellow paint. Soon, waxy green leaves sprout around them that are completely water-repellent.

Some of the arums have characteristic arrow-shaped leaves. Arrow arum (*Peltandra virginica*), so called for its attractive, fifteen-inch-tall foliage that grows from a rhizome without stems or branching, imparts a tropical feeling to a watery planting.

Arrowhead (*Sagittaria latifolia*) has edible tubers that were cultivated by Native Americans as food, and is also one of the most handsome species for an aquatic habitat garden. Complementing its shiny foliage, spikes of showy white three-petaled flowers with yellow anthers are produced midsummer to fall.

Lizard's tail (*Saururus cernuus*) could be grown for its

lush, spade-shaped foliage but also boasts curious fuzzy flower spikes that lend its descriptive common name. Peltandra, sagittaria, and saururus like to grow covered with about a foot of water.

At one time, a trip to a bog or marsh, the drainage ditch along a roadside, or beneath a bridge would have revealed exceptional flowering plants, and even today you may sight the garden-worthy *Chelone* spp. (turtlehead) or the gaudy flowers of *Hibiscus moscheutos* (swamp mallow). More often than not, however, you'll come upon acres of *Phragmites australis,* or giant reed, a plant with worldwide distribution that unfortunately takes advantage of many wet situations, particularly in disturbed areas, and chokes out everything else. An even more noxious plant, an alien, never fails to elicit as many oohs and aahs from the uninitiated as a fireworks display. The plant that has supplanted most other wet wildings in northern sunny places is purple loosestrife (*Lythrum salicaria*).

In the 1980s growers

claimed that the hybrids sold on the commercial market were sterile (and I showed them in *The Natural Garden*), but apparently some hybrids produce pollen viable enough to cross with wild stands and create even more tenacious offspring. It is disappointing to see the plant for sale in a nursery today, but even worse to see it in the border of a gardener who should know better.

Some plants called loosestrife, however, such as fringed loosestrife (*Lysimachia ciliata*), have gardenworthiness and far less potential for disaster. *L. ciliata*'s pretty yellow flowers last for several weeks, but what's best is the maroon-leaved selection, *L. c. purpurea*, a colorful foliar accent for the damp garden or native border.

This summary of the beauties of the wet would be incomplete without a mention of a particular favorite of mine, swamp or red milkweed (*Asclepias incarnata*). It is an essential in the repertory of every habitat gardener with a moist spot—gorgeous, and an important butterfly host plant, too.

ABOVE, LEFT TO RIGHT: *Indian pond lily* (Nuphar polysepalum); *western skunk cabbage* (Lysichiton americanum); *marsh marigold* (Caltha palustris). LEFT: *Hardy water canna* (Thalia dealbata). RIGHT: *Arrowhead* (Sagittaria latifolia).

She could simply have cleared out the unwanted plants, including lots of multiflora rose, and encouraged the "keepers" from among the existing wildings, but she went a step further and also excavated to create the ponds. She then encouraged the natural plant cover from sedges (*Carex* spp.) and rushes (*Juncus* spp.) and moisture-loving shrubs like winterberry (*Ilex verticillata*), which also provides wildlife food in the form of berries.

By opening up the space and making the ponds, mosquito and fly populations have been reduced. Air circulation is better, and more animals seem to be able to make use of the area. A functioning wetland, with a system of insect and animal predation intact, will not be an insect breeding ground. Stocking the ponds helped, since fish feed on the bug population while also attracting hungry herons and the like.

Besides maximizing food and cover from natural features, Tyree erected man-made houses for the birds. She and her neighbors, who have followed Tyree's lead and created ponds on their properties—now there are five in the immediate area—have had

ABOVE: *One of America's most versatile and beautiful shrubs, winterberry* (Ilex verticillata), *revealed by Kate Tyree to best advantage.* RIGHT: *Tyree also capitalized on the wet lowland behind her house by scooping out two ponds—linked by a waterway, spanned by a bridge.*

UP WITH INSECTS

The most evolved form of wildlife gardening is gardening to lure insectivores, designing your landscape deliberately to attract spiders, birds, and small mammals like bats, moles, and shrews along with toads, frogs, and fish (the latter, of course, only where feasible). Once you begin to appreciate the workings of the food chain, as the savvy insectivore gardener does, planting for a continuous bug buffet will be far from repellent, and instead seem the most natural way to garden. Without insects, there is no food chain, without the food chain no life. Suddenly pollen plants, nectar plants, and host plants (the preferred diet of larval forms of various moths and butterflies) start to head your list of desirables.

Someone ought to rewrite the books on plants for wildlife so they list the plants that insects prefer. Perhaps prairie ecologist Neil Diboll says it best: "Like birds?" he quips. "Then you better get used to bugs."

the good fortune of attracting aerobatic troupes of purple martins. Catalogs offer multiple-dwelling martin houses, promising that they're a sure thing for attracting these voracious insect-eaters. But Tyree knows the most important element to lure and keep these special swallows is water.

The gardener's role in the protection or development of the wetland habitat could be seen as an unnatural intervention. Yet wetlands are often in varying states of transition, evolving because of weather, changes in the water table, human impact (pollution, dredging, etc.), and even a natural element like fire, which affects certain wet systems, too.

Some wetlands are only seasonally wet—flooded in the spring, for example, and then dry in the warmer months. At Tower Hill Botanic Garden in Massachusetts, a wildlife garden was created around a seasonal wetland, technically called a vernal pool, where red maples dominate the magical low-lying point in the landscape where the wet meadow meets the forest.

Some wetlands are freshwater, others salt; some have currents, some tides, and in still others the water moves very little.

With all these disparate qualities, it is difficult to define wetland simply. Many professional organizations, from the Army Corps of Engineers to each recent presidential administration, have offered versions. Generally accepted is this one: wetlands are places where the soil is saturated at least seven consecutive days a year, and/or where the water table comes within a foot of the surface and stays there for seven days a year. In other words, wetlands are all around us.

OPPOSITE, ABOVE: *A familiar "good guy," daddy longlegs.* BELOW: *Purple martins are attracted to bird-apartment dwellings placed near water. They consume countless mosquitoes.* LEFT: *Fern crosiers and skunk cabbages—spring in the wetland at Garden in the Woods.*

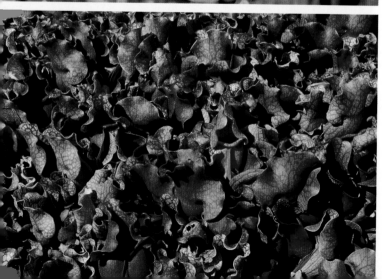

CARNIVOROUS PLANTS

Some plants grow in places where the soil is so acidic and nutritionally poor that they have evolved other ways to get nourishment to survive. Carnivorous, or meat-eating, plants live on insects. Many are native Americans, from the Venus flytrap (*Dionaea muscipula*) of the Carolinas to the cobra lily (*Darlingtonia californica*) of the West Coast. Only 3 percent of their habitat in the United States remains.

Carnivorous plants have specialized attracting and trapping mechanisms that make them good hunters. Some stalk and snare passively: pitcher plants (*Sarracenia* spp.), for example, have vaselike leaves lined with downward-facing hairs. Victims finding their way into this "pitcher" cannot turn back and eventually make their way to a pool of water collected at the bottom, where they drown. Others are active, like the sundews (*Drosera* spp.), which react to contact with prey by actually moving. The best-known active hunter is the Venus flytrap, a "steel-trap" type plant. Carnivorous plants also have the means of digesting what they catch—with the aid of bacteria, enzymes, or both.

Flytraps and cobra lilies sold as little hothouse novelties don't make good houseplants. Most have a requirement for winter dormancy, and want more humidity than an average home can provide. Climate-controlled terrarium collections are a possibility with the cobra lilies, but they do best in outdoor bog gardens in northern California, Oregon, and British Columbia.

The carnivorous plants that hold the most promise for home habitat gardeners are the pitcher plants. Among the species to consider are pale pitcher (*Sarracenia alata*), yellow pitcher (*S. flava*), white trumpet (*S. leucophylla*), and the naturally occurring subspecies northern pitcher (*S. purpurea* subspp. *purpurea*) and southern pitcher (*S. purpurea* subspp. *venosa*).

The sarracenias hybridize freely—constantly pushing the boundaries of evolution. A collection of *Sarracenia leucophylla* will soon exhibit variations in leaf color and flower as surface-sown seeds sprout and grow. This white trumpet looks delicate with its tubular leaf, flared and hooded at the top and etched with red and green veins. This plant, little-known to American horticulture despite its native status, is grown as a popular cut flower. Actually, it's the leaves that are used. This is the species to try in Zones 7 and south. *S. flava* is alleged to be hardy in Zone 7, too,

TOP TO BOTTOM: *A fading autumn leaf (pitcher) of the yellow pitcher plant or huntsman's-horn* (Sarracenia flava); *S.* flava *with flowers; southern pitcher plant* (S. purpurea *subspp.* venosa) *in a dense planting at the Atlanta Botanical Garden.* OPPOSITE: *The northern pitcher plant* (S. purpurea *subspp.* purpurea). OVERLEAF: *A marshy field of blue flag iris* (Iris versicolor) *and cinnamon ferns* (Osmunda cinnamomea) *in Rhode Island.*

but it grows happily at Garden in the Woods in Framingham, Massachusetts, in Zone 5. (In severe climates enthusiasts report that they mulch with straw and pine needles and boughs up to a foot thick over winter.) Right up into Zone 3, the hardiest candidate is *S. purpurea* subspp. *purpurea*, named for its flower color though its leaves, too, are tinged purple.

If their needs are met, pitchers are not hard to grow in a boggy site, natural or man-made. Keep the crowns at the surface, above the normal water level, and give them sun—six hours or more in the north, a bit less in the south, where they will tolerate some shade. Generally speaking, grow them in an acid medium like sphagnum moss, or sphagnum mixed with peat. *Sarracenia purpurea* subspp. *purpurea* is more tolerant of a pH closer to neutral than the rest, which may prefer a mix of sphagnum and peat with one fifth coarse sand. Water with collected rain, and don't worry about fertilizer —they won't need any.

Pitcher plants can be increased by division once you have a stand of your own, or from seed, and I am encouraged to see that some native-plant nurseries are growing them ethically this way to offer to gardeners. Kim Hawks of Niche Gardens nursery in Chapel Hill, North Carolina, for example, has obtained seed from curator Rob Gardner of nearby North Carolina Botanical Garden and is offering both *purpurea* and a variable mixed species with genes from *flava, leucophylla,* and *purpurea* for a vivid display.

GRASSY PLANTS FOR THE WET

Many grasses are adapted to regions of the country with hot, dry summers like the prairies, but there are grasses for wet areas in gardens, too. Salt-marsh cockspur (*Echinochloa wateri*), variegated manna grass (*Glyceria aquatica* 'Variegata'), variegated ribbon grass or gardener's garters (*Phalaris arundinacea* 'Picta'), and fowl meadow grass (*Poa palustris*) are among them, and another is an important wildlife food and favorite of human gourmets—*Zizania aquatica* (wild rice).

Often, though, what look like grasses in the wet are really sedges, rushes, or other plants. Grasses have round, hollow stems with solid joints. Rushes, too, have cylindrical stems, but sedges have angular ones, hence the naturalist's mnemonic "Sedges have edges, rushes are round." As their uses for home landscapes are explored, many of these will certainly become important ornamentals, but perhaps their greatest asset, especially in the wetlands, is as food and cover for wildlife.

Rushes are members of the *Juncaceae* family, and al-though numerous plants are called rushes, they frequently turn out to be sedges—another example of why common names fall short. Several true rushes, members of the genus *Juncus,* are attractive in flower: *Juncus tenuis* (path rush), a swampland species, has full flowerheads with graceful bracts on two-foot plants. *J. gerardii* (black grass) is from the salt marsh, with magenta flowers and fruits that make it appear brown from afar.

Sedges are members of the *Cyperaceae* family. They have very ornamental flowerheads that are formed like umbrellas above triangular stems, particularly apparent among plants in the genus *Cyperus*. The *Scirpus* genus, which includes bulrushes, encompasses beautiful grass-like plants.

Carex is the sedge genus that shows the most promise for future home landscapes. I have seen carex growing by the woodland edge in Pennsylvania, some deep in shade in Illinois, and still another in full sun in Texas, where it was used as the dominant plant in a deerproof garden.

The tussock sedge (*Carex stricta*) is just what it sounds like: a big hummock, or tuft, of a plant—a handsome specimen, and unforgettable en masse. A sedge meadow during the relatively dry season may appear as a humpty-dumpty terrain. The fresh growth emerges each spring when the water is high, but because it is produced on top of the tussock, it is spared from "drowning."

I have seen eleocharis growing in drainage ditches by the Ithaca, New York, airport and in a roadside trench alongside a bluestem prairie in Austin, Texas, but this same plant is sold for a pretty penny in water-garden catalogs. *Eleocharis acicularis* (spike rush, or fiber-optic plant, in California) is a favorite grassy plant.

Cotton grass (*Eriophorum virginicum*), another sedge, has wonderful woolly puffs above straight stems. Cattails (*Typha* spp.) also form cottony masses when their seedheads ripen. Besides making fine wildlife food, they are favorite nesting perches for the red-winged blackbird, which attaches its nest to last year's flower-stalks.

ABOVE: *Soft-stem bulrush (Scirpus validus); sedges in rows at Country Wetlands Nursery.* RIGHT: *A great blue heron takes off in the marsh.* OPPOSITE, ABOVE: *Giant reed (Phragmites australis);* OPPOSITE, BELOW, *Nursery owner JoAnn Gillespie's license plate.*

WETLAND TIPS

Relatively few wetland restoration firms work on the residential scale—as a rule, they talk in square miles, and wear scuba gear when they work.

But you don't need fancy equipment to plant a home-sized wet meadow, or make a small water garden with an inground plastic liner, soft or rigid. Restoring a large submerged wetland or developing the littoral zone, or wet edge, can be more rigorous, but even these can be undertaken by gardeners.

To increase the wildlife potential of a pond by developing its edge plantings, what Country Wetlands Nursery of Wisconsin calls aquascaping, keep these considerations in mind:

Determine the appropriate plantings by noting the size of the pond—its open area and water depth. Observe the contours of the edge and slope toward the water. What is the water course; how often does it flood; how long do areas remain submerged? What is the nature of the soil? What plants are there now?

Only use native, noninvasive plants. That means that although giant reed (*Phrag-*

mites australis) is indigenous, it is too aggressive to introduce. Never use purple loosestrife (*Lythrum salicaria*) or reed canary grass (*Phalaris arundinacea*), either. If you want cattails, for wildlife food value, remember that they can get out of hand.

Use started plants for residential applications; seeding is much slower and can frustrate the beginner.

Check purchased nursery stock carefully. Too many growers ship wetland plants covered with undesirable hitchhikers, like duckweed (*Lemna* spp.). Rinse the plants before introducing them.

Plant sparsely. Wetland plants are great colonizers. Use a diversity of species, and plant the way nature does with several of one kind in clusters, not rows.

Plant the higher ground first as a hedge against settlement and instability of the edge soil. After these are established, there will be less danger of losing plants placed closer to the water.

In spring, remove undesirables when young and easy to grab. In fall, cut off and discard seedheads of undesirables before they ripen and blow around.

THE NEW YORK
BOTANICAL GARDEN
NATIVE PLANT GARDEN,
WET MEADOW
BRONX, NEW YORK

VISITORS TO THE NEW YORK
Botanical Garden's Native Plant
Garden meadow in April may
think the wooden viewing tower
looks decidedly out of place—
who needs an elevated platform
to observe barely six inches of
unidentifiable scruff growing out
of the ground? But come August, the tower provides an
amazing perch for surveying the
likes of New York ironweed
(*Vernonia noveboracensis*), Joe-pye
weed (*Eupatorium maculatum*),
and cup plant (*Silphium perfolia-*

IT'S WET AND WILD

*The wet meadow at the New York
Botanical Garden is the home of
many plants that love this
environment, including turtlehead
(Chelone lyonii),* BELOW, *and*

*the magnificent swamp rose mallow
(Hibiscus moscheutos),*
OPPOSITE, *with Joe-pye weed.*
RIGHT, TOP TO BOTTOM: *In
1993, permission was granted for a
rare spring burn; the same area in
summer; a familiar common cattail.*

tum), each topping out at up to
eight feet.

The quarter-acre meadow in
the Bronx is wet, particularly in
spring, which has dictated the
maintenance schedule. Were the
gardeners to wait until spring to
mow down last season's spent
growth, they might lose a tractor
in the mire. So the meadow is
typically mown around Thanks-
giving, but only after seeds have
ripened and been dispersed. The
debris is allowed to decompose
on-site.

Then, in late April and early
May, the emerging meadow is
mown twice more with a light-
weight push mower, effectively
retarding the flowering time by a
week or two and also promoting
stout, storm-resistant stems. The
later it flowers, the longer the
flowers remain, since at night-
time temperatures are generally
cooler. Care is taken to time the
mowings before the Turk's-cap
lilies (*Lilium superbum*) and false
indigos (*Baptisia pendula* and *B.*

australis) are in active growth, since neither of these important members of the community can tolerate mowing.

A third, and final, mowing is undertaken in mid-May to cut the pathways that allow visitors to move through the planting.

If it weren't mowed (or burned—not the easiest thing to accomplish in the middle of a city environment), the meadow would begin to evolve into woodland. A meadow is a transitional community, and human maintenance—in this case mowing—is what stops the natural succession from proceeding, by preventing young woody plants from getting a hold on the area.

Sometimes, exceptions have to be made in the schedule to accommodate unexpected developments in the meadow itself. The use of heavy mowing machinery season after season has resulted in some areas of soil compaction, for instance, which must be addressed and not aggravated further. And in recent years a parasitic plant called dodder, which looks like a tangle of orange string, has invaded the area, threatening the desirable plants. In order to eliminate the dodder, which twines around a host plant and intercepts food and water from its tissues, the gardeners have been mowing less and doing more hand cutting to eradicate it. All debris is removed during this period, because so much of it contains dodder, too.

By August the wet meadow is in its prime—and the viewing tower is not only right in scale with the planting, but also the best seat in the house.

The meadow is perhaps most beautiful in mid- to late summer— a time when flower gardens have usually passed their prime. TOP: *Cup plant flowers turn to equally ornamental seedheads.* CENTER: *The cardinal flower's cousin, great blue lobelia (Lobelia siphilitica).* BOTTOM: *Joe-pye weed and cup plant (Eupatorium maculatum and Silphium perfoliatum).*

ABOVE, TOP TO BOTTOM: *The meadow in autumn; the birdhouse was a gift to the Native Plant Garden; Carolina rose (Rosa carolina) has single pink flowers in summer, but grow it for the birds—they love the hips.* OPPOSITE: *The meadow as the birds view it—above the sweet gum (Liquidambar styraciflua) treetops.*

Plants that grow in the drier areas surrounding the wet meadow would be welcome in any flower garden.

OPPOSITE: *The NYBG gardeners call a hill near the entrance "the prairie." Among the plants that grow there are members of the mint family* (Labiatae, *typified by square stems), including pink false dragon's teeth or obedience* (Physostegia virginiana); *the buttons of faded wild bergamot* (Monarda fistulosa); *and the multitiered horsemint* (M. punctata). CLOCKWISE, FROM ABOVE: *Northern (or inland) sea oats* (Chasmanthium latifolium); *a view toward the "prairie"; and the scene from within it; sneezeweed* (Helenium autumnale); *floral wands of southern* Gaura lindheimeri; *the aromatic foliage of sweet fern* (Comptonia peregrina), *a deciduous shrub; New York ironweed* (Vernonia noveboracensis).

PATTI GOLDSTEIN
LONG ISLAND,
NEW YORK

DIVINING INTERVENTION

Patti Goldstein was inspired by her neighbor, Kate Tyree, to transform the sodden ground behind her Long Island house into a naturalistic pond, OPPOSITE. *To stabilize the*

edge, she transplanted shrubs and perennials from adjacent thickets. A mowed path cuts through this shaggy hedgerow and leads to a bridge of her design, ABOVE, *that crosses to an island.*

"I ONCE SAW SOME OLD PIC-tures of this place," says writer Patti Goldstein about the Long Island property she shares with Sandra Powers. "There was water here—probably an inlet that connected the bays—but I guess that was before the roads were put in." However, she didn't need that confirmation to know there was water here; it was always muddy. Inspired by her neighbor, Kate Tyree (page 141), Goldstein decided to try to make a pond.

"We just dug down six inches, and it was water." The pond was dug with a backhoe, and it was done quickly, forming a quarter-acre pond fed by two natural springs. "There was a willow tree in the middle of the site, and I didn't have the heart to cut it down, so I decided to make an island to save the tree." Gold-stein's West Highland terrier, Wallis, claimed the island for herself.

Herons and egrets visit fre-quently. The pond was stocked at the outset to control mosqui-toes, but now there are some fish that weren't introduced. "I guess they came as eggs on duck feet, or something." An air pump at-tached to a bubbler oxygenates the water in summer for the fish. Three merganser ducks also made the pond home. And the property, named Rabbit Run, has its share of bunnies.

The balance of nature can seem daunting. Along with the wel-come pets, there have been un-welcome pests. The muskrats are the worst. "There's a natural muskrat run back there. We can't have waterlilies—they eat them all." Still, Goldstein is unwill-ing to exterminate. "The ship-ping lanes are open. We just have to learn to live together," she says. There are a few other problems. Algae can really get going in a hot summer. Aqua-shade is a product that is like "sunglasses" for the pond. It dyes the water blue, excluding some sunlight from the depths. "It looks like Lake Como; but the color dissipates quickly." Fortifying the pond edge has also been a concern. At one place, a large naturalized plant-ing of fiddlehead ferns (*Osmunda cinnamomea*) runs down to the water. Mallows (*Hibiscus moscheu-tos*) have filled in well with their overseer's help, and most of the rest of the edge is held by what amounts to a hedgerow of Joe-pye weed, goldenrod, rhodo-dendron, phragmites, and *Rosa multiflora*.

Some problems seem to solve themselves. For a while, there was a family of Canada geese on the pond. Geese have benefited from all the development on Long Island; they used to mi-grate, but many are now year-round residents. "At first, they were so cute—just like rubber duckies in a bathtub. But then they turned into adolescent gangsters, rooting, honking, messing up the place. Then they suddenly departed. They're mo-nogamous, and I guess one of the parents must have died. Now only an occasional kid comes by for old-times' sake."

THE BLOEDEL RESERVE
BAINBRIDGE ISLAND,
WASHINGTON

"THE BLOEDEL RESERVE IT-self should be an example of man working harmoniously with nature; where his power to manage is used cautiously and wisely," wrote Prentice Bloedel, in archival material in The Bloedel Reserve collection. His vision over several decades turned a former family estate on Bainbridge Island, Washington, into a splendid sanctuary glorifying both gardens and nature. Today, the reserve is open by appointment, managed by the Arbor Fund that was set up for the purpose.

WISDOM IN THE WOODS

Creating an attractive environment for birds has always been one of the goals of the Bloedel Reserve. The bird marsh, RIGHT, *is a managed wetland habitat. Red alders (*Alnus rubra *or* A.

oregona), *the dominant trees, are thinned from time to time, and several flowering and fruiting shrubs, such as the white spring-blossoming thicket serviceberry (*Amelanchier canadensis), ABOVE, *have been planted.*

It was appropriate—if perhaps a bit ironic—that the estate stood on cutover forest land, logged by a former owner. The Bloedels were longtime members of the lumbering industry, too, and in their life among the former forest they learned a new relationship to trees, walking the old logging roads of the land where they had come to live.

"We discovered that there is grandeur in decay," wrote Bloedel about such forays into the young mixed conifer-hardwood stand, "the rotten logs hosting seedlings of hemlocks, cedars, huckleberries, the shape of a crumbling snag. . . . Out of these experiences came an unexpected insight," he continued. "Respect for trees and plants replaces indifference; one feels the existence of a divine order. Man is not set apart from the rest of nature."

The reserve is by no means a purely native landscape; formal areas include a Japanese garden,

and a long reflection pool flanked by lawn and framed by hedges. Even more arresting than these handsome features is the moss garden—though man-made, it evokes the character of a rain forest like the greater landscape of the Pacific Northwest. Paths are safe and dry, but the visitor still feels that at any moment he or she might sink ankle-deep into the sodden carpet—warm slippers formed by stalagmites of pure jade.

Habitat for birds has long been a point of emphasis on the property. When trees were thinned, trunks were left standing up to fifteen feet to attract cavity-nesters. A university ornithologist advised designating a bird sanctuary around a pond dotted with alder islands, a carpet of ferns and sedges thriving beneath the trees. Once, it had been choked with cattails, but now it is a more balanced community with open water that birds can move through easily. Native blood currant (*Ribes sanguineum*), western azalea (*Rhododendron occidentale*), red osier dogwood (*Cornus stolonifera*), and moosewood viburnum (*Viburnum edule*) are among the plants used to enhance the site.

OPPOSITE: *A unique double western* Trillium ovatum, *discovered in 1949, grows in redwood sorrel (Oxalis oregana). The Moss Garden,* TOP RIGHT, *is home to the deer fern (Blechnum spicant).* CENTER RIGHT: *The western skunk cabbage (Lysichiton americanum) glows among tree trunks,* CENTER LEFT AND BELOW, *where hemlocks (Tsuga heterophylla) are shrouded by the thick carpet.*

PRAIRIE DOCK
LAKE FOREST, ILLINOIS

TURTLES SUN THEMSELVES on the little island in the pond at Prairie Dock, a private home in Lake Forest, Illinois, where waterfowl also like to stop and scout out nesting sites.

Neither the pond nor the island existed when the owners hired designer P. Clifford Miller to make the most of their wet, five-acre homesite, but their creation has been central in the success of their habitat, both aesthetically and in wildlife-value terms. A boardwalk runs from a deck outside the back door of the

ISLAND IN THE POND

Yellow-flowered prairie dock (Silphium terebinthinaceum), BELOW, *lent its name to this rejuvenated wetland. A boardwalk leads from the*

house, OPPOSITE ABOVE, *to the pond,* BELOW, *created by designer P. Clifford Miller.* RIGHT, TOP TO BOTTOM: *The front yard is higher and drier. Steps offer a visual invitation. Prairie dock grows throughout the property, and by the pond.*

house to the edge of the pond, bringing human and animal habitats together.

The pond was dug by machine and lined with flexible sheets of heavyweight PVC. Because it was too large for a single sheet, the crew unrolled the pieces in place, laid them out, and then "what we call field-seamed them," says Miller, as if they were sewing together a giant rubbery quilt.

The island is actually a floating device, fastened to two fifty-five-gallon plastic drums. Miller's crew made it from three black locust logs (black locust offers good rot protection without chemical treatment) fashioned into a triangle, and stapled plastic mesh underneath. Next, a geotextile fabric was attached to the top, and a wetland-type soil mix was heaped up on the island and planted.

"The spoils from the pond ex-

cavation were spread across the front yard to form a reconstruction of a hill savanna," says Miller. The hill was planted with purple prairie clover (*Petalostemum purpureum*), goldenrod (*Solidago* spp.), New England asters (*Aster novae-angliae*), panic grass (*Panicum virgatum*), big bluestem (*Andropogon gerardii*), and little bluestem (*A. scoparius* or *Schizachyrium scoparium*).

"And, of course, lots of prairie dock," says Miller, referring to *Silphium terebinthinaceum,* the imposing composite-family plant for which the place is named.

SANCTUARY ESTATES
FRANKLIN, WISCONSIN

FIVE YEARS OF BASELINE studies preceded the start of construction at Sanctuary Estates, a five-home housing development set beside sensitive wetlands. Today, not only is the complex of wetlands preserved, but residents live in a sixty-five-acre sanctuary for foxes, great blue herons, and other wildlife of all kinds.

The Monastery Lake area, where Sanctuary Estates is situated, includes a marsh, a tamarack swamp, and also a rare

AMONG PEACEFUL WATERS

Wetland preservation often results as a concession between developers and environmentalists. Some farsighted builders, however, recognize the aesthetic,

economic, and ecological value of these habitats. Sanctuary Estates, RIGHT, *is a development of grand houses surrounding a restored wetland in Wisconsin. Raised walks and bridges provide access between properties without disturbing the delicate ecosystem,* ABOVE.

fen where water comes from mineral-rich groundwater.

"Everyone has become a real protector of the environment," says JoAnn Gillespie, of Country Wetlands, who was called in by owner-developer Gerry Ritzo to perform studies and restoration.

White sweet clover (*Melilotus alba*), a formidable opponent, is best pulled at petal drop and the pulled plants removed from the site. But canary grass (*Phalaris arundinacea*), which forms some of the worst monotypic stands of any choking plant, has been the chief opponent. Burning has not proved effective, so a mowing program has been developed to overcome the invasion. "By timing the mowing correctly, we have been able to bring back fifteen species of plants that had been present before," says Gillespie. Spring (prior to meristem, or new plant, development) and fall mowings over a three-year period were the key. A newly developed hover-mower may prove to be an important tool.

THE NEW ENGLAND WILD
FLOWER SOCIETY—
GARDEN IN THE WOODS
FRAMINGHAM,
MASSACHUSETTS

IN 1931, WILL C. CURTIS began a garden of wild plants in Framingham, Massachusetts. Later he was joined in the effort by Howard O. Stiles, and on this naturally wooded site of very varied topography, the two built a collection of plants—wild, but not necessarily indigenous. This is not a habitat re-creation or restoration, nor does it have the synoptic or systematic assemblies of plants of a botanical garden. It is built around botanicals and its mission is to share the knowl-

THE GARDEN
IN THE WETLANDS

edge of these plants and insight from years of growing them. In this living museum, every plant is clearly labeled with Latin and common names, country of origin, and its status if rare, threatened, or endangered.

Today, the garden is run by the New England Wild Flower Society, and members and staff are faced with a dilemma: Should the garden remain preserved as a memorial to its founders, or should all the exotic plants be removed from the forty-eight-acre grounds in the name of purity? A likely outcome is that all new plantings will be of natives, with the original gardens maintained as their creators intended.

The shady sylvan gardens for which Garden in the Woods is famed are still a major attraction, particularly when most of the ephemerals bloom in May. In recent years, the society has introduced habitat-style plantings of meadow and shaded rock gar-

"Garden in the Woods" aptly describes this place's best-known feature, but the wetland plantings are equally rich. In autumn, the

Pondside, ABOVE RIGHT AND OPPOSITE, *Shady Brook,* CENTER RIGHT, *and Sunny Bog,* BELOW RIGHT, *are filled with colors from residents such as the amazing yellow pitcher plants* (Sarracenia flava), ABOVE.

den, and there is still room to grow. Among the most fascinating areas are the wet ones: the sunny bog garden, the pondside, and the shady brook.

Curtis and Stiles fashioned the original bog after wet spots in the New Jersey Pine Barrens, a generally dry plant community with very acid, often sterile soil. The uneven topography had made it possible for plants with differing moisture requirements to coexist—winterberry holly (*Ilex verticillata*) in the medium-wet areas and wild calla (*Calla palustris*) in the lowest, wettest ones, the shallow pools that

OPPOSITE: *A rivulet runs through the Sunny Bog garden— by a planting of self-hybridizing sarracenias and to a tussock sedge* (Carex stricta). ABOVE: *Winterberry* (Ilex verticillata) *has a handsome vase shape, silvery bark with age, plus berries that are the last to be eaten by the birds in winter.* ABOVE RIGHT: *A humble bridge spans Hop Brook— a managed but not meticulously maintained area.*

aquatics adore. The stars of the garden are pitcher plants (*Sarracenia* spp.) and sundews (*Drosera rotundifolia*), which grow where the water table is just below the soil surface and the nutrition-poor soil is acidic.

Other herbaceous plants include sedges (*Carex* spp.), skunk cabbage (*Lysichiton americanum*), globeflower (*Trollius laxus*), and orchids—purple fringed (*Habenaria psycodes*), white fringed (*Habenaria blephariglottis*), and grass pink (*Calopogon pulchellus*). Around these are shrubby plants including members of the heath family (*Ericaceae*) including highbush blueberry (*Vaccinium corymbosum*), sand myrtle (*Leiophyllum buxifolium*), Labrador tea (*Ledum groenlandicum*), and sheep laurel (*Kalmia angustifolia*).

The pond at Garden in the Woods was a feature from the start, but in recent years the staff has somewhat systematically filled in with more and more natives. By the waterside, *Helonias bullata,* swamp pink, originally a denizen of New Jersey swamps

where much of its habitat has been altered or destroyed, is thriving, and other natives— blue flag (*Iris versicolor*), turtlehead (*Chelone glabra*), Canada lily (*Lilium canadense*), bluestar or dogbone (*Amsonia tabernaemontana*), closed gentian (*Gentiana andrewsii*) ferns, and lobelias (both great blue, *Lobelia siphilitica,* and cardinal flower, *L. cardinalis*)—add to the show.

Near the northwest boundary of the property little has been developed, or will ever be. Here a beautiful woodland (where a stream called Hop Brook winds its way along through the brush) is managed, but not meticulously maintained. When an old pine fell, it was left in place and a path was made to run along its downed trunk. The soil here is nearly always moist, and in early spring, actually underwater. Native beeches and pines thrive on a slope beside the sodden earth and in their shadows, the two eastern clintonias bloom: speckled beadlily (*Clintonia umbellulata*) and blue beadlily (*C. borealis*).

GEORGE PURMONT AND
DAUNE PECKHAM
LITTLE COMPTON,
RHODE ISLAND

GARDEN OF FOUR PONDS

REMNANTS OF SOME OLD stone walls in what is now woods tell George Purmont and his wife, garden designer Daune Peckham, that the land behind their home was probably once farmed. But that was long ago, Purmont says—look at the girth of some of the second-growth trees—and probably not so successful, since the tract of land in Little Compton, Rhode Island, is too wet even to build on.

On the site, which has been in the family for more than a

century, Purmont's grandfather built a pond about the size of a house many years ago. Thus began Purmont's love of water.

"My brother Wayland and I used to play in the swampy places and crawl through the tall grass," he recalls. "I can still remember the odor of blue clay."

When the boys were in their early twenties, they decided to build ponds in the wet land to make it more accessible for recreation and attractive to wildlife and so they could stock the water for fishing and to help reduce mosquitoes. The ponds were designed in place by bulldozing the scrub and small trees into windrows or berms that defined the shapes of the ponds-to-be. Then the sodden earth was scooped out, piled up on the berms, and smoothed.

The first pond was built next to the existing one and connected with a slim waterway spanned by a bridge. There are now a total of four. The property has

What started out as a place for recreation became much more—a wetland habitat replete with all the life that accompanies this exuberant

community. A few of the ponds have islands or peninsulas. This one, RIGHT, *is blessed with white waterlilies* (Nymphaea odorata). *Many shrubs have found this place, such as black chokeberry* (Aronia melanocarpa), ABOVE.

no defined aquifer, but the boys located underground springs that support the ponds. Today, local regulations might dictate how and where such ponds could be created.

Several islands built within the ponds add visual interest and more edge for bird habitat. Wood duck boxes on the islands drew tree swallows (and a few raccoons)—common subtenants. Owls favor the pond area, too.

The vegetation is natural; some waterlilies had inhabited the original pond, and a chance pink form was encouraged to naturalize in another. Now there are cattails (*Typha* spp.), wild iris (*Iris versicolor*), asters (*Aster* spp.), goldenrods (*Solidago* spp.), Joe-pye weed (*Eupatorium maculatum*), and phragmites.

"The phragmites is a problem," says Purmont. "It has been pushing out all the other plants." Burning and a few other techniques have failed, and Purmont will not use herbicides. "We'll probably get in there and dig them out with machinery at some point."

The woody plants don't present such problems, and the master pond builders are proud of their naturalized collection, including clethra, bayberry, highbush blueberry, and deciduous holly, with princess pine on the ground below.

RIGHT, CLOCKWISE FROM TOP: *Another sculpted landform; waterlilies and other rich plantings; sensitive fern* (Onoclea sensibilis) *and blue flag iris; a wood-duck house hanging on an island tree.* OPPOSITE: *The oldest pond is sheltered by trees and hosts pink waterlilies.*

THE NORTH CAROLINA
BOTANICAL GARDEN
CHAPEL HILL,
NORTH CAROLINA

THE MICROCOSMIC COASTAL plain, sandhills, and mountain demonstration gardens are perhaps the smallest treasures of North Carolina Botanical Garden's 598 acres of natural and cultivated land, where hillsides of *Rhododendron catawbiense* and a seven-acre pond enjoyed by mink and beaver are more the normal scale. But because of careful planning and maintenance, a whole region's environmental lessons are revealed in these miniature communities.

NATURE CONDENSED

Totten Center is the smallest part of the university's 598-acre botanical garden. A boardwalk through the demonstration garden allows visitors close-up views of maple and dogwood (detail OPPOSITE*); pine bark*

(BOTTOM RIGHT); *dead tree "homes"* (CENTER). *The area is especially handsome in fall when the first frost turns southern shield fern* (Thelypteris normalis) *nearly black* (ABOVE RIGHT). *The garden's prize pitcher plants, including* Sarracenia leucophylla, ABOVE.

Instead of a conventional footpath, a boardwalk lifts the visitor up high enough so that the sometimes-soggy ground is not an impediment, a strategy that might improve the design and enjoyment of a moist home landscape, too. On a dank fall afternoon, the trees and shrubs drip with moisture, and the only brightness is from a reddening oakleaf hydrangea (*Hydrangea quercifolia*) and the droopy golden leaves of bluestar (*Amsonia tabernaemontana*). Yet a few months later, two of these gardens are burned. Without the cleansing effects of fire, the coastal plain garden in particular would not remain open enough for fringed orchids (*Habenaria* spp.) and pitcher plants (*Sarracenia* spp.).

The botanical garden's ethic: conservation through propagation. A specialty is carnivorous species. Hybrid pitcher plants from this program are distributed to native-plant nurseries so that widespread losses in their wild habitat can be offset.

W O O

*"*I *speak for the trees,*

for the trees have no tongues."

~ The Lorax,
A DR. SEUSS CHARACTER

I LOVE TO VISIT THE WIDE-OPEN SPACES; I'M transfixed by the vision of the expansive amber prairie in autumn and the seamless sea of desert. And yet the sight that heartens me most is sheltered and snug: I love the woodland best.

Beneath the spires of the towering trees, I feel as if I have entered a cathedral built by nature for worshiping these grand totems of my faith. My fantasy home landscape would be a mixed hardwood forest with native rhododendron and rocky, fern-covered terrain traversed by a stream—not unlike the woods of North Carolina.

The forest's majesty is unmistakable, whether seen from the air in fall, ABOVE, *or from right in among the trees, such as in Muir Woods north of San Francisco,* RIGHT. *In that cathedrallike setting stand some of the planet's largest citizens, the giant redwoods (Sequoia sempervirens),* guardians of a complex forest community.

When conditions in a woodland change, some animals never get a second foothold. Amphibians and birds are particularly vulnerable, LEFT AND ABOVE. *Others such as woodchucks,* RIGHT, *and deer seem invincible. Electric fencing and nylon net barriers are the safest, most effective methods to keep out deer.*

The woodlands of the United States—the eastern hardwood forests, the coastal conifer forests of the Northwest, the oak woodlands of central Texas and California, the pine forests of the Northeast and the Rockies—are exemplified by their enduring woody perennials, the longest-living creatures on earth. In Muir Woods, north of San Francisco, visitors can see some of the planet's largest beings, the redwoods (*Sequoia sempervirens*), in whose shade an old and complex community of plants and animals thrives, protected since around the turn of this century.

"Any fool can destroy trees," wrote John Muir, the great champion of wild spaces. "They cannot run away; and if they could, they would still be destroyed —chased and hunted down as long as fun or a dollar could be got out of [them]."

Today, Third World rain forests are falling to slash-and-burn tactics, and the United States' trees (even ones in some national forests, sold off like so many cattle to logging interests) are still dropping, though most were scraped right off the face of the emerging nation in our own eras of settlement and development. Little remains in the East, for example, and what is there, besides fragments of virgin woodland, is really new hardwood forest, regrown as the forest-turned-farmland was abandoned and young trees moved back in.

Unfortunately, the new forests are an unbalanced tangle of natives and exotics, not the same mix as the originals at all, and all too often dominated by opportunistic weedy species that don't always support the native wildlife very well.

Once the trees are cut, letting the sun in, the underlying soil quickly dries and compacts, altering— perhaps permanently—what can and will grow on the site. It can be many decades before enough leaf litter builds up from the young pioneer tree species, opportunists who jump into the cleared site, for conditions on the ground level to be right for ferns and woodland wildflowers to repopulate; some may never do so. Likewise, many animal inhabitants never get a second chance.

Recent efforts to save the habitat of the spotted owl, a native of the Northwestern woods, made its protectors the brunt of political jokes. Yet anyone who fails to recognize the pertinence of every last organism, from microbes to mankind, is in danger of sharing the owl's fate. If logging had continued, the forests the spotted owl inhabits would have been gone by the year 2000, and the owl with them.

Already in the Northwest, some trees have been felled that had been standing for more than a millennium when Christ or Buddha lived—three-thousand-plus-year-old giant sequoias, *Sequoiadendron giganteum.* These trees were America's pyramids, a true wonder of the world, and their destruction will be recalled as a memorial to the death of reason.

SAFE, SHADED HAVENS

Although I grew up in a 1950s-vintage ranch house in a typical New Jersey suburb, what I recall most vividly were the nearby places left from the pre-tract-home days—traces of a nineteenth-century Romantic landscape in which grand mansions once stood. In a vast wasteland of lawns a fifteen-foot rhododendron and mountain laurel beneath a towering hemlock formed a darkened "fort." I shared this magical playground with companions like nightcrawlers and an occasional salamander.

No wonder, then, the feelings that were stirred when I was invited into Evelyn Adams's Massachusetts garden, a hidden hollow among the trees where each spring the ground bursts forth with trillium and Virginia bluebells. Or when I was allowed to poke around in the many hidden corners of the Pennsylvania garden of Dr. Richard Lighty, where one narrow path leads to a patchwork of many distinctive forms of foamflower, *Tiarella* spp., another down into a depression bright with yellow western skunk cabbage, *Lysichiton americanum,* beside a little stream.

Trees and their understory—the kinds of places where Adams and Lighty make their gardens—are bonded to my memory. As a teenager, I traveled with my parents to the Great Smoky Mountains and saw bright orange-red carcasses of chestnut trees littering the forest floor. These trees succumbed to a devastating blight that slipped into this country in the

When an opening in the forest occurs, or when pasture land is left to revert to woods, young trees move in to fill the gap, as in this New England scene, ABOVE. *But too often the new population doesn't accurately represent the former generation and includes aliens. Good woodland management would prescribe the removal of so-called trash trees.* BELOW: *What could replace trees so precious as the giant redwoods? Just imagine if weedy eucalyptus trees were to overrun this sylvan spectacle.*

early part of this century from Asia; by the 1950s it had infected and destroyed virtually every mature tree. The American chestnut, an important link in the food chain, fed countless animals like squirrels and black bears, whose numbers continue to decline.

Even the smallest details—the delicate textures of leaves, the intricate sculpture of flowers—are too important to overlook. Every element of the forest, right down to the exquisite fungi and plush, vibrant mosses, have considerable value, just as much as the giant living trees themselves. Learning to look in the cracks, along the floor, out of the way—not to let your attention be captured by just the obvious, dominant plants—these are important lessons for the natural habitat gardener wishing to initiate a plant community in his or her landscape.

"The worship of leaves, trunks, twigs, shoots— that's real gardening," says Lighty, who has made his life work taking notice of the details, developing and introducing "better" native plants to the nursery trade by careful selection.

TREES AT WORK

The forest is the model for habitat gardens in places that favor tree growth. If you imagine a woodland, the vision probably will depend on the part of the country in which you were raised or where you live today—a picture of fiery sugar maples in New England's fall, the dark and quiet of a mature northern conifer forest, the scaled-down image of dwarf pin-

CLOCKWISE FROM OPPOSITE FAR LEFT: *Each forest is distinctive, such as that of the Smokies in the Southeast. Chestnut trees once filled this woodland, but now only carcasses are reminders of the accidentally imported blight that took virtually every mature tree. Pay attention to detail: the sculptural quality of flowers such as bicolored bergamot; American turkscap lilies; red bergamot flower; and the textures of ferns.*

yon and juniper in a southwestern canyon. Even the floor of each is different in the mind's eye. One might be spongy, dark, and moist where leaf litter is built up, the other a rusty color and drier with the crunch of brittle pine needles underfoot.

The sparse, sometimes scrubby oak woodland of Portola Valley, California, and the dense New England forests are too disparate for generalizations, and it would be no easier to make sweeping conclusions that embrace the sandy-soil Pine Barrens of New Jersey and Long Island with the continually wet rain forests of the Pacific Northwest.

What they all do have in common, of course, is trees—the most obvious element of the woodland habitat. It is hardly necessary to make a case for them; beauty is reason enough to command their planting and preservation, but they also work hard for the benefit of life on earth. Besides taking in carbon dioxide and putting out oxygen, trees have an enormous impact on temperature. As much as 90 percent of the solar energy is absorbed, making the shady place below a tree a fine spot indeed. But trees also cool by transpiration, the evaporation of water from their leaves. A medium-sized tree can move more than five hundred gallons of water into the air on a hot day, thereby reducing air temperature. Trees are living air conditioners. The importance of reducing fuel consumption, and its resultant pollution, by planting deciduous trees to the south and west of a home cannot be overrated.

Trees also moderate winter temperatures. When evergreens are sited on the side of the house from which winter winds prevail, the energy savings can be enormous. Trees planted for windbreak purposes should not be placed close enough to block the warming effects of sunlight, but, depending on local topography, as many as one hundred feet away. An evergreen windbreak several trees deep can reduce

There is beauty in small things in the woodland, such as an exquisite fungus, ABOVE; the highly pleated leaves of American false hellebore (Veratrum viride), OPPOSITE; and in the velvety texture of even the tiny moss plants, RIGHT, which can be cultivated as here, in Carol Mercer's Long Island garden. Generally, moss wants a very acidic (pH 5.5), clayey, and compact soil. Scrape away any remnants of grass, rake stones and debris away, and sweep. Compress the surface by rolling or stamping on a flat board. If you live near a woodland where moss grows, just keep the spot damp for several weeks, and spores in the air will probably settle and grow. You can also transplant moss. If it is sheet moss, it will peel up in a solid mat. If it is the kind of moss that falls apart when you lift it, that's fine, too. Place the collected moss in a plastic bag to transplant as soon as possible. Scratch the surface of the prepared site with a hand fork. Place bits of the moss, green side up, around the area, about one in the center of every square foot of space. Press the moss firmly into the soil and keep it watered for a week—longer in hot weather.

wind impact on the structure by as much as half. Instead of planting in a straight line, soften the near side of the windbreak with a mixed planting of evergreen and deciduous trees, shrubs, vines, and herbaceous plants.

Trees also buffer traffic and other noise pollution; they can intercept dust with their leaves, and their roots conserve soil that might otherwise be eroded as it washes or blows away. They mediate the impact of raindrops on the soil surface, a major cause of soil compaction that too few gardeners recognize. When water (whether rain or snow) falls first onto trees, it will drip more slowly and gently onto the ground from their leaves, needles, or branches.

If you live on or purchase a property that is wooded, you might think your work is done, and I suppose that in a few places still left on earth that would be the case. But in most situations you will be facing, at best, a second-growth woodland in need of rehabilitation, a place of Japanese bittersweet and honeysuckle perhaps, or numerous seedlings and saplings of trash tree species. A chain saw, as well as several handsaws and pruners and a pole saw/pruner, will be essential to almost everyone who sets out to garden a woodland habitat, but these tools must be used with caution and common sense. Never remove a tree without a lot of thought—even dead trees have value as shelter for such prehistoric treasures as pileated woodpeckers. Remember the sentiments of the poet William Blake: A tree is an object that moves some to tears, to others it is only a green thing that stands in the way. Gardeners should find themselves in the former category.

When Sara Stein came to her New York property,

already profiled in the grasslands section, she couldn't even get through the woods. The understory was choked by catbrier and poison ivy; many of the trees were weedy species. She has spent years clearing the undesirables from the underbrush, but just as soon as she finished the last area she had to start over again, where the aggressors were already getting a renewed foothold. Planting acceptable species on the woodland floor helped discourage them, but a regular ongoing maintenance program will continue to be necessary. Gardening in the woods is a commitment to woodlands management.

Do not go overboard. Clearing all the brush from beneath the trees indiscriminantly might cause the ultimate destruction of the community, eliminating conditions that foster welcome seedlings and even the older trees. Do not rake out the litter on the forest floor, either; it is nature's compost. Forests collect their debris and break it down slowly. For example, soils in conifer forests, in particular, are acid to very acid and therefore nutrient-deficient. The soil life is limited by the acidity, and as a result litter can remain a decade or more before decomposition is complete.

A WOODLAND INVENTORY

Before setting out armed with tools, it is wise to catalog all existing trees. Using a comprehensive field guide, key out and list or map all the trees. Note the natives, and also which plants are not just American but local—those that are indigenous to your area. You might even consider a system of tagging the trees with ribbons color-coded by species, or simply by which ones stay and which ones go.

The goal is not so much to tally the natives as to rogue out the weed species, trees whose propensity to seed or otherwise spread themselves around makes them gluttons of the landscape. In the mid-Atlantic states, that might be *Ailanthus altissima,* the tree of heaven, brought to the United States in the eighteenth century in an ill-fated attempt to establish a silk industry here. Silkworms turned up their noses at ailanthus leaves, but the tree loved America, and

The trees of New England, ABOVE LEFT, *just before the leaves drop to replenish the dark and moist forest floor,* OPPOSITE, *where life in the woodland begins and ends. Other trees, such as the weeping Brewer spruce* (Picea brewerana), ABOVE, *from the Siskiyou Mountains of Oregon, leave the crunchy sound of needles underfoot.*

now it deposits its progeny in every last nook and cranny of urban zones like the New York metropolitan area. (Ailanthus is the hero of the story *A Tree Grows in Brooklyn*.)

Elsewhere, the culprit might be buckthorn (*Rhamnus frangula*) or boxelder (*Acer negundo*), white mulberry (*Morus alba*) or Chinese tallow (*Sapium sebiferum*), mimosa (*Albizia julibrissin*) or Siberian elm (*Ulmus pumila*). It might even be Norway maple, *Acer platanoides,* a weed tree that is still sold and even recommended by "environmentally conscious" gardening books. Not only does Norway maple seed itself, it also has a chemical, or allelopathic, effect on the soil its roots stretch into, preventing other plants from growing by secreting a toxin. Ask your local agricultural extension service or botanical garden, particularly one with a native-plant area that will have combated such pests, to provide you with a list of weedy species.

Categorize your trees and other woody plants according to the forest's natural layers: Group the tallest under the heading of *canopy* and the intermediate-height trees as *understory*.

After you finish listing the trees, move on to the *shrub layer,* the midrange shrubs and vines as well as the low-lying plants of the forest floor. Use a notebook for this process, detailing all ornamental and wildlife benefits of each plant in every season—

meaning you'll have to either look it up and/or repeat your note-taking over the course of a full year. Examine the views from inside and outside your woods (or potential woods, if you are planning a mini-reforestation), and note visual impediments and assets.

In your tree inventory, pay special attention to the condition of each individual: Is its bark intact and healthy-looking; are roots badly exposed because of erosion; is the crown full or sparse; is it free from dead and diseased wood? If the tree is stressed, perhaps from crowding or light deprivation, or from a change in the water table or increase in air pollution, can this be corrected?

Remember before making even one change that with each opening made in the canopy, and the resultant light increase, the underlying plant palette will change, sometimes quickly and dramatically. Take care to protect even the tiniest seedlings of the trees of the future; and do not trample or otherwise harm them. If you are grading or constructing on the property (putting in a driveway, for instance), and some woody plants must be sacrificed in the process,

The first step in woodland management: an inventory of existing treasures, ABOVE. *Be careful when clearing brush—keep an eye out for seedlings,* ABOVE LEFT. OPPOSITE: *Staghorn sumac* (Rhus typhina). FAR RIGHT, TOP TO BOTTOM: *Cutleaf sumac* (R. typhina *'Laciniata'*); *smooth sumac* (R. glabra); *staghorn fruits.*

think of the area as your very own nursery source. List worthy ones to be saved from the bulldozer for relocating elsewhere in the landscape.

When you have completed this thorough inventory, begin to remove weed trees, shrubs, and vines, according to the best methods for each species. Those that will resprout from their roots cannot simply be cut down; again, the local extension service or botanical garden may be able to suggest the least-toxic method of eliminating such plants.

Always evaluate the amount of damage that uprooting a tree will do to its neighbors—not just whether its trunk will strike another on the way down, but whether its extraction will damage the roots of other desired plants. Some people take trees out gradually over several years, cutting them to about two feet the first year. If the plant doesn't sprout a year later, you might then choose to leave the stump for good, and even incorporate it into a permanent bench or table design. If it does resprout, rub off the new growth a few times and see if it

finally succumbs. If not, it will have to go by pulling, burning, or some other method—stick to those that are environmentally safe.

If you own or purchase a wooded site on which you plan to build, you may have to do your inventory quickly, before a single piece of equipment rolls onto the land and over tree roots. Identify the trees you want to save, then make this a priority by writing it into the construction contract.

The hazards to trees from building (or paving, or excavating for a drywell or cesspool, or even from parking a car on their unseen underground root zones) cannot be overstated. Besides the obvious damage from impact with heavy machinery (including the family car!) soil compaction kills trees. Have your contractor erect a sturdy fence around each tree

Many trees enjoy the company of their kin, such as ponderosa pine (Pinus ponderosa) *from the Rocky Mountains,* ABOVE. *Some redwood trees grow vegetatively from the burls that surround the base of old trees. Now these giant sequoia,* ABOVE LEFT, *form a circle around the spot where their long-gone parent stood.*

to be saved, not right up against the trunk but as far out as the dripline, an imaginary line corresponding to the circumference of the branches. Plan to supervise the process, since damage may not be visible until a tree dies a year or two later.

The effect on trees from chemicals used during construction, like pH-altering concrete and paints, is significant. Piling up soil over a tree's roots, or against its trunk, during grading work is also inviting disaster. A mere six inches more or less of soil can have catastrophic consequences.

If the grade must be changed near a tree, bring in a tree surgeon or landscaping professional with expertise on protecting trees during construction. Landscape architect Ron Lutsko of San Francisco was brought into a project because some California live

Fallen pine needles, ABOVE, *form a wonderful mulch. Their coarse texture and low moisture, combined with a high acid content, allow them to last for years: It can take ten years for them to decompose.* ABOVE RIGHT: *The perfect place to rest and relax may already exist in a wooded spot, such as this one at Tower Hill.*

oaks were dying more than a year after construction was complete on the client's new home. He discovered that as much as six feet of rubble and soil had been moved onto the trees' root zones, cutting off oxygen and water, and began excavating to try to save them. He built retaining walls around their bases, then filled the outside space with gravel to allow for good drainage where the accumulation couldn't be removed—and most of the trees survived.

Just as trees do not want to grow half submerged in rubble, they would not volunteer to a life as soldiers, all lined up single file. Look at natural places where trees grow, or at paintings and historic photographs of the ancient forests before they were cut. They hardly resemble rigid plantings on graph paper. Leave such orderly layouts to the tree farms.

"Trees are much like human beings and enjoy each other's company," wrote Jens Jensen, ". . . with their branches interlaced they give an expression of friendship."

MIXED FRUIT

When planning a biohedge, or any other use of berried shrubs and trees in the natural habitat garden, consider the birds' needs carefully. Summertime food and wintertime food requirements may be very different; the fruit that suits one bird in summer may not be its wintertime choice at all.

High-lipid fruits (those that include fats) like spicebush (*Lindera benzoin*) and sassafras (*Sassafras albidum*) are ideal for the premigratory phase since they are intensely calorie-rich, perfect for storing up reserves for birds' incredible long-distance journeys. In spring and summer, high-sugar fruits like blackberry, elderberry, raspberry, and cherries are more to birds' liking. And wintertime food in cold-winter areas must be high in carbohydrates. Winterberry (*Ilex verticillata*), poison ivy (*Toxicodendron radicans*), and sumac (*Rhus* spp.) are ideal for meeting these needs. Too many gardeners wishing to welcome wildlife focus only on birds' wintertime feeding requirements. Refer to birding books, or contact your local Audubon Society chapter or the National Wildlife Federation for further help in designing a locally appropriate, year-round avian food supply.

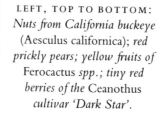

LEFT, TOP TO BOTTOM: *Nuts from California buckeye* (Aesculus californica); *red prickly pears; yellow fruits of* Ferocactus *spp.; tiny red berries of the* Ceanothus *cultivar 'Dark Star'.*

WOODLAND TIPS

Plan for a smooth transition to your woods, both for aesthetic reasons and wildlife benefits. Develop the intermediate level between lawn or low-growing herbaceous plants and trees with smaller trees and shrubs.

Creating paths, rather than allowing random movement through the wooded area, may prove beneficial in rekindling the plants of the floor, like sedges, ferns, wildflowers, and mosses.

If the soil needs improvement, try to stick to amendments that are as close to the natural forest elements as possible: leaf mold, for example, particularly from trees similar to those in the planting, should be used instead of peat moss or some other foreign substance.

Spacing is critical when planting trees, and to only a slightly lesser degree shrubs. These are long-term additions to the landscape. Plan for their eventual size, and space accordingly.

Cutting back and pruning woody plants yields woodchips, which should be composted before they are used in the landscape. Uncomposted chips rob nutrition from the underlying soil. When mulching with composted chips, use a thin layer, and never pile them up against tree trunks.

Don't haul away all the debris; fallen trunks are beautiful, and invite diversity in the form of fungi, mosses, lichens, and their companion insects into the woodland.

Use some of the brush from the clearing of the woods to create a brush pile, a favorite haunt for birds and other animals.

Where there is a soil-compaction problem, which can mean death to trees, the best antidote is a mulch of leaves. An appropriate organic mulch encourages an abundance of soil-aerating lifeforms beneath the surface.

Where trees will remain in a lawn area, remove the sod from underneath them, all the way out to the dripline. Replace it with a thin layer of appropriate mulch (leaf mold, pine needles, composted chips), or a ground cover.

Never flush-cut a tree when pruning; flush cuts injure trunk tissue, which can be devastating to the tree's health. Do not leave long stubs that encourage disease, either. Never damage the branch collar, in most species a raised ring that differentiates trunk from branch.

Never paint a pruning cut or a wound to a tree; let the tree heal itself.

Transplanting can be a money-saving strategy, and many seedlings, in particular, are easily moved. While still in leaf, mark the trees to be moved, and prepare the holes. Then, when the leaves fall (November in many areas), transplant the tree.

When tree roots are damaged from construction or transplanting, be sure to recut them cleanly with a pruner before replanting. Crushed or shredded roots don't take up moisture effectively.

Some tree work, especially on older specimens, is not for the gardener to do, but for a professional. Hire a licensed, insured arborist who demonstrates a strong knowledge of native trees:

OPPOSITE, TOP TO BOTTOM: *False Solomon's-seal* (Smilacina racemosa); *highbush blueberry* (Vaccinium corymbosum); *gray dogwood* (Cornus racemosa); *American highbush cranberry* (Viburnum trilobum). COUNTERCLOCKWISE FROM TOP: *Berries are as ornamental as they are edible, but some, such as poison ivy and baneberry, are toxic to humans. Baneberry* (Actaea rubra) *and doll's-eyes* (A. pachypoda) *in Judith Stark's wildlife garden; doll's-eyes (detail); fragrant thimbleberry* (Rubus odoratus); *sugarbush* (Rhus ovata) *is a frost-tender cousin of the sumacs.*

AMERICA'S OWN RHODODENDRONS

In much of America, rhododendrons and azaleas have become synonymous with spring and are a mainstay of nearly every home landscape. Unfortunately, the majority of home owners have overlooked the native American rhododendrons, many of which are beginning to be promoted in nurseries.

Most of our native rhododendrons come from the Southeast and the Pacific Northwest, where soil and climate conditions are ideal for them. Because rhododendrons are acid-loving plants, they are not appropriate for many central areas of the nation, where alkaline soil is common.

Among the North American species are many evergreens, including *Rhododendron chapmanii,* which grows in the Florida sand dunes in conditions that could not be more unlikely for a member of this genus. At the top of the continent, *R. lapponicum* thrives in the Arctic tundra near the pole and down to the northernmost forests.

The Southeast is practically synonymous with the genus. It is the home of the twenty- to thirty-five-foot *R. maximum,* the rosebay rhododendron, a familiar evergreen of the Great Smoky Mountains that blooms early to midsummer, and whose range extends into Massachusetts and up to Maine. In Newport, Rhode Island, for example, the mansions are sheltered from the street by giant specimen rosebays.

From the Carolinas come *R. minus* and the very similar *R. carolinianum,* with flowers in white or shades of pink in late spring. There are many cultivated varieties, including one with blotches of yellow on the white flowers and narrow leaves (*R. minus* 'Album'). One of the sturdiest of all the southeastern rhododendrons and parent to many hardy hybrids is *R. catawbiense,* another Smoky Mountain native. Large, mounded shrubs cover the rolling terrain of central to western North Carolina in June with drifts of lilac-purple to pink, and sometimes white, at elevations as high as six thousand feet.

About the hardiest native rhododendron is *R. vaseyi,* the pinkshell azalea, and it is also very showy, blooming pink or sometimes white before the leaves emerge. It also offers red fall foliage.

In the Northwest, *R. macrophyllum* is the Catawba's western counterpart. This species, which grows along the coast, blooms in late spring and has voluptuous, bell-shaped flowers of rose-purple with brown spots. *R. albiflorum* grows in the mountains of the Northwest and into Colorado, but hasn't found its way into many gardens yet.

Rhododendron occidentale, the western azalea, is a deciduous species appreciated by sophisticated English gardeners for over a century. It is most valued there for the role it played in the development of numerous prized hybrids—many of which came back to adorn American gardens in the West. It is a medium-sized shrub with leaves and flowers coming at the same time; the flowers are creamy white to pale pink and

pale to chrome yellow at the base. The leaves turn yellow to orange to ruby in fall.

There are more than a dozen deciduous azalea-type rhododendron species native to Georgia alone.

The deep coral flowers of *R. prunifolium,* the plum-leaf azalea, are produced from August to September in my garden, earlier in its native territory. But it is the early spring species, particularly the fragrant ones, that are more popular.

The sweet azalea (*R. canescens*) is the first to bloom in March to April in Georgia, along with another fragrant species, the yellow-flowered *R. austrium.* In mid-April, *R. flammeum* (syn. *R. speciosum*) produces its yellow, salmon, or pink blossoms; from the lowlands of Georgia and South Carolina, it is not as hardy as some and is not fragrant.

Rhododendron periclymenoides (syn. *R. nudiflorum*), the pinxterbloom or honeysuckle azalea, is better known as a parent of the popular Ghent hybrids. It is floriferous (April), producing pale pink blooms with a red tube that are honey-and-spice scented, and survives with minimal care in an extensive range of hardiness up through Massachusetts.

Rhododendron prinophyllum (syn. *R. roseum*), rose-

shell azalea, a very hardy species that ranges to Quebec, offers its pink, intensely clove-scented flowers from April to May in Georgia. *R. albamense,* Alabama azalea, is a fragrant white species blooming around the same time. *R. atlanticum* hails from along the Atlantic coastal plain; it is a small, stoloniferous shrub whose bluish green foliage is a fine contrast to the fragrant white to pinkish blooms.

One of the most brilliant Georgians is *R. calendulaceum,* the flame azalea, whose flowers (May and June) range from yellow to orange to scarlet. It also has fine fall color, making it one of the nation's showiest all-around rhododendron species. About two weeks later than *R. calendulaceum,* look for the outstanding red or orange-red blooms of *R. bakeri,* the Cumberland azalea, which is less heat tolerant than its close relative.

The swamp azalea, *R. viscosum,* grows by freshwater ponds in Cape Cod and down to the Alabama swamps—a star for wet-soil areas. Its clove-scented flowers are white to light pink, May to June.

Some southern individuals of *R. arborescens,* the sweet azalea, bloom late—July, and perhaps even August—though others bloom in early summer. The range of this plant is wide, from Georgia up into Pennsylvania and New York. The fragrant, white funnel-form flowers are set off by a reddish style (the elongated part of the pistil). *R. serrulatum* is about the last to bloom, often into September, its fragrant, white flowers sometimes blushed pink.

Some of our native rhododendrons include: ABOVE, LEFT TO RIGHT, *pinxterbloom* (Rhododendron periclymenoides *syn.* R. nudifloram); *the mid- to late-summer-flowering plum-leaved rhododendron* (Rhododendron prunifolium); Catawba rhododendron (R. catawbiense); *western azalea* (R. occidentale), *prized for its fall color; pink-shell azalea* (R. vaseyi).

DICK AND SALLY LIGHTY
KENNETT SQUARE,
PENNSYLVANIA

WHY THERE IS NOT AN AMERI-
can plant bearing the specific epithet *lightii* or at least one called
'Lighty's Gem' or some such
thing is hard to understand, for
Dick Lighty is a champion of our
native flora.

Dr. Richard Lighty has been at
the native game since at least the
day in 1958 when as a young
plant geneticist, he collected a
solitary trillium plant from the
woods of the Pocono Mountains
and carried it home. Today,
more than fifteen hundred stems
from that *Trillium grandiflorum*

TWO WORLDS, ONE GARDEN

*There's an arresting planting
in the Lighty garden,*
BELOW. *It's a circle of
native Allegheny spurge*
(Pachysandra procumbens),

framed by a wreath of Asian
Pachysandra terminalis
'Variegata'. *East meets West
here—except over the bridge
in the all-native garden
where,* RIGHT, *spectacular
wildflowers can be found, such
as yellow lady's slipper orchid*
(Cypripedium calceolus).

fill the garden that he and his
wife, Sally, have built over
thirty-plus years near the Delaware border in Pennsylvania.

Trilliums are notoriously slow
to multiply, and have therefore
been shunned by the nursery industry as noncommercial. But
this variety, which Lighty has recently named 'Quicksilver', re-
produces three or four times
faster than other clones. Lighty
has begun to distribute 'Quicksilver' to native-plant nurseries
so that the consumer can have
ethically propagated trilliums at a
reasonable price for the garden.

The story of the trillium and of
Lighty's career are one: a commitment to bringing better selections of native plants to our
gardens. The former administra-
tor of the Longwood Graduate
Program at the University of
Delaware, Lighty has been the
director of Mt. Cuba Center for
the Study of Piedmont Flora
since 1983.

Even such a dedicated native-

plant type as Lighty suffers from a bit of horticultural schizophrenia. The symbols of his split passion are evident at Springwood, the undulating seven-and-a-half-acre property he and his wife so aptly named, for it is a woodland rich and moist with the presence of underground springs.

Plants of Asia share the stage with Americans—a wave of variegated Asian *Pachysandra terminalis* with a dollop of native American *Pachysandra procumbens* in its midst about sums things up. As if to find a way to manage his dual botanical enthusiasm, Lighty built a little footbridge over a stream that crosses the place, officially marking one bank as the international side and the other Americans-only.

On the native side, a frothy crazy quilt of foamflowers, each displaying a different leaf shape or surface pattern, coaxes visitors down a path. Around a corner, a clump of golden *Deschampia flexuosa* 'Aurea' positively glows a luminescent chartreuse in a shaft of light.

A favorite feature is the Lightys' "symbolic meadow," a kind of king-sized perennial garden made up of herbaceous giants

In some ways this appears to be a conventional landscape, LEFT, *but the Continental contrast can be seen again,* ABOVE LEFT, *where American pachysandra is separated by an ocean of lawn from its Asian mate.* OPPOSITE, CLOCKWISE FROM NEAR RIGHT: *Phlox and trillium; woodland natives; a selection of foamflower* (Tiarella cordifolia) *isolated for leaf shape and markings;* Deschampsia flexuosa 'Aurea'; Cornus sericea 'Silver and Gold'.

typical of meadows and grass-lands. In the grass-dominated mix, color is not the guiding element, though *Eupatorium fistulosum,* liatris, *Vernonia altissima,* cassia, and coreopsis are represented. Texture and form are all-important here, a revealing lesson in design.

A walk in the Lightys' garden is like that: bits of botany and horticulture gently interspersed throughout the beauty. A tip on how to divide a trillium might be offered ("Right after bloom when foliage is hard, and they will suffer no setback," he says), or propagating that luscious native pachysandra said to be so difficult ("In early July, grab hold of the new shoots when they are reasonably hard and jerk them out, then plant as you would rooted cuttings").

Several decades of life with deer has yielded lessons, too. A seven-foot fence of plastic netting hung between the trees has finally given way to barriers of chicken wire and a heavier cable.

Soil preparation is a well-oiled routine at Springwood, where the Lightys smother a new area to be planted with ten inches of woodchips, and then use a glyphosate herbicide to knock down anything that dares to push through. "The chips mean fewer chemicals are needed to kill existing vegetation; they enrich the soil; and they act as mulch until the desirables fill in," he says.

Not all the plants get names, and some will never be seen beyond the Lighty garden. A lipstick-pink selection of the trillium, for instance, will probably never make the catalog headlines, as pretty as it is.

"I would have to call that one 'Molasses'," Lighty says with a laugh, "because it's slow as molasses in January to propagate."

One planting dominates the landscape, LEFT, *in the sunny open area beyond the swimming pool. It is the "symbolic meadow"—a perennial bed occupied by the behemoths of the meadows and prairies, including Joe-pye weed and tall ironweed* (Vernonia altissima), *which shoots up through lower plants in late summer, along with some cultivated ornamental grass varieties.* ABOVE LEFT: *Wild senna, or cassia* (Cassia marilandica), *flowers on one side of the Joe-pye weed; northern sea oats bears its animated chevron-shaped spikelets on the other,* ABOVE.

MT. CUBA CENTER FOR
THE STUDY OF
PIEDMONT FLORA
GREENVILLE, DELAWARE

IT HAS BEEN THIRTY YEARS since Pamela Copeland set about to bring the wildings closer to home. The surrounding woods on her Delaware Valley estate, Mt. Cuba, were rich with colonies of wildflowers, but closer to the house, extensive formal gardens dominated the scene.

The large naturalistic garden she added in the early 1960s made a perfect counterpoint to the formality, and also something more: a landscape that could silence even the harshest

BUILDING BETTER NATIVES

The woodland path at Mt. Cuba Center is in its prime in mid-spring, RIGHT. *Under a spreading American dogwood* (Cornus florida), *herbaceous*

perennial natives bloom, such as blue wild sweet William (Phlox divaricata), *columbine* (Aquilegia canadensis), *and a tiny white-flowered native sedum, wild stonecrop* (Sedum ternatum). *A wooden bench makes a place to sit among the wildflowers,* ABOVE.

critic, the kind who dismisses native-plant gardening as either too wild-looking or too limited in its choice of plants.

It did not take long for Copeland to learn where native plants came from: namely, that they are plucked unscrupulously from the wild to be offered up for sale. In that sad realization, a conservationist was born.

Today, the Mt. Cuba Center for the Study of Piedmont Flora is a living native-plant guidebook, revealing a select portion of America's great natural diversity. Whole glades of flowering native shrubs—rhododendron, fothergilla, and kalmia among them—are underplanted with a tapestry of wildflowers. Phlox, foamflower, dicentras, and ferns are planted in sheets. Here and there along the broad, mulched paths are some less-familiar faces, like a native astilbe (*Astilbe biternata*), taller than the typical Asian garden varieties with stately cream-colored plumes, or

a flowering native sedum (*Sedum ternatum*), a carpet of frothy white beneath the trees.

Mt. Cuba Center was established on the site to select and promote desirable varieties of flora native to the Piedmont, the foothills region of the Appalachians that runs from New York to Alabama. Under the direction of Dr. Richard Lighty (see pages 198–203), a plant geneticist who has worked for Copeland since 1983, Mt. Cuba has already introduced many gardenworthy forms of native species, including *Cornus sericea* 'Silver and Gold', a variegated yellow-twig dogwood that is highly showy in every season.

Asters and goldenrods are among America's great plants, adding late-season color to the landscape, but many of the straight species are simply too rank for garden use. So Mt. Cuba introduced a dwarf, mounded *Aster novae-angliae* 'Purple Dome' along with its ideal goldenrod companion, *So-*

ABOVE RIGHT: *Yellow daisylike ragwort flowers* (Senecio aureus) *bloom among the lavender-blue phlox and occasional alien primroses.* CENTER LEFT: *Bluets* (Houstonia caerulea) *will grow right up to a high-limbed tree trunk.* CENTER RIGHT: *Foamflower* (Tiarella cordifolia) *and maidenhair fern* (Adiantum pedatum). RIGHT: *Yellow lady's slipper orchids* (Cypripedium calceolus).

lidago sphacelata 'Golden Fleece'. *Heuchera americana* 'Garnet', another Mt. Cuba product, turns a garnet-purple in fall through winter, and new spring foliage is similarly colored.

Attention has also been turned to wildflowers that have been thought of as difficult, namely orchids and trilliums, so that these delicate creatures that are among Copeland's greatest gardening treasures could be shared with others. *Spiranthes odorata* 'Chadds Ford', whose spiraling flowers smell of vanilla, is already finding its way into commerce, and Dr. Lighty has also promoted 'Quicksilver', a *Trillium grandiflorum* that is especially quick to reproduce for sale as a nursery plant.

At present, Copeland's garden is open only to groups by appointment, for springtime tours, but upon her death, Mt. Cuba will become a public garden, another gift from a dedicated plantswoman to lovers of native plants.

ABOVE LEFT: *Yellow trillium* (Trillium sessile *var.* luteum). CENTER: *Pitcher plants* (Sarracenia *spp.*) *by the pond.* FAR LEFT: *A very uncommon yet familiar-looking flower reminiscent of many wildings is Barbara's buttons* (Marshallia graminitolia). LEFT: *A vanilla-scented cultivar of the native orchid ladies'-tresses* (Spiranthes odorata 'Chadd's Ford').

PORTOLA VALLEY RANCH
PORTOLA VALLEY,
CALIFORNIA

A CENTURY OF OVERGRAZ-ing had thwarted the emerging oak seedlings on the land that was to become Portola Valley Ranch, a progressive residential community and nature preserve in the foothills of the Santa Cruz Mountains, about thirty miles south of San Francisco.

It was the oaks—young and old representatives of six species of the genus *Quercus*—around which the plan for building on the rolling site was formed after developer Joseph Whelan pur-chased the 450 acres of coastal

ACORNS TO OAKS

In the mid-1970s, a pioneer experiment in controlled-use development was begun in the coastal hills south of San Francisco. Every effort was made to cause the least disturbance and even to restore the grassland,

chaparral, and oak woodland while constructing two hundred homes. The benefit has been exquisite settings with native plants, RIGHT, *and spectacular uninterrupted views,* OPPOSITE. *But the landscape still functions "normally." People who wanted lawn have native-grass plantings,* ABOVE.

oak woodland in 1974. It was on these acres that he created an early foray into controlled-use development. The landscape architect Nancy Hardesty was brought in to create a strategy for accomplishing this, and that would also protect wildlife habi-tats of more than 125 resident an-imal species, stabilize the soil, and recharge existing water-sheds. About 200 homes were to be clustered on 76 of the 450 acres so that the whopping share would remain open, traversed with nature trails. Although the oaks are the main focus, chapar-ral, grassland, mixed evergreen forest, and other habitat com-munities also exist on-site.

The oak woodland environ-mental ethic Hardesty devised protected existing trees (each one was numbered, evaluated, and given the care required) and re-newed the oak forest, which in-cludes coastal live oak (*Quercus agrifolia*), canyon or golden oak

(*Q. chrysolepis*), blue oak (*Q. douglasii*), California black oak (*Q. kelloggii*), and valley or Cali-fornia white oak (*Q. lobata*). Her-itage trees, some of them gnarled and four hundred years old, are treated as esteemed members of the community. Home owners, as well as their children, have been educated in the protection and regeneration of the oaks, in-cluding how to plant and nurture acorns into young trees.

Hardesty wrote a newsletter called "Nature Notes," which was distributed periodically to home owners to teach them to care for the environment's other inhabitants, both plants and ani-mals, offering guidelines on everything from local plant com-munities for help in choosing landscape plants to wise watering practices and feeding of birds.

Even the views are safe here. With houses nestled below the ridgelines of the hills and even open-sided carports built instead of traditional garages, the award-winning community is meant to stay as is, or better.

EVELYN
(MRS. ERNEST) ADAMS
WELLESLEY HILLS,
MASSACHUSETTS

THE SECRET GARDEN

*The path through Evelyn
Adams's garden forms a circle
around a solid blanket
of plants dominated by
wake-robin* (Trillium
grandiflorum) *and Virginia
bluebells* (Mertensia
virginica), RIGHT.
However, many other trillium

*species and North American
ephemerals live there, too.*
ABOVE: *"The thinking
stone" was christened years
ago when Adams's husband
came out to the garden to find
a little boy sitting on the large
rock. When asked what he
was doing there, the boy
replied, "Thinking."*

MANY DECADES OF FOOT-
steps have worn smooth the narrow pathways through Evelyn
Adams's hidden little garden, a
naturally secluded corner of the
property with an errant tree
branch "gate" that must be lifted
to gain access.

Adams, a native Vermonter,
began making the garden in
Wellesley Hills, Massachusetts,
nearly fifty years ago, beginning
with four trilliums passed along
to her from family land, along
with some daffodils. As her interest in the daffodils waned, her

love of the trilliums grew, and
she has divided them faithfully
every spring since, just after they
stop blooming, and also gathers
and scatters their seed to help the
incredible colony grow. In it are
represented more than half a
dozen of the thirty or so American species including literally
thousands of individual plants.

Also from Vermont, from the
basement of her husband's
grandfather's home, came a
large, rectangular rock that the
Adamses set into the garden as a
feature. One morning, Evelyn's
husband went out and found a
young boy sitting upon it.

"What are you doing?" he
asked the boy.

"I'm thinking," the child replied, and ever since it has been
called the thinking stone.

The native canopy of dog-
wood (*Cornus florida*) is under
stress from *discula,* the anthrac-
nose-type fungus threatening
this cherished native tree, but a

unusual pink-flowered form of Carolina silverbell (*Halesia carolina*) and volunteer crab apples (*Malus* spp., probably not natives) are doing a nice job of carrying on the symbolic flight of butterflies above the garden. On ground level, foamflower (*Tiarella cordifolia*), Virginia bluebells (*Mertensia virginica*), and trout lilies (*Erythronium* spp.) join the trillium-dominated planting below the house.

Today, gardeners wishing to grow trilliums must not take their first plants from the wild, of course, but purchase their initial stock from a nursery that does not wild-collect, or from a native plant society sale. Then they can join Adams in the practice of conservation through propagation—creating safe havens for these delicate wildings in our own nature-inspired garden designs. Evelyn Adams didn't set out to create a native habitat. She just prefers this kind of wild garden to the calculated organization of a perennial border.

"Flower gardens are beautiful," says Adams, "but they don't look like the Lord made them."

The stars of the garden, wake-robin and Virginia bluebells, OPPOSITE. *Years of propagation have led to this unbelievable spectacle. The soil and leaf-litter paths through the garden,* ABOVE AND RIGHT, *provide access to view the exquisite jewels of the forest understory.*

THE NEW YORK
BOTANICAL GARDEN
FOREST
BRONX, NEW YORK

IT STANDS IN DEFIANCE OF all around it, as if the last several centuries—from the arrival of the first Old World explorer on the Hudson River to the enduring age of high-rises—had not even happened.

The New York Botanical Garden Forest, 40 acres at the heart of a 250-acre, century-old institution, has managed to hang on as the largest remnant of the forest that once covered much of the metropolitan area. It has never been cut, neither for agriculture

A GENTLE HELPING HAND

When people hear that there is a forty-acre untouched woodland in New York City, they are incredulous. But it's true. Within the 250-acre, 100-year-old New York Botanical Garden is a

managed, but not maintained, forest; the glittering attraction is the Bronx River, RIGHT. *Foliage color comes from maples, oaks, tulip trees, sycamore, and sweet gum. Glacier-deposited rocks are features as well,* ABOVE.

nor for development. Some trees within the rugged, hilly tract of mixed hardwoods and hemlock are as old as three hundred years, living on despite air pollution, trampling by many millions of feet—and the pocketknives determined to leave their messages in the bark.

This forty acres is not a garden, the staff members who manage it are quick to point out. It is a living organism, protected and examined by them in extensive studies of the forest ecology. Their basically hands-off policy means that here, disease, damage, and even death are recorded but almost nothing is removed—snags (dead standing trees) are left as insect food and animal shelters, for instance. Even the great old hemlocks (*Tsuga canadensis*), besieged by the potentially deadly pest, the woolly adelgid, that is devastating the region's hemlocks, are monitored but not treated.

The native canopy of towering tulip trees (*Liriodendron tulipifera*),

birch (*Betula* spp.), sweetgum (*Liquidambar styraciflua*), cherry (*Prunus* spp.), oaks (*Quercus* spp.), and hemlock provide cover for increasingly large natural stands of trout lily (*Erythronium americanum*), mayapple (*Podophyllum peltatum*), and other ephemerals. But until a path system was established (mulched with woodchips to fit into the forest as well as possible) to limit visitor impact on the greater area, ground-level vegetation was having a hard time. Now, stress to the floor has been greatly reduced and the wildflowers, sedges (*Carex* spp.), and even grasses like little bluestem (*Andropogon scoparius* or *Schizachyrium scoparium*), in areas that get relatively high light, are rebounding nicely.

Besides stabilizing the floor, a prime objective of woodland management is to get the native canopy reestablished. Opportunists like Amur cork tree (*Phellodendron amurense*), a Chinese species, and Norway maple (*Acer platanoides*) have seeded themselves into the mix and shut out native seedlings.

Though the overall policy is one of nonintervention, some removals of trash tree species like these are performed, but carefully. Weighed into the decision of whether to remove even a modest-sized tree is the degree of disturbance it will cause. When the additional light reaches the forest floor, what will its effect be? All too often, says Ed Roy, manager of the Forest Project, such light increase favors the exotic species of the forest floor.

"You have to be really careful,

case by case, to understand the impact," he explains. In some cases, it's architecturally impossible to get the tree out without damaging the root system of another.

"And in other cases," says Roy, "the tree is performing a function that needs to be addressed." Introducing small native trees and shrubs to shade the ground where the tree was removed can mediate the impact.

The signs that this kind of management works abound on the forest floor: the little bluestem and increased population of seedlings are encouraging.

"Our job is a difficult one," says Roy, "to use management practices that enhance native species over nonnatives." The fact that this undertaking occurs in a small pocket tucked into one of the most populated urban centers on earth should steel the habitat gardener. Preserving and protecting one tree or a small woodlot should seem a little less daunting.

The river flows to a series of falls, which are popular attractions, RIGHT. *Some of the best views of the falling water,* ABOVE, *are afforded from elegant bridges.*

WING HAVEN, FORMER
GARDEN OF EDWIN AND
ELIZABETH CLARKSON
CHARLOTTE, NORTH
CAROLINA

ELIZABETH CLARKSON WAS A habitat gardener from the beginning, although when she began her formal garden in the 1920s, on bare red clay scraped clean for farming, that horticultural concept did not exist. It would be more than half a century before the native-plant movement really arrived, but by then Clarkson and her husband, Edwin, had hosted uncountable numbers of birds on the three acres they called Wing Haven. More than

PLOT FOR THE BIRDS

Habitat-style gardens are not necessarily new or informal. Wing Haven is devoted to birds. Nearly all the plants have been selected to provide shelter or food. Mahonia flower buds, BELOW, *will*

eventually produce berries that are favorites of cedar waxwings. RIGHT, TOP TO BOTTOM: *A mirror set into a brick arch is covered with netting to keep the birds from flying into the glass. The view from the bench across the garden's formal axis. Wood-duck boxes hang from trees. Carolina snailseed (Cocculus carolinus).* OPPOSITE: *The path continues to wilder parts of the garden.*

140 distinct species were recorded in the Clarkson years.

Wing Haven, now a public garden in the quiet Charlotte neighborhood where the Clarksons lived until 1988, was not just ahead of its time. It is proof positive that a structured design can be a thriving habitat.

Despite the extensive system of symmetrical brick paths, boxwood parterres, and other traditional elements, wild is the overriding word at Wing Haven. Muscadine grapes, mulberries, wild cherries, and privet (today, *Viburnum rufidulum* [rusty blackhaw] or *Vaccinium arboreum* [farkleberry] could be substituted for that exotic) grow together in a delectable jumble. Elsewhere, wild grape, trumpet vine (*Campsis radicans*) and greenbrier (*Smilax rotundifolia*) tangle their way over dogwoods and cherries. Holly, elderberry, pokeweed, mahonia, viburnum, and eleagnus (again, one to avoid because of its propensity to self-sow) contribute to the picture, too.

The place is like a living fruit salad served up in thicket form, precisely geared to avian tastes.

The Clarksons catered to their birds, not just with seed-filled feeders, but with natural features chosen to give them both food and shelter: berried plants at every turn, snags (dead trees) left standing, fallen trunks left to decay in place, piled-up brush for a safe hiding place, just enough thorns to deter predators, numerous small pools—and dripping faucets everywhere, for nothing fascinates, or satisfies, a bird more. The Clarksons first erected a wood duck box in the 1950s, and mating pairs have fledged young nearly every year.

Elizabeth's greatest vision may have been her stand against chemicals. She knew better, and so her birds survived. In the 1940s and 1950s, during municipal DDT-spray programs to reduce insects, Elizabeth went out in her nightgown in the predawn hours and stood in the road to stop the trucks from spraying her block, a proper southern housewife's brand of passive resistance. Her cul-de-sac was eventually taken off the spray route.

Indeed, Wing Haven grew wild, perhaps to a fault. Elizabeth Clarkson didn't even like to pull volunteer seedlings since her darling birds had planted them. As nature would have it, the thinning took place anyway, if belatedly and anything but gradually: In 1989, Hurricane Hugo devastated the region, taking down more than seventy-five trees on the Clarksons' small property alone. And so the habitat continues to evolve.

SAM AND BEV RYBURN
DOVER, MASSACHUSETTS

WHEN SAM AND BEV RYBURN first saw the site of their future home some thirty years ago, they were smitten—although friends, family, and even the real-estate broker warned that they were in for trouble with such a "difficult" piece of land. But it was the imposing rock outcropping and the many large boulders that attracted them to the suburban Boston property.

To the Ryburns, then novice gardeners who had been living in the congestion of New York City, this wooded land seemed

BUILT ON SOLID ROCK

Few set out to make a museum garden, but the Ryburns have created a place where native plants are thoughtfully displayed and accurately labeled. This garden lies across a bridge,

ABOVE RIGHT, *in a hollow below the house and is home to blue dogbane* (Amsonia tabernaemontana), ABOVE, *and trillium,* CENTER RIGHT. *A stream trickles through the garden,* RIGHT, *and into constructed pools.* OPPOSITE: *Blue phlox bask beneath thousands of dogwood bracts that hover like butterflies.*

like paradise. It turned out that there were reasons why the spot had never been developed; what finally became the Ryburns' land had served as the local rock depository for farmers clearing their own acres. However, even in the early days, before the couple began gardening, the property had more than thirty wildflower species growing in the moist, thin soil.

The Ryburns' initial goal was to make a beautiful wildflower garden, but soon it became building a showcase—a museum, perhaps—of the wild woodland flora of their region. The basin-shaped garden in the hollow below the house today contains winding gravel pathways that take the visitor to within inches of nearly every plant, all clearly labeled with tags that rival any botanical garden's.

Twenty years after the Ryburns started, 270-plus herbaceous species of plants coexist on

the same "difficult" site, including remarkable stands of pink lady's slipper (*Cypripedium acaule*)—plants the Ryburns didn't purchase (and couldn't, since even today it defies propagators) but simply encouraged so that existing colonies now produce up to 175 flowers at a time. Unfortunately, unless like the Ryburns you "inherit" such treasures, they must be admired in botanical gardens and the wild for now. Instead, start with easier ones such as *C. calceolus pubescens,* the yellow lady's slipper, which is slowly becoming available in number from ethical commercial sources. Or start as the Ryburns did by purchasing a single plant at a wildflower society sale and exercising the key trait of the wildflower gardener: the virtue of patience. Today, their once-solitary plant has grown to bear sixty-five flowers.

The garden is also home to enormous stands of single and double bloodroot (*Sanguinaria canadensis* and *S. c. multiplex,* or 'Flore Pleno'), mayapple (*Podophyllum peltatum*), and wild ginger (*Asarum canadense*). Seven trillium species, violets, and phloxes add to the spring color.

Close to the house, Sam, a for-mer chemical engineer who in his retirement gardens full time, has made a more formal rock garden representing the flora of many lands. A path leads up through the giant outcropping to a flat pad covered with the tiny native bluets (*Houstonia caerulea*) and down the other side, across a bridge over a series of pools. The water moving from one pool to another draws a wide variety of birds. This is the Ryburns' collector's area, where exotics such as Japanese jack-in-the-pulpit are contained in a carefully managed space, peacefully commingling with their native cousins.

OPPOSITE, ABOVE FAR LEFT: Viola labradorica *climbs some rock below* Iris cristata *foliage.* NEAR LEFT: *Rock doesn't thwart interrupted fern* (Osmunda claytoniana) *to the left of a dwarf hemlock.* OPPOSITE, BELOW: *The rare pink lady's slipper* (Cypripedium acaule) *should not be purchased or transplanted.* ABOVE, CLOCKWISE FROM LEFT: *Three flowers repeat trillium's leitmotif; a mature colony of bloodroot* (Sanguinaria canadensis); *an eternal sign of spring: cinnamon fern crosiers; the venerable yellow lady's slipper orchids.*

THE ARTHUR L. MENZIES
MEMORIAL GARDEN OF
NATIVE PLANTS
SAN FRANCISCO,
CALIFORNIA

EPILOGUE

Quaking aspen (Populus
tremuloides), OPPOSITE,
*provide patterned gray bark
for winter interest after silver-
dollar leaves turn yellow and
drop. But the spring sea of
meadow foam* (Limnanthes

douglasii) *beneath them,*
ABOVE RIGHT, *steals the
show. A stream, crossed by
bridges,* BELOW RIGHT,
winds past flowers of
Darmera peltata *or*
Peltiphyllum peltatum,
CENTER, *and cow parsnip*
(Heracleum lanatum), ABOVE.

THE EXQUISITE CLIMATE OF
California represents different
things to different people. To
farmers, it's a land of nearly un-
limited agricultural potential; to
gardeners, it is a paradise found,
where nearly any plant can survive outdoors—providing there
isn't a five-year drought. To naturalists and native-plant lovers,
California is the last Eden,
though an endangered one. The
incredible diversity of the plants
in the land west of the Rockies is
staggering, and the many habitats within the state and niches
within them present both opportunity and challenge.

"One thing that grows won-
derfully in one place won't do
well ten miles away," says Ron
Lutsko, who is noted for creating
natural landscapes throughout
the state, including the redesign
of the Arthur L. Menzies Memorial Garden in Golden Gate
Park's Strybing Arboretum, San
Francisco. The four-acre Menzies
garden is a condensed look at
that wide range of California's
possibilities—and it won Lutsko
the National Award of Merit
from the American Society of
Landscape Architects in 1991.

The Strybing Arboretum, of
which Menzies is just a part, is
dedicated to plants suited to what
is called a "Mediterranean" climate, with low rainfall, hot days,
and cool nights—the kind of
general conditions experienced in
much of California. The four-
acre Menzies garden, however, is
planted purely in California natives—846 species. But unfortunately, there are few such
enforced protected areas as Menzies, and indigenous species have
been pushed out by similar plants

from the Mediterranean region, Australia, and South Africa.

In 1986, when Lutsko began to rework the garden first dedicated in 1973, it was overgrown. "You couldn't see ten feet in front of you."

Lutsko began to design a garden that would make as much use of the existing flora as possible and strive to express the habitats and vegetation typical of certain of the state's plant communities. Within the larger plan he developed a coastal scrub, a freshwater marsh, stream and bog, a pond, a home for bunchgrasses and mountain wildflowers, a stand of mixed evergreens, chaparral, arroyo (wash), and a rock garden, created in collaboration with Phil Johnson, a rock-garden architect. According to Walden Valen, director of the Strybing, the next garden at Menzies will be made up of San Francisco native plants.

There is much that makes Menzies so successful besides its California palette. Beyond a collection, it is perhaps the most beautifully planned and maintained public garden in the country dedicated to habitat-style planting.

The entrance is one of the most colorful areas, with herbaceous flowering selections of the

April is the most colorful month in the Menzies garden.
CLOCKWISE FROM ABOVE: *Flowers line the streambed; pale yellow meadow foam and palmate-leafed lupine* (Lupinus polyphyllus); *white-flowered currant* (Ribes sanguineum *var.* glutinosum); *California poppies and Douglas iris; yellow monkey-flower* (Mimulus guttatus) *and more lupines; Douglas iris; blue ground-covering* Ceanothus impressus *'Santa Barbara'.*

Northwest coast and oak woodland edge, such as a variety of white and pale to dark blue Douglas iris (*Iris douglasiana*), orange California poppy (*Eschscholzia californica*), and blue-eyed grass (*Sisyrinchium californica*). The centerpiece is a grove of quaking aspen (*Populus tremuloides*) underplanted with meadow foam (*Limnanthes douglasii*), growing in a stand as they do in many parts of the country. This poplar relative is one of the most widely dispersed trees in North America, and a recently discovered forest of them is thought to be the largest living organism on earth, since all of the trees proved genetically identical, growing from a common rootstock.

Winding through the entry area is a stream, crossed by three bridges, that spills into a pool and overflows into an arroyo that is dry except in the winter months. This has become a wildlife haven. Along the pool's edge, giant cow parsnip (*Heracleum sphondylium*) bloom. The rocks here look completely at home, but they, too, were carried in from a construction site and installed. Everything fits— but keeping it that way against the efforts of people, birds, wind, and other forces that carry incongruous influences is the Men-

zies' heroic gardener, King Sip.

Late fall is the beginning of her crew's busy time, when faded grasses are cut back into tuffets, their tops raked and collected with the rest of the season's debris. A burn would be helpful, but it is highly unlikely that it could take place in this town. Weeding of the meadow is probably three quarters of the work.

In winter, Sip makes three sowings of the native annuals that form the visual amalgam of the colorful plantings. The meadow foam, in particular, is a knitter, with cheerful yellow and white blossoms that can still be seen when the grasses are cut back. In time, Sip hopes, the annuals will self-sow with enough regularity to make them permanent members of this ever-evolving community.

The Menzies is one of a very few gardens that attempts to interpret some of the plant communities of a place as huge and diverse as California. The fact that it can teach so much in a relatively small place is miraculous. The fact that this has been done so beautifully is the pleasure of visiting this garden. It is a prototype for what botanical gardens should do, and what American gardeners can learn to do, too.

LEFT: *The view across the meadow to the aspen grove.*
OPPOSITE, CLOCKWISE
FROM BOTTOM LEFT:
Chaparral is represented by shrubs and subshrubs; the bunchgrass meadow features pink Pacific Coast mallow (Sidalcea malviflora); *rushes, sedges, and grasses such as* Juncus patens, Carex fissuricola, *and* Calamagrostis nutkaensis; *meadow flowers.*

Autumn at the Menzies.
<small>OPPOSITE, CLOCKWISE
FROM BOTTOM LEFT:</small>
California fuchsia
(Zauschneria cana);
*detail; yellow-twig
dogwood* (Cornus stolonifera
or C. sericea *'Flaviramea'*);
rush (Juncus patens); *Saint-
Catherine's-Lace*
(Eriogonum giganteum),
*native to Santa Catalina and
San Clemente islands; the
view across the meadow to the
aspen in fall; the silvery bark
shimmers when they become
the focal point of the garden
as winter approaches.*
<small>OVERLEAF:</small> *The winter
rains fill the arroyos that run
through the bunchgrass
meadow and produce the
spring explosion that plant
collections manager Barbara
Keller considers the crescendo
of the garden year. Then
the water pools in a basin
of cattails surrounded by
meadow foam.*

SOURCE GUIDE

INTRODUCTION

The following section of this book contains, among other things, specific how-to information to help create gardens and restore plant communities in four habitat types—grassland, dryland, wetland, and woodland—along with guidelines for accessing sources for the detailed plant and soil information you will need as you begin landscaping with native plants.

FIRST THINGS FIRST

The first step of the process is to evaluate what you already have; that is, to positively identify all plants currently growing on your property and to gauge soil conditions. In other words, determine the type of habitat that is natural to your property. The Peterson Field Guides are excellent "in hand" references for identifying wildflowers and trees; there are two basic editions, one for eastern states, and the other for western. There are more specific guides also: *Pacific States Wildflowers*, *Rocky Mountain Wildflowers*, and *Southwestern and Texas Wildflowers*. *Newcomb's Wildflower Guide* is very good for states east of the Mississippi from Maine to North Carolina. *Grasses: An Identification Guide* by Lauren Brown, while not all-inclusive, is also a valuable aid.

As for positively identifying invasive species, more and more valuable plant information becomes available on the Internet every day. Visit the Web sites listed in the "Invasive Plants Primer"; here you can find help with identification and methods for eradicating invasive species. Although there are no local-specific Web sites or published guidebooks to invasive species as of this printing, the lack of sites and guides will, no doubt, change.

KNOW YOUR SITE

Several factors enter into the decision to make grassland, woodland, wetland, or dryland garden: location, location, location. If you live in Arizona, a dryland garden will probably be in your future. In much of the Northeast, where there is often more rainfall than places we think of as wet, such as Seattle, woodland and wetland gardens dominate. Climate, and more specifically, rainfall, determines your natural habitat garden type.

In natural grasslands, which range in central states from Ohio to the eastern steppes of the Rocky Mountains, there is moisture, but less than in the Northeast or Northwest, where trees dominate the landscape. In addition to moisture, wind and cold keep plants short, or thwart woody shrubs and trees from taking hold, preventing the grassland from becoming woodland. In some cases, the moisture is locked up in snow or ice. In parts of Texas, Nebraska, the Dakotas, and Montana and nearby states, short-grass prairies grow. These places are typified by scruffy low-growing grasses, and in the old days, bison. In states with more rainfall, tall-grass prairies

once thrived. And there are pockets within the tall-grass prairies where trees grow, such as the oak savannahs, where moisture collects. Natural fires also keep woody plants from becoming established.

In addition to climate, soil types direct the habitat types. The clay soil of the Midwest encourages the plants that evolved there, such as the grasses and non-grass flowering herbaceous plants called forbs. The plants in this region have developed roots able to penetrate the hardpan and travel deep—often many times deeper than the plants are tall—to find moisture and survive brutal winters.

In the deserts, a lack of rainfall combines with fast-draining sandy soil to make the dryland habitat. Places with poor drainage may be wetlands, whether they are tiny year-round marshes or vernal pools. So, know your climate, and also get to know your soil.

KNOW YOUR SOIL

Some people say good soil looks like chocolate cake. But soil quality cannot be judged by its appearance. Then there is the squeeze method, when a handful of soil is closed in a fist. The hand is opened, revealing a clod of earth. If the clod breaks easily when poked, the tilth is pretty good. But you still will not know the makeup of the soil.

Knowing your soil goes beyond the squeeze or chocolate cake tests. Soil-testing kits are available from nurseries, and state extension offices provide soil-testing services. Testing will reveal the contents of the nutritional elements nitrogen, phosphorus, and potassium (NPK), and the soil's acidity or alkalinity, noted as a number on the pH scale (pH 7 is neutral; lower, acidic; higher, alkaline). It will still be helpful to discover the relative percentages of the key ingredients of loam: clay, sand, and decayed vegetation—organic matter or humus.

Author Sara Stein outlines a similar method in greater detail in her book *Planting Noah's Garden: Further Adventures in Backyard Ecology*. Paraphrasing her instructions: fill a quart jar with soil (sifted clean of twigs or stones), water, and a few drops of dish detergent, to act as a surface-tension breaker, or a surfactant. Close the jar and shake vigorously; view the contents after one minute and throughout one day. The first material to settle to the bottom of the jar is sand. After one hour, the humus settles. When the water is clear, the fine particles that make up clay will be visible as the top layer.

Good garden loam has a balance of all three ingredients. Clay soil is what is found in grassland areas. The desert may have more sand than the other components. A wetland may have clay that remains sodden, or a high amount of organic matter (humus). Woodland "soil" is made mostly of humus and is very shallow—sometimes only 4 or 5" deep. Bear in mind that soilless media, popular for container gardening and sometimes pushed on the public as "garden soil," has little to do with what we hope to find in the ground.

Stein also writes:

"Good garden soil" and "rich woodland soil" is considered a balance of all three components. "Thin" soil has little organic matter, and "hard" soils are comprised of clay that dries brick hard. You may discover that you have several inches of good garden soil on top of a layer of rocky subsoil with hardpan at the bottom. If there has been construction on the property recently, subsoil, or gravelly fill may be what the construction crew has left behind.

It is also important to know how quickly water passes through the soil, or, said another way, how well the soil retains water. To test how well water drains in your ground, dig a hole. If water seeps in, the soil is wet or saturated; if it is full of stones, it is obviously rocky. Continue digging until you have gone about 18" deep. Fill it with water and observe it over the next few hours. If it drains at the rate of about an inch an hour, this is considered well-drained soil.

For woodland and grassland habitats, "good, well-drained garden soil" is preferable. Wetlands exist where the soil can hold moisture for a long time, and drylands are defined by fast-draining or "thin" soil. Different plants thrive in different types of soil.

BLACK GOLD
Humus is another word for organic matter in soil. Start a compost pile now if you haven't already, so it will be ready when you need to amend your soil. If you need some now and cannot wait, contact your local recycling center. Most municipalities have compost piles they have made from collected grass clippings, leaves, and brush, and it is all free for the taking. The good steward reaches for compost—"black gold"—instead of peat moss.

PLANTS
When purchasing wildflowers for your garden, be sure they are nursery propagated, not just nursery grown. Look for that specific phrase, "nursery propagated," when you see threatened species for sale, for example, at the big box retail stores—and if you don't see it, don't buy them. The best way to obtain wildflowers is through one of the societies listed on pages 246–248 and through sales at conservation groups and botanical gardens.

If you see a potentially invasive plant for sale, at a nursery or a botanical garden, inform the proprietor. When I see a plant such as purple loosestrife for sale at a nursery, I will not shop there. I simply and politely point out the fact that they are selling environmentally harmful material as I'm walking out the door. It is important to have standards and rules, and the best way to have an impact with retail outlets is with our purchasing power.

COPING WITH PESTS
Good stewardship of the land includes a deep respect for all living organisms. When life in the garden falls out of balance, choose the mildest methods for correcting the problem. Insect and mammal pests often pose a huge threat to our gardens. Most areas of the country have problems with deer, raccoons, groundhogs, rabbits, and rodents. Mosquitoes carry dreaded diseases, some caterpillars destroy trees.

Get to know your insects as well as the other animals in your neighborhood. And teach your children and visitors not to slap or step on every "bug" they find in your garden. Many insects and bugs are beneficial. Integrated Pest Management (see page 244) is the logical and, in the long run, most practical way to keep insects from becoming a problem. IPM promotes a healthy environment, whereas toxic "quick fixes" possibly endanger all living things, not just insects.

Overpopulation of deer and other animals is a huge problem in most areas of the country. We human beings are responsible for the changes in their environment that have led to this serious situation. Now that there is a significant economic impact, governmental agencies are finally beginning to realize they need to address the issue. Conservation groups have been crying for aid for years. Those of us who embrace nature must also take responsibility for helping to find humane solutions for saving healthy populations of our wild animals, not simply protect our own grounds. Hunting permits are not the solution, since there are far too few hunters to manage the herds. Join (i.e., give financial support to) those groups that fund research for humane solutions.

Adequate fencing is the only way to keep grazing animals out of the garden. When this is not possible, try one of the several deer and small animal repellant sprays that have been tested in university and public gardens and agricultural sites, and by me, with good results.

Some animals, like groundhogs and rabbits, cats, and dogs, seem unfazed by most deterrents based on smell. As one nurseryman in the Northeast put it, "I'd rather have ten deer in my neighborhood than one groundhog." Anecdotal evidence seems to indicate that spray repellants can be effective for keeping deer away, but groundhogs and other small mammals are much more difficult to discourage. In these cases, fences, netting, and humane trap-and-release methods are the alternatives, if local law allows that practice. Many suburban and rural areas allow critters to be captured, but not released. They must be disposed of by the property owner, on the property. Gulp.

Poisons are out of the question.

Placing chicken wire or hardware cloth fencing on the ground around plantings may repel rabbits, groundhogs, cats, and dogs since they do not like walking on these surfaces.

Protect young trees from animal damage either with deer- and bear-proof fencing that surrounds the entire area or with a protective trunk wrapping that allows for air circulation and trunk growth expansion.

WHERE ARE THE PROFESSIONALS?
In your efforts as a responsible steward you may try to hire a professional to help you identify any problem plants on your property, but I am sad to report that it is still difficult to find very many knowledgeable professionals who are committed to using native plants and removing harmful, invasive species from the environment and marketplace. Nurseries continue to sell bamboo and promote the use of *Vinca minor* and English ivy, while some certified arborists in the Northeast still suggest Norway maples for home gardens, even as the beloved sugar maple remains threatened by road salt and development.

In the "hard to believe but true" department: the titles of

"landscape architect" and "landscape designer" imply that these certified individuals possess a knowledge of plants; however, most college and university programs *do not* require landscape architect or design students to take more than a single plant course. In your interview, before you hire any designer or gardener, ask him or her what native plants they like to use; if they hesitate, or have very few suggestions, excuse yourself politely and move on.

The best way to locate professionals you can trust is by word-of-mouth recommendations from other homeowners and gardeners on the same mission. You may find some names through a nursery that carries or specializes in native plants and through wildflower societies. Find and join your state and local chapter (see "Native-Plant Societies," page 246). Get to know the people in your town who have joined the movement to protect endangered species and "go native." And, just as important, spread the word. Share what you learn with garden friends, and, especially, tell your favorite nursery owners that you need and want to buy and learn about more local plants. The journey of discovery is as exciting as the acquisition and growing of plants. Join and be counted; let your voice be heard while making a difference in your own backyard.

INVASIVE PLANTS PRIMER

Would you knowingly welcome a plant into your garden if you knew it was going to become a menacing weed that you will spend the rest of your life trying to get rid of? Ridiculous question you say? Then why do gardeners continue to buy and nurseries to sell hundreds of flats of English ivy and vinca, or welcome *Ranunculus repens* 'Buttered Popcorn' and, coming soon to a seller near you, *Ixeris*? English ivy (*Hedera helix*) and vinca and periwinkle (*Vinca minor, V. major*) have invaded woodlands near neighborhoods all over America. Anyone who has moved to a new landscape where the former owner planted and encouraged English ivy as an easy, no-mow ground cover, and who hopes to have a garden knows how difficult if not impossible it is to eradicate this plant. Most chemicals do not work, and hand pulling may cause serious allergic reactions.

Every place seems to have its own favorite nemesis. In parts of the Midwest, it might be buckthorn or purple loosestrife. In New York City, the tree of heaven (*Ailanthus altissima*), although beloved by some as the woody plant that grows in Brooklyn, thrives nearly everywhere else.

When you meet with your garden club, or visit a friend and hear the phrase "pass-along plants," take a moment and think. Make sure that you do not unwittingly continue to pass along pests. We gardeners have a responsibility—now more than ever—to pass along our special consciousness, our commitment to protect our delightful, valuable, precious, and threatened local species. When you meet a new gardener, share knowledge and experience along with rooted cuttings. Do not allow your enthusiasm for new plants to override your common sense.

WHAT IS A WEED?
In the simplest definition, a weed is any plant growing in the wrong place. Therefore, a sturdy oak seedling, destined to become a stately specimen, is a weed when it sprouts in a crack between the paving stones of the patio.

WHAT IS AN INVASIVE PLANT?
Weeds that spread aggressively to the detriment of other local or native species are said to be invasive. They consume all the resources—light, nutrients, water, and soil, to the extent that other plants are eliminated.

WHERE DO INVASIVE PLANTS COME FROM?
The New England Wild Flower Society reports that approximately 60% of the invasive species are a result of horticultural activity in the form of introductions by arboretums, botanic gardens, and gardeners. Another 30% of species now considered invasive were introduced by the Department of Agriculture in its conservation activities for windbreaks and erosion control and to supply food and cover for wildlife. Purple loosestrife is counted among the 10% that were introduced accidentally: it was transported in the ballast water of a cargo ship but was then spread throughout the country by the horticultural industry. But it is important to realize that invaders are not always exotic aliens from other countries. They may be natives from one region of the United States that grow out of control in another.

The very clear lesson to be learned from these statistics is this: we must "test grow" any new exotic, nonnative introduction for several years before we embrace it. "Test grow?" nursery owners ask. "Are we supposed to put a plant in an isolation bed for twenty years to see if it is going to pose a problem?" I tell them that they can guess which plants might pose problems. If a plant spreads naturally, in its homeland, to colonize vast areas, such as grasses, these plants could be a problem elsewhere, especially if their natural controls are not exported along with them. If a plant is a vine that covers the treetops in its native land, it could do that when exported, as well, to the detriment of local species. If a plant has berries that are eaten by birds, it could be dangerous. If a plant's seeds are picked up and carried on the wind, such as a dandelion, why wouldn't it escape in its new homeland, too?

WHAT'S SO BAD ABOUT INVASIVE PLANTS?
People often ask, "Isn't it natural for plants to move around from place to place?" The answer is a qualified "Yes, but . . ." Plants do migrate through natural processes and expand their range—usually along with climate changes over hundreds of years. The plants we are concerned with are those that humans have moved around the world, plants that, when moved to certain new environments, threaten the biodiversity that currently exists. In the past, plants might have crossed oceans as stowaways on ships. Then the Concord came and went, but air travel still poses potential problems.

So what? So what if a beautiful plant covers your garden, neighborhood, state, region, country? Only one plant can live in one spot at one time; therefore where every invasive exotic plant grows, the local native has been pushed out. That indigenous plant might have been a food source for a local animal, which is also impacted. The Nature Conservancy's Wildland Invasive Species Team Web site (http://tncweeds.ucdavis.edu/worst.html) describes it clearly: "Some of the worst invasive species are those which alter normal ecological processes. For example, in some deserts fire is rare. Exotic annual grasses may form a flammable carpet that can spread fire easily, and as a result the frequency of fires increases. The native plants are soon killed, and the invasive species spread even further. As a result, what was once a biologically diverse desert may become a solid infestation of just a few invasive species."

Some vines, for instance, may grow up into a tree's canopy and block sunlight from indigenous plants and the emerging seedlings of precious plants we wish to preserve. Other plants, such as the Norway maple, have chemicals in their leaves and seeds that inhibit the germination or growth of other plants, either killing existing vegetation or preventing new natives from sprouting.

WHAT NOT TO PLANT

Some states, after realizing the damage plants can cause to the economy by threatening crops of timberland, are proposing to ban the sale of plants proven to be invasive. New Hampshire, for example, lists barberry, oriental bittersweet, water-flag iris, blunt-leaved privet, four different honeysuckles, purple loosestrife, "burning bush" euonymus, and Norway maple, while restricting porcelain-berry, knapweed, Canada thistle, crown vetch, Russian olive, wintercreeper, common privet, white poplar, black locust, and Siberian elm, among many others.

My intention was to include a list of invasive plants in this source guide, but in the compiling of the list it soon became very apparent the list was too long to be published here. The list will be posted from time to time, along with updates, at www.kendruse.com.

In his book *Native Trees, Shrubs, and Vines*, William Cullina includes a very helpful list, "Alternatives to Invasive or Potentially Invasive Exotic Species." I also urge you to visit other Web sites for important and valuable information regarding this issue. Some very good ones are posted by the Exotic Pest Plant Council (state and local chapters with Web sites are easily reached via any search engine); Montana Noxious Weed Trust Fund (http://invader.dbs.umt.edu/default.htm); New England Wild Flower Society (http://www.newfs.org/coserve/invasive.htm); Northeastern Weed Science Society Northeastern Weed Science Society (http://www.newss.org/index.php) (good for weed identification); Plant Conservation Alliance (http://www.nps.gov/plants/alien/index.htm); Wildland Invasive Species Team of the Nature Conservancy (http://tncweeds.ucdavis.edu/index.html); and yes, the U.S. government (www.invasivespecies.gov). These sites post free, downloadable lists—many with illustrations and/or photographs for positive identification—that you can print out for your own use and pass along to friends and your favorite nurserymen and -women.

The importance of the lists to gardeners is that first and foremost, we should not welcome these plants into our gardens by purchasing them from garden centers and nurseries or mail-order sources. Very few plants are actually banned from sale. The restrictions are determined state by state. And keep in mind, a plant that is a menace in one state, may not be a problem in another.

MORE HELP

While conservation organizations dedicated to the promotion of native plants and the control of dangerous ones are doing their best to educate and inform us, it still requires individual research to find the information we need. Perhaps there will come a day when nurseries and post offices will display posters profiling the "Ten Most Dangerous Garden Plants" to our local habitats, but even then it is our individual responsibility to obtain accurate information.

Your best source for finding a reliable professional will be recommendations from fellow native-plant enthusiasts, from local chapters of the Nature Conservancy and extension agents, and from local colleges with programs in conservation, environmental sciences, and botany.

GRASSLANDS

The word "prairie" conjures up images of waving golden grasses stretching to the horizon, or an endless sea of wildflowers, but I hope the chapter on grasslands has made it clear that, while a true prairie is a complex ecosystem, a prairie garden can be created almost anywhere conditions are compatible, whether it is in the suburbs or a tiny vacant city lot surrounded by asphalt and concrete.

Prairie only exists in the United States—it is a unique habitat type. What then is a meadow? A meadow may look like a prairie, but it is an interim or transitional plant community. When a woodland has been cut or burned in a moist area, a meadow may develop or be planted. Unless the meadow is cut or burned for maintenance, the planting will evolve into woodland in places where moisture is ample and there is less wind than on the open plains.

PATIENCE

The first step is to acknowledge that the process of creating a prairie or grassland garden can take two to three years. Clearing the site of unwanted plants and weeds takes time; perennial wildflowers and grasses take two or three years to establish their deep roots when using plants, longer if grown from seed. But the gardener can take great satisfaction in knowing that the investment yields gratifying dividends: a healthy site that will flourish for decades to come.

SITE SELECTION AND EVALUATION

Grasslands thrive in full sun with excellent air circulation, so while the site does not have to be large, it should be bathed in full sun all day, and brushed by the wind. While prairie topography is generally flat or rolling, it is possible to create the desired effect on ground that includes a steep bank, but if you choose to plant with seed, the timing and method of sowing are essential to erosion control.

Once you've picked a site, examine all the plants that grow there now and the soil type. Determine what plants, if any, can remain as part of the new habitat and what plants need to be removed. See the recommendations for guidebooks to help in the identification process (page 251) or contact a reliable professional who can help with positive identification.

Even in small spaces, and certainly in larger tracts of soil, texture and condition will vary. It may be sandy, or loaded with clay. It is important to determine what your soil is made of and what, if any, amendments should be added. The grassland habitat planting will thrive on its own—once established—and to speed up the process, some soils will benefit from being scratched open for seeding, and rolled like a grass lawn sowing, or organic matter can be added to retain moisture for young plants as they grow.

Carefully controlled lawns where broad-leaf herbicides were employed are ripe for conversion to a grassland habitat. So are former farm fields where herbicides kept weed populations from taking over. (Except where Atrazine has been used in the past two years: if you suspect it has, sow and grow corn the first year until it has broken down; see Prairie Nursery's Web site, www.prairienursery.com, for more details.) After removing all the lawn grass and any remaining "crops," water and let the ground lie for a month or two to make sure no new weeds are growing.

PLANT SELECTION: RESEARCH AND DREAM IN REALITY

As soon as you have determined soil type and environmental conditions contact native seed and plant suppliers for copies of their catalogs and/or start studying Web sites to determine what you want to plant and when it should be planted. Like all gardeners, you will change your mind several times as you become more knowledgeable about the choices available.

Your budget will most likely decide for you whether you will start with seed or transplants—or a mix of both. When creating a small prairie garden on a town or city property it may be advantageous to use some plants, to achieve a more immediate result. But transplants should be separated from seeded areas since the mowing maintenance schedule for the more mature plants will differ from the seedlings' schedule.

The smaller scale of a city or suburban plot where less than an acre is planted would be overwhelmed by the taller prairie grasses but is perfect for the shorter grasses such as little bluestem, or prairie dropseed. These clump-forming grasses will also leave more space for flowers in a smaller site.

Be sure to consider early spring flowers, which are often short-growing and finish their cycle before taller summer species emerge or mature. Study flower charts carefully so that you achieve a succession of bloom throughout the entire season, remembering that grasses will change their color in the fall and winter as well.

Many of us get excited about using plants that will attract birds, forgetting that while the birds will eat the seeds eventually provided, they also come to eat the insects that are lured in by those flowers. Be prepared to see more crawling and flying visitors to the garden, learn to identify beneficial insects, and encourage family and friends not to be put off by these sometimes creeping allies.

Most nurseries selling seeds for prairie habitats offer prepackaged combinations of flowering plants and grasses. This is economical, but a custom seed blend created with your specific goals and conditions in mind is just that, customized for you, and your planting schedule.

Different species germinate under different conditions. Some seeds will germinate when given warmth and water; others require cold, moist stratification, in other words, exposure to damp winter conditions. The two categories are divided into spring-sown species and fall-sown species. Most wildflower seeds have a higher germination rate when planted in the fall. Pretreated seed—seed that has been properly dry refrigerated by the nursery—will simplify your job greatly, and moist stratification is accomplished with fall planting. Talking with a nursery professional who specializes in prairie planting will help you sort out your plant selections and determine your sowing calendar. Prairie Nursery's catalogs and Web site provide a chart that lists wildflowers and grasses and the preferred sowing/propagating methods for dozens of species. On pages 46–47 you can find some specific plant suggestions listed by soil type. The *Prairie Propagation Handbook* by Howard W. Rock details specific information for growing hundreds of prairie plants, both common and rare.

Included in many seed mixtures are "nurse crops," like annual rye grass or oats. These are fast growing and used to fill the void that weeds would occupy before desired plants are established. These nurse crops generally die over the winter and do not reseed.

Neil Diboll, owner of Prairie Nursery in Wisconsin, warns against using winter wheat, winter rye, or perennial rye as a nurse crop. On the nursery's Web site this warning is posted: "Studies have shown that wheat and rye produce chemicals in their roots that can suppress germination of other plants. Perennial rye is a fast growing cool season rye that can out compete your prairie seedlings, and should never be used as a nurse crop."

If you are preparing a steep slope, schedule it so that it will be planted by September 15th in the northern states (USDA zones 4–6) so that plants can grow and mature in time to control erosion over the winter. If it is an especially steep gradient, you might want to consider using erosion blankets, specially constructed fiber mats that will hold the soil in place through heavy rains and strong winds until plants are well established. The mats eventually disintegrate.

And you thought it was going to be a boring year while you wait for the weeds to die. Beginning your research a year in advance gives you the opportunity to talk with or e-mail the experts and get most of your questions answered before mistakes get planted in the ground.

SITE PREPARATION

Add organic matter to the soil only if the ground is excessively sandy or compacted clay that cannot support plant life. Growing a crop of "green manure" can condition clay, but will add another year to the process. Sterilized organic compost and manures will bring essential elements to barren ground without importing more weeds.

Removal of all weeds and undesirable trees and shrubs is essential. Without question, starting with a blank slate is the surest bet for establishing a grassland planting.

Every square foot of earth that has not been treated contains a host of viable weed seeds that will spring to life as soon as the earth is disturbed and a bit of moisture is added, or even more threatening, a stronghold of rhizomatous perennial weeds—ones that can regenerate themselves from the smallest bit of root left in the earth when they are yanked out. Failure to remove all weeds and weed trees and shrubs from the site is the main cause for failure in new prairie or grassland plantings, and the hidden truth only faintly hinted at on those tempting "meadow in a can" products.

Getting to know the weeds in your ground, and how to get rid of them, is key, the first step to a successful prairie garden. State fish and wildlife agencies can be helpful, as can national forestry and conservation centers. Studying the information available on Exotic Pest Plant Council Web site for your state or region or the USDA's Web site (contact information on page 236) can help you determine just what needs to go. On land where weeds are firmly established, one entire growing season is required to ensure weed extermination.

After identifying all plants worth saving, tie bright ribbons of weatherproof material around trees and shrubs. Set stakes around worthwhile herbaceous plants and flag those as well.

Unless you are a professional, or an experienced amateur, it might be too dangerous to cut down trees yourself. In any event, take all precautions. Tree parts can be chipped or shredded by professionals to use as mulch or compost. Arrange in advance to add your cleared brush to the chipper. But keep weeds that sprout from bits of root or twig out of the chipper.

After all the woody material has been removed, mow the area on the lowest setting and rake the area clean. (Do not put the weeds and their roots and seeds in the compost pile.) The ways to kill well-established weeds are burning, cultivating, applying herbicide, and smothering (or solarization). Most prairie restoration projects begin with the application of a chemical herbicide, and to some, this seems to fly in the face of environmentally appropriate gardening. Products with glyphosate such as Roundup are considered the safest (but should never be used near water, i.e., streams, ponds, bogs, etc.). If you choose not to use any herbicides, you still have to "clean out the weeds," and there are various ways to accomplish this, without chemicals. Burning is nature's method, and still most efficient, and several burns over the course of a few years may be required. But burning in some communities may not be safe or even legal. Do not attempt burning without proper permits.

If you use herbicide, a solution of glyphosate (Roundup, Rodeo) can be brushed on cut surfaces immediately to prevent the trees and shrubs from resprouting. This works most efficiently late in the season when sap returns to a tree's root system.

For small areas, the process of smothering or solarization can be used. This involves covering the area to keep light, moisture, air, and new weeds from reaching the soil. Thick-gauge, black plastic film will work, so will clear plastic. Some prefer the clear, feeling it kills plants more efficiently by intensifying the suns rays, much like a magnifying glass does.

Lawn grass is easy to kill and takes as little as two or three months during the growing season if there are no broad-leaf weeds present. If there are weeds in the lawn it can take a full year. I have smothered grass and weeds by laying newspapers, at least four sheets thick, or corrugated cardboard down over weeds and soil, moistened with a hose and then covering it

all with sterile compost, soil, or mulch. After six to twelve months, depending on when the project is started, the soil can be turned under and seeds sown or plants installed.

Smother the lawn as described above; then in the fall you can sow your seeds directly on the dead sod, killed by solarization, without cultivating. This is particularly effective with seeds that need cold and wet treatment to germinate. If you must wait until the following spring, the dead sod must be tilled before sowing. Tilling will be needed for newspaper and mulch-covered areas, unless the paper products have fully broken down over the season.

Cultivating is the most labor-intensive method and may require a full second year to successfully exterminate weeds. You must begin tilling in the spring and continue throughout the year, every two to three weeks at a depth of 4–5". And you must obey the calendar religiously. Waiting any longer than a couple of weeks will allow perennial weeds to recover and regrow. Cultivating also exposes weed seeds and promotes their germination. Cultivating is not recommended for slopes or other erosion-prone areas.

A combination of *shallow* cultivation to just 2–3", and judicious application of glyphosate as weed seeds germinate in spring and summer and again in the fall is usually a successful method, but you won't know for sure until the following year. It may be wise to sow a "nurse crop" the first year, until you determine just what is left behind.

SOWING SEED

Sowing seed is simple, yet there is a technique that involves more than pouring the seed into your hand and scattering it across the prepared soil.

For small sites, hand sow:

1. Save tiny seeds for last, sowing larger seeds first.
2. To ensure an even distribution, thoroughly mix the seed in a bucket with a carrier like sand, or dampened sawdust and divide the mixture in half, to sow in two separate passes across the site.
3. Walking at a slow pace in one direction, scatter the first half with a wide, sweeping motion evenly across the entire site. To sow the second half, begin walking perpendicularly from the starting point of your first pass, broadcasting in a similar manner.
4. Rake in the seed lightly. Sow fine seeds after raking in the larger seeds.
5. Firm the surface of the soil by walking over the entire site.

For large sites, use mechanical seeders, often available from rental shops, following the manufacturer's directions. "Rake in" the seed with a drag bar or section of chain-link fence, then firm the seed in with a lawn roller unless the seeder you use firms the seed as it sows. Detailed information on types of seeders can be found on Prairie Nursery's Web site.

Mulch the entire surface with clean, weed-free straw. Covering the straw with plastic netting will keep the wind from carrying it away. Water plantings only if regular rains don't do it for you, particularly in warm, windy weather. Timing is important. Irrigate for 15 minutes to half an hour, just to keep soil moist, and in the morning rather than the heat of the day or evening. Watering late in the day increases the risk of fungal growth that will destroy seedlings.

And here's another warning about "meadow in a can" and other wildflower seed mixes. Some of them contain fillers, perhaps as much as 90%, things like rice hulls. Worse, many contain exotic plant seeds, such as Queen-Anne's-lace, a plant many people believe to be native. This wild carrot is not only nonnative—it is invasive. If you have a lovely meadow with Queen-Anne's-lace, in a few years, you may have an all-Queen-Anne's-lace meadow. You may be sowing some of the same plants you are desperately trying to eradicate.

ONGOING CARE

Nature used to "manage" her prairies with grazing animals, fires started by lightning, blistering winds, and freezing winters. Her natural cycle of gentle seasons balanced by fierce weather extremes, and an array of creatures from buffalo to bumblebees are what shaped the evolution of the grasses and forbs.

If you live in a rural area it may be possible, with the permission of local fire agencies and under the guidance of professionals, to conduct a "controlled burn" of your large prairie landscape. However, please remember that "controlled" is a risky proposition and fire can quickly get out of control. Sometimes the fire department may participate in the burn as a training exercise.

Regular mowing of the grasses and forbs can do nearly the same job that fire and grazing animals once provided: stimulating growth of desired plants and controlling weed species. But the hard truth is, despite your best efforts for the first year or two—until the perennial species are well established—your prairie garden will look a bit sparse, with lots of open spaces for weed seeds "on the wing" or those in the ground that toughed it out to take hold once again. (If necessary, read the "Patience" step once again.) On small sites, hand weeding may take care of the problem, but mowing is still advantageous.

For seeded meadows:

First year: Mow small sites with a weed whacker or reel mower to a height of 4–6" once a month during spring and summer before weeds flower, and certainly before they set seed. At the end of the season, mow to a height of 8–10". Taller stubble will help protect the roots through the winter, hold insulating snow in place, and help to limit frost-heaving.

Second year: Mow in the spring, 4–6" high. Rake off the debris. If weeds appear, mow again before they flower, but at least before they set seed.

Third year and ever after: Mow each spring when cool-season grasses are 6" tall. Rake away the debris the same day. You want the sun to warm the soil and promote the growth of your prairie plants.

Never, ever spray Roundup after the planting is established. There is no way to control spray "drift," which can kill the desirable plants. Only when it is absolutely necessary, apply glyphosate with a brush only to those stubborn tap-rooted or rhizomatous weeds that cannot be removed by hand.

DRYLANDS

Just as the ocean is the ultimate wetland, the desert is the most extreme dryland. When we hear the word "desert," we may picture the sands of the Sahara. But there is a huge range of plant and animal communities in places with less than 25" of rain per year. The arid areas of California, just ten miles east of the San Francisco Bay, fit this description. Oregon has deserts. We are talking about available moisture, so the cool, high valleys of the Rocky Mountains—often buried in snow through April—are drylands. When the snow melts, the thin layer of rocky soil bakes in the sun and turns to dust.

If you live in an arid region, you must consider dryland gardens. The pour-water-on-it mentality of a golf course is simply too wasteful. In recent droughts in the Tucson area, around 10% of water resources were directed to golf courses while residents were under severe mandated water restrictions.

But a lack of soil moisture is not restricted to arid climates. Even where the average annual rainfall is relatively high there can be long periods of time when the soil is dry. Take for instance a summer morning along any seacoast. Dew drips from the porch roof before the thick morning fog finally gives way to brilliant sunshine. Soon a warm breeze becomes a stiff wind, perfect for sailing, but the sandy soil of a seaside garden is almost instantly dried out. A wide swath of shale runs close to the earth's surface through New Jersey, "The Garden State," and when rains disappear, lawns in this region instantly crisp yellow.

Even in those areas blessed with deep layers of soil full of moisture-retaining organic matter, shifts in the jet stream often carry beneficial snow and rainstorms along a different arc, leaving normally moist regions suffering with drought. During the latter half of the 1990s and the first years of the new millennium, most of the United States experienced drought conditions, with some regions forced to implement water use restrictions. Even the mighty Colorado River cannot keep supplying a burgeoning population when year after year winter monsoons do not arrive to replenish the earth of the Desert Southwest.

Here are some suggestions for creating and maintaining attractive habitat gardens in dry regions while conserving as much water as possible.

GET TO KNOW THOSE CLOSEST TO YOU

Plants native to your region are species that have adapted to local climatic extremes and soil conditions. These plants, once established, require less water, less fertilizer, and less maintenance than do many exotic imports, or even domestic imports—natives from dramatically different habitats.

THROW AWAY YOUR SPRINKLER?

All plants do need some measure of regular moisture, particularly when young and/or newly planted. Regular—but not necessarily frequent—watering is essential for deep root development, which is essential for surviving long dry periods. In the domestic landscape, particularly desert gardens, plantings are usually more intensive than found in the wild, making even dry-tolerant plants compete with each other for moisture, making necessary some type of irrigation system.

But sprinklers that throw the water through the hot, dry air are the most wasteful form of irrigation. Much of the water is lost through evaporation before it has a chance to soak into the soil and down to plant roots.

EXAMINE YOUR SOIL

Soil type and condition are critical factors in determining just how much supplemental watering will be required. Very sandy soils drain quickly and do not retain nutrients very well either. While clay soils retain moisture longer, they turn hard and impenetrable when dry, cracking in the intense heat of the sun and often exposing plant roots. But perhaps worst of all, as clay dries it can actually draw moisture out of plant roots, a process known as reverse osmosis.

Both soil conditions can be improved by adding organic matter, but avoid using too much compost. A ratio of 1 part compost to 2 parts garden soil should be adequate for most situations. Clay will retain moisture if it is not exposed to drying winds and sunlight. Mulch will help. Adding coarse sand (grit or even crushed stone or gravel) to heavy, sticky clay will help to open it up and allow roots and moisture to penetrate more easily.

The most challenging soil has to be caliche, a combination of calcium carbonate and clay. As described in the March 2002 "Xeriscape Gardening News," an Internet newsletter produced by High Country Gardens (the mail-order arm of Santa Fe Greenhouses in New Mexico), caliche "forms a layer of very poorly draining white chalky alkaline clay. A caliche layer will typically occur 6 to 12 inches below the surface soil layer. Dealing with it isn't easy—often requiring a pickax and a ferocious battle of wills." If you have inherited a landscape with large areas of caliche, very precise plant selection may be one answer. Professional excavation may be required to treat and/or replace the soil, allowing for a wider selection of plants.

MULCH

A 2- to 3-inch layer of mulch wherever soil is exposed will greatly reduce evaporation so moisture stays in the ground longer, and keep roots cool during the hottest temperatures.

CATCH EVERY DROP

Making the most of the rains that do come is a must for dry gardens. Install a rain barrel at each downspout, and you will collect many gallons of water in a brief rain shower. It has been calculated that 1,000 square feet of roof area collects 625 gallons of water from one inch of rainfall.

Create earthen "bowls" at the base of trees and shrubs so any rainfall will collect and soak in. When it is necessary to irrigate, use a slow stream of water from the hose with a bubbler attached, or place the mouth of the hose on top of a flat stone to disperse the flow, which will help prevent erosion of the soil; the earthen "bowl" will keep the water in the root zone and prevent it from running away.

So-called gray water—household water collected from bathtubs, washing machines, kitchen sinks, but not toilets—can be recycled to the garden when conditions become extreme. (In some communities it is illegal to use gray water, so check your local ordinances first, and work to change the law in your town, if necessary.) Do not use any water that has been "softened," as it may contain harmful salts, or any that has been mixed with household cleaners. Recycled household water should be used immediately and not stored in containers since bacteria in the water would multiply quickly. Gray water should not be used if anyone in the household has an infectious disease.

GO DEEP

Deep soaking is far more important than how often you water. Shallow watering forces plant roots to stay near the surface where they are more vulnerable to drying out. Periodic soaking encourages plants to establish deeper roots. Also, the deeper the roots, the stronger the plant; and strong plants have the greatest chance for survival in extreme conditions.

GO UNDERGROUND

Rain barrels are great when filling cans for watering container gardens, but not always the most practical solution for large gardens. Drip irrigation systems, while initially expensive to install, deliver water right where plants need it most—at the root level—and there is little, if any, water wasted to evaporation or runoff. Permeable rubber soaker hoses (made from recycled tires) laid just under the soil, or buried underneath mulch are less expensive than drip and nearly as efficient. They are, however, prone to clogging or the accidental piercing from trowel or spade; and the plastic or rubber may break down over time.

The savings make the initial financial investment and labor worthwhile since either one of these hose systems will use up to 50% less water than overhead sprinkling. And since they can be set up on timers, watering can be done at regular intervals, which is critical for newly planted specimens. Once plants are established, be sure to adjust the timers to a new, less frequent schedule, particularly during seasons when rains are expected. Moisture sensors are also available to automate an irrigation system's timer and turn it on only when water is needed.

LISTEN TO SMOKEY BEAR

Dryland habitats are, by their very nature, highly susceptible to fire. Even though fire is an essential fact of life and part of the natural cycle of renewal, it is a dangerous force no homeowner should attempt to use in a dryland habitat. One of the most important lessons learned from the frightening western wildfires in very recent history is that dead wood and underbrush in dryland forests and woodlands is dangerous fuel that can turn a wild fire into a cataclysmic conflagration. All shrubs and trees must be carefully pruned and all dead wood cleared out religiously—especially close to the house and any outbuildings.

People who live in fire-prone areas can learn from the wild also. The plants that naturally grow in these regions often burn faster and for a shorter duration than do exotic bushy ornamental shrubs or trees such as oil-rich eucalyptus—the ones that exploded like firebombs during the Oakland, California, fire of October 1991.

If your home is in a fire-prone region, seriously consider having emergency sprinklers installed outside your home, all around the perimeter. At the very least install two or three spigots on each outside wall so you can set up a tall sprinkler system that could keep your roof and walls drenched if wildfires do endanger your neighborhood.

REDUCE LAWN

Nonnative turf can be responsible for 75% of a homeowner's water usage during the summer months. Reduce the lawn to just the amount needed for recreation, and let that Kentucky blue die out; replace it with buffalo grass or other less thirsty natives like red fescue (*Festuca rubra*) or sheep's fescue (*F. ovina*).

Buffalo grass (*Buchloe dactyloides*) is native to plains, from cold northern regions including Minnesota and Montana and down south in Mexico. It stands up to minor foot traffic and has a fine texture that is comfortable to bare feet. It needs little or no water or fertilizer (it will turn a golden buff color when it goes dormant in winter or severe drought) and infrequent mowing. Though not for everyone, it is worth investigating. The fine-leaved red and sheep's fescues do not want fertilizer and are only 12–18" high at maturity. When a more manicured look is desired, only two mowings are required, once in June and again in September.

The well-designed and thoughtfully planted drylands habitat garden relies on native plants. Once established, these species stand the greatest chance of performing beautifully through all but the worst droughts with remarkably little supplemental watering. Check with your state's native-plant society to discover where there are display gardens you can visit. Better yet, become a member and help save endangered habitats and species.

WETLANDS

Wetlands exist when the water supply stays ahead of evaporation and drainage. Pools and ponds are de rigueur in gardens today. If you can take on the work to maintain an artificial pond, few things will be as satisfying as the light, color, and sound of a naturalistic water feature. Much has been written about pool and pond construction. Materials suppliers also feature instruction in their catalogs and online sites. For that reason, that information is not repeated here. However, information on making bogs, which are less common and arguably less work to maintain, is harder to come by.

Bogs form as ponds and wet depressions fill with sediment and plant material over time. Fed by streams, rainfall, or underground water sources, bogs support an astounding array of plant and animal life. For those who embrace the natural world, constructing a bog will enrich the gardening experience like nothing else can. They are much easier to build and maintain than a pool or pond since no pumps, filters, or electrical wiring is required. If you love birds in your garden, water features will attract more species than any feeding station ever will, and that goes for bogs, as well.

If you have a pond, creating a bog is a natural next step. Or perhaps there is an area on the property where water collects and is slow to drain away after every rainstorm. This is the perfect place to create your new bog, whether you have many acres in the country, or work the earth of a smaller suburban or city lot.

While natural bogs develop in shallow depressions over hundreds of years, you can build a small one in a few weekends, employing some of the same tools and methods used to make artificial ponds.

Yes, a healthy bog does attract insects—fascinating, quizzical, unbelievable species you did not know existed in your neighborhood. When the habitat includes a pond stocked with fish along with plants that attract a variety of birds and bats, worrisome mosquitoes and other biting insects are kept under control to some extent. By definition a bog is a wet area characterized by poor drainage. There is some water exchange, and if the edge of the bog liner is below grade, there may not be enough standing water to support mosquitoes, but at times, there may be. When necessary, nontoxic *Bacillus thuringiensis* may be used in all garden water features to kill mosquito larvae before they become adults. See "Mosquito Control" below for more information.

LOOK BEFORE YOU LEAP

If you are building a bog starting from scratch, you will be creating a sizable hole, so it is important to know ahead of time where you plan to put the soil you remove. Perhaps building a berm or creating raised beds in another location may be a good idea, or not; just make sure to determine where it will go before you pick up the shovel.

If you do not wish to, or simply cannot do the physically demanding work of digging the hole yourself, ask at local nurseries that feature pond plants and supplies for a list of contractors that can help with the heavy work.

SITE AND SIZE

Evaluate your property to determine where a bog is best suited. It will blend in most naturally where growth tends to be lush. Bogs occur naturally in both sunny and shady locations. For ornamental plants, however, full sun is required. Try to site the bog in a spot that receives at least eight hours of direct sunlight in summer.

Your bog will need regular water replenishment when it does not rain, so install a rain barrel, or system of several connected barrels to use during extremely dry periods. Do not plan on using municipal tap water since it contains minerals and chlorine that are harmful to the bog plants and is generally neutral in pH; bogs are composed of highly acidic soil.

For do-it-yourselfers, an area of 25 to 50 sq. ft. and 12" deep is a doable size. Lay garden hose out along the ground—the same way you would to create a new garden bed—to help you visualize how the finished size and shape will fit into the scheme of things. Round, oval, or amorphous shapes are most natural. If the water table is high, plan the bog so that the soil level is at least 6" above the water level for plant crowns.

THE HOLE

The sides should slope gradually toward the center; in other words, a bowl shape without perpendicular edges around the perimeter. Dig the deepest part first (it does not have to be in the exact center), this makes it easier to create a slope toward the rim. Line the hole with a one-inch layer of sand, which will protect the liner from being punctured. Excavate so that one end or side is slightly lower than the surrounding ground, which will allow for overflow during heavy rains.

Wait to cut the liner for your bog until the hole is finished. It may change in size and shape as the earth is removed.

THE LINER

The liner will be the foundation of your bog. The liner is often made with a single piece of rubber or plastic sheet. The liner can be made with overlapping layers of the material, however, since unlike a pool holding water is not the goal. The idea is to hold enough water. Frankly, you can make a bog from any waterproof material, but the best ones are composed of fabric bonded to rubber and vary in thickness from 32 to 60 ml. The thickest are worth the investment, since the liner will be impossible to replace without remaking the entire bog garden. A 40-ml liner will us ually serve. Check the product's guarantee. Most often, the liners succumb to exposure to ultraviolet light, but if the material is covered with soil or planting medium, it can be kept from all light.

Measure the length, width, and depth of your hole, and your supplier will help you calculate the right size.

Enlist the help of friends, or the professionals who dug the hole for you, to lay the liner into the hole; the liner will be too heavy to handle alone. Fill partially with water and pull on the edges to get the pleats that form to lay flat. Secure the edges temporarily with stones or soil. Lay in the irrigation line if you plan to use one.

In the Brooklyn Botanic Garden's publication *The Natural Water Garden: Pools*, C. Colston Burrell writes, "Some drainage is necessary to keep the crowns of the plants (the point where the roots meet the top growth) from rotting." Burrell's garden at the time was located near Minneapolis, where winter temperatures reach ⁻30 degrees F. Winter ice would also threaten his plants, so he "placed drainage holes around the periphery of the liner, a foot below the soil surface. By duplicating the conditions under which many plants grow in the wild, I ensured that the top of the soil—where the crowns are—remains relatively dry, while the roots are kept moist."

Jeff Jabco, horticulture coordinator at the Scott Arboretum of Swarthmore College, in Pennsylvania, has more ideas. He dug a bowl-shaped hole 24" deep. Instead of piercing the liner or using overlapping scraps for drainage, he simply made one side lower than the ground surrounding the bog so that water would overflow the bog and drain into the garden. Jabco used a medium of 3 parts premoistened peat moss to 1 part coarse sand. He created a higher mound at the center of the bog, having observed that plants, such as the carnivorous pitcher plants, grow on hummocks in natural bogs. The crowns of these plants, where the roots meet the stems, are very susceptible to rotting. The roots want to be moist at all times, but not so the crowns.

The problem I have is that since I have pretty much weaned myself off peat moss, I need to find alternative materials.

SOIL

Bogs are as much about organic matter as they are about water (remember where peat comes from?). In her book *Planting Noah's Garden*, Sara Stein has an excellent chapter on creating a wetland habitat. For a bog, Stein recommends mixing 1 part soil from the excavation, 1 part peat, and 1 part commercial organic compost. Fill the hole to the top with the soil mix. "Walk over the soil to settle it in," she advises, "then overfill the hole somewhat with more soil. When wet, the fill will settle even more, but if you irrigate it to a muck at this point, you'll sink into the bog when you try to plant it."

Again, peat moss is not the product of choice for my gardening, and one cannot imagine how hard it is to do without this product. Peat moss is a renewable resource, but it takes thousands of years to renew it, and delicate plant and animal communities are disturbed and destroyed whenever a new peat "mine" is excavated. Of course, all natural habitat gardeners make compost, but more and more municipalities are making and giving away or selling compost, too. Bogs should be acidic, and peat moss is acidic. Ideally, replace the peat moss with compost. If the compost was made with acidic oak leaves, pine needles, or even chopped pine bark and wood, the resulting material should be as good as peat moss.

WATER SOURCE

If there is no natural water supply for your bog—a stream, pond runoff, or consistent rainfall—and you must use household water on a regular basis to replenish it during dry spells, it is a good idea to have your water analyzed to know just what you are adding to you bog. The pH of the water supply will affect the bog environment. So will chemical additives such as chlorine, salts from water softeners, and other chemicals—and possibly pesticides—that have leached from the ground in wells and public waterworks. Do-it-yourself water-testing kits are available at nurseries that offer water gardening supplies, but for a full analysis of all chemicals in the water, a laboratory test would be useful. Also, save every drop of rainwater that you can for the bog and other watering needs.

Some people who have made bogs have rigged up connections to the rain gutters on their houses so that water drains directly to the bog.

MOSQUITO CONTROL

Any pool or pond can be stocked with fish that will eat mosquito larvae. The cure may become a preventative, with water attracting mosquitoes and fish gobbling up the eggs or larvae and, in many cases, jumping out of the water to eat the adults as well. In the case of a bog, there is not enough water for fish. Mosquito dunks, small doughnut-shaped cakes containing *Bacillus thuringiensis* (Bt) kill mosquito larvae, allowing us to have our garden water features safely. Nontoxic Bt is safe for humans, animals, fish, amphibians, and other, beneficial insects. But the dunks must be administered correctly to work on the first larvae hatched. The doughnuts work slowly; as they absorb water the Bt is released, so they must be in place whenever mosquitoes are breeding. The dunks can be crushed and sprinkled over the surface or wherever water collects; but the product is also available in a granular form called Mosquito Bits, which the manufacturer says will kill mosquito larvae within twenty-four hours. Testimonials regarding the efficacy of this product abound, and it is available at most nurseries and stores selling garden products.

PLANTING

Sarah Stein recommends doing planting before saturating the soil so that you don't sink to your knees. At the Atlanta Botanical Garden, gardeners lay pieces of plywood over the new bog gardens to stand or kneel on without sinking. Like Jabco, they use peat moss in Atlanta.

There are many more sources for bog plants than there were just a few short years ago. Search engines on the Web will provide many nursery names for suppliers of plants such as the carnivores. Planting is just like planting any other garden area. Remove plants from pots, loosen roots, excavate a hole in the muck, insert the plant, and water well.

MAINTENANCE

Check the water level regularly—daily during hot, dry weather—and never let the soil dry out. As plants die back at the end of the season, let the organic matter remain, as it would in the wild, to keep replenishing the planting medium of the bog. Mulch with leaves, and protect the crowns of the plants from heaving due to freezing and thawing by covering the bog plants with a thick but loose layer of pine boughs around December to shade the frozen bog. Remove weed or tree seedlings as soon as they appear. The soil will continue to settle, especially during the first season. Add rich compost mixed with coarse sand to keep the surface of the medium at the right level. For carnivorous plants, that is above the ground level. Some bog gardeners also recommend a yearly dusting of lime each spring.

Plants in bogs are used to very lean nutrition. That's how the carnivorous plants evolved to digest insects for food. As a bog gardener, you can augment the nutrition with a little bit of water-soluble plant food. But use the fertilizer at about one-quarter strength once a month during the growing season. Stop fertilizing by August to discourage any new growth that might be damaged by cold.

WOODLANDS

The woodland habitat may be filled with "giants"—trees being the largest living organisms in our gardens—but they are, nonetheless, delicate ecosystems. The hidden world beneath the leaf "litter" and the decomposing logs and branches, mosses, ferns, and stones is a complex composition of minerals, microorganisms, humus, insects, animals, and the roots of all those trees, shrubs, and wildflowers. Many trees, like beeches, have surface roots that can be easily damaged; and it is a myth that a tree's roots are contained within the drip line of the canopy: fine feeder roots often extend many feet beyond. And some of our most precious wildflowers are spring ephemerals, species that flower and set seed before the forest canopy leafs out then disappear as larger plants leaf out, or as they go into dormancy. Valuable seedlings you will want to encourage can appear throughout the growing season.

Before embarking on any major restoration project, and particularly before constructing any buildings, pathways, or roadways, spend one year carefully observing everything that grows and lives in your woodland, hiring a professional botanist if necessary, to help determine which species and locations might require special attention and protection.

The urge to explore the woods is irresistible, but tramping through underbrush is hardly enjoyable or advisable, nor is it good for the earth beneath your stumbling feet. Generations of deer, bear, fox, sheep, cows, and school children usually create pathways through woodlands, and if one or more of these "natural" pathways already exist, consider this your starting point for creating a woodland walk that will allow you and visitors to observe and enjoy the seasons among the trees.

AT THE EDGE

The transitional area from lawn or garden to the woodland is important to consider and certainly an opportunity for creating a woodland garden walk. Shrubs such as blueberries and rhododendron could line the edge where sun fades to shade. Or, in a spot between grass lawn and wooded edge, a meadow could be planted and maintained.

A strip of native grasses and wildflowers—the meadow—can provide a soft break from the lawn to the strong vertical lines of the trees. Meadows are transitional plant communities in the process of evolving. If left alone, a meadow will change into woodland. First, shrub seedlings will sprout among the meadow plants, followed by tree seedlings that grow into saplings that will one day be a forest. If your goal is to maintain the meadow as a meadow, shrub and tree seedlings must be weeded out as they appear. One way to do this is with a yearly mowing.

Most of our meadow plants are warm-season plants. Unlike European and Eurasian weeds, our natives sprout late, either from seed or from the dormant roots and crowns of established herbaceous perennials. The opportunistic weeds sprout early in the spring and shade our natives out. A late spring mowing thwarts the early weeds while encouraging the yet-to-emerge natives. In New England, for example, the mowing may be done as late as mid-May.

The very edge of the woodland is also an ideal spot for sun-loving shrubs, herbaceous perennials, native roses, or grasses. Many shade-tolerant flowering shrubs, such as Pinxter azalea (*Rhododendron periclymenoides*), appreciate more sun exposure and will provide a profuse display on the edge of the forest rather than tucked away in the understory. Little bluestem (*Schizachyrium scoparium*) tolerates dry conditions once established and offers bright green or glaucous summer color, followed by lovely autumn colors ranging from tan to bright red-orange. Rick Darke writes in *The Color Encyclopedia of Ornamental Grasses* that those cultivars with the strongest blue or purple coloration provide the deepest fall colors. The edge of the woodland is a perfect place for a collection of asters, one of the most important nectar plants flowering in the fall. They attract a variety of pollinators with their late, colorful blooms.

UNDERFOOT

When mulching your pathway, choose material that blends well with the woodland floor. When using stone, try to use that which is native to the site. If it is a moist environment where mosses flourish, let them edge the pathway and take over from the sunny, grassy path extending from lawn into the trees. Remember: when pathways run up steep gradients any loose material, but small stones particularly, can be very unstable underfoot. In these situations it is usually best to lay stone or wood "stepping-stones" into the ground to provide firm footing.

STOP, LOOK, LISTEN

As you get to know your woods you will begin to notice that you pause along the pathways in certain spots, places where light, foliage, flowers, or animal or bird activity capture your interest each time. These spots are perfect places for chairs or benches. An old stump, perhaps, or large, flat stone could serve as well as a manmade piece.

LIKE A LOG

Recognize dead trees as part of the woodland composition and a very important link in the life of the woods. Remove only those that would be considered fuel for a fire or that threaten human safety, other trees, or buildings and fences.

NEW LIGHT

It is important to remember that when you remove weed trees and shrubs you alter the environment. More light will now reach the forest floor in this spot and will affect all the smaller plants growing there. Take this into consideration; you may not want to plant anything here immediately, until you see what happens as a natural response to the change.

WOODLAND FLOWERBEDS

Keep in mind that the soil on the woodland floor is naturally thin, and it is not a good idea to bring in loads of soil or humus. And do not be heavy handed if/when applying mulch. Nature's natural mulch beneath trees is several inches of leaf "litter," decomposing woody branches and twigs, bark, etc. It is relatively light and airy for several inches; very different from the heavy wood chips usually chosen for garden mulch.

When it is necessary to bring in a little soil or mulch, add only a thin layer. Tree roots require oxygen and piling a thick layer of soil or mulch over the root zone could literally smother the tree to death.

If the spot you choose has had a bit of suffering lawn, deprived of enough light to make a lush cover, then you may want to create a small bed. One way is to cover an area with four layers of moistened newspaper or one layer of corrugated cardboard, which can then be covered with a mulch of leaves, shredded bark if available (from all those trash trees you had chipped and composted), well-aged manure, compost, or a combination of these.

The beds can be raised a bit over the soil and edged with fallen logs, rocks, or similar materials. If the trees are close to the beds, or are shallow-rooted kinds, such as maples, you may have to do a little more research as to which plants can tolerate dry shade. Remember: do not cover existing tree roots with too much new soil or mulch. A shallow raised bed (4–6" thick) over a small area of the roots will not hurt the tree. The bed should be no more than one-quarter of the tree-roots area. In all cases, adding a little bit of material to the top will do far less damage than excavating into the ground—cutting tree roots.

PLANTS AND PLANTING

Grow some of the wonderful spring ephemerals, plants that sprout, flower, and set seeds before all the leaves on the trees have fully emerged. This is a perfect opportunity to increase populations of those that have lost their natural homes to development. Examples include *Trillium* spp., bloodroot, May apple, *Vancouveria*, and more. We think of plants like trillium as being East Coast only, but there are members of this genus in many other regions of the United States.

As leaves fill out in the canopy and the floor turns shady, Bowman's root (*Veronicastrum virginicum*) will flower in the summer, ferns fill in, and in the fall the blue *Aster cordifolius* and white *A. divaricatus* will lighten the forest edge.

Plants that may have been collected by organized plant rescue groups could find a home in your backyard habitat. Many of the plants we would like to grow are available from wildflower society plant sales and specialty nurseries.

When planting new wildflowers or larger shrubs and trees, use only small hand tools for digging around trees and shrubs. *Never* use any type of tiller, which could permanently damage root systems.

Look beyond the area immediately next to your pathway when planting new material. The goal is to create a natural-looking habitat, not an artificial-looking flower-lined path. Be sure to plant a few colonies of your favorite flowers and woody plants in areas where your eyes alone will travel.

Expect some summer dormancy—that's the nature of the ephemerals: here today, gone tomorrow, but, with your help, not gone forever. This may not be the spot to guide guests on an August garden tour. But there will be something for you to look at all summer, and perhaps, all year. In some areas, evergreen wild ginger might be suitable. You might even try the native Allegheny spurge (*Pachysandra procumbens*).

Growing wildflowers, growing them well, and even propagating them is one of the best things you can do as a natural habitat gardener.

LET IT RAIN

No irrigation system is required for restored woodland, once it is established. New plants, however, will need regular rain or watering for a year or two until they have developed mature root systems. If you plant new wildflowers and shrubs with the spacing that occurs when nature seeds the forest floor—that is widely scattered, or small groupings—you still will not have to worry about watering after they are mature, except during extreme dry, hot spells. Species that tend to colonize will do so according to their own timetable, which follows climate and seasonal variations.

On the other hand, if you make an intensive planting with a lot of species—a woodland flowerbed—you will have to treat it as any other garden and irrigate during dry spells. It is best to think of this planting as a garden, because it is. We can try and mimic nature, but it is nearly impossible to create a thriving, independent community in an artificial setting—a garden in a home landscape.

INTEGRATED PEST MANAGEMENT (IPM)

Conventional horticulture has traditionally recommended a regular preventive spray schedule for gardens. Likewise, green-grass lawn was thought to be dependent on tons of water, herbicides, and fertilizer. The promise for natural habitat gardening lies in something called Integrated Pest Management (IPM), an enlightened approach for controlling diseases, weeds, and insects in the garden, farm, and even the home, which advocates a series of decision-making steps to arrive at the least-toxic solution possible. Soon these unfamiliar initials will be as well-known as the letters of their biological antithesis, DDT. We may not have any choice. More farm and garden chemicals are being banned every year.

THE RIGHT PLANT IN THE RIGHT PLACE

IPM's step-by-step approach begins with planting "correctly." Plants that are in stressful situations because of improper siting are the ones most likely to succumb to problems. When a plant has evolved to cope with the conditions in a certain area, then, obviously, it will be the best choice for that place. Taking IPM to its ultimate conclusion—the most surefire solution of all—*don't plant the wrong plant in the wrong place.*

PREVENTION

Sanitation is extremely important, as both prevention and a control. Remove damaged leaves, and continue to monitor the problem. See what can be done culturally. Reducing the desirability of the environment for a given pest is a good way to limit its effects. In the case of mildew, for example, air movement helps. Attempt to improve air circulation by removing obstacles, such as solid fences, or trimming overgrown shrubs. Then comes diligent observation.

STEP BY STEP

When it comes to insects, the stepped approach continues with an unappealing environment—using insect-resistant cultivars, for example. Then there's hand picking—remove individual insects as they are discovered. If the problem will get out of control without more serious intervention, there are barriers, such as netting. Sometimes traps are used, with synthetic pheromones (sex attractors), or those baited with fragrant lures that resemble the insect's favorite meal. Place these traps upwind and as far away from the host plant as possible. You could place a beetle trap, for example, with its collection bag removed, over the stocked pool or pond. Beetles fly toward it and crash into the yellow trap and fall into the water to be gobbled up. Remember, these traps *attract* pests.

Other visual devices, such as sticky red balls to hang in crab apple trees early in the season, attract and catch apple-maggot flies. Sticky yellow flags are effective for houseplants and ornamentals outdoors. Yellow draws many flying insects; it works, just like old-fashioned flypaper.

There are biological controls, too—germ warfare on pests. In the 1970s, many people sprayed poisons for gypsy moths, but some enlightened homeowners realized that spraying would throw off the balance of nature by starving the moths' natural predators. Eventually, nature's balance would prevail. In the wet summer of 1990, a naturally occurring fungal disease had the gypsy caterpillars dropping like flies.

Certain pathogens are easily introduced. *Bacillus thuringiensis* (Bt) can be bought at the garden center as a powder or a liquid; this bacterium kills nearly all caterpillars but will not harm adults of the same species, or other insects for that matter. It sounds like germ warfare. It is. But this selective bacillus will not harm anything else. Certain insects have been able to develop immunity to some of the new bacilli. Every year new host-specific remedies become available; *Bacillus thuringiensis israelensis*, for example, controls mosquitoes.

You might have to turn to a naturally derived toxin or degradable fatty-acid soap, for example, that will not harm the environment. And these are pest-specific, that is, they kill only the invader and leave the beneficial insects, family members, pets, and produce alone. Whenever curatives are called for, aim directly at the problem area, in a pinpoint spray, and never broadcast all over creation.

Horticultural oil, or "sun-oil," smothers pests, like the woolly adelgid, when they are active, just as dormant oil has in winter for decades. Dormant oil is used when plants and pests are in their rest cycle. This material will smother the problem insect, such as scale, without harming either the tree or other insects that do not hibernate in this manner.

Botanical pesticides derived from plants, such as rotenone, pyrethrum, ryania, neem, sabadilla, and nicotine, are real poisons; nicotine sulfate, for example, is toxic to mammals. But they break down rapidly, unlike synthetic insecticides. Sorptive dusts, such as boric acid, sodium bicarbonate, silica gel, and diatomaceous earth, work by destroying the protective wax or mucous coating of many insects. However, care should be taken to avoid inhaling the dusts or rubbing eyes, and always stand upwind. Again, read the label and only apply to the affected areas.

Some of the safe materials, such as baking soda, might be nearly as unsightly as the mildew they are used to control, but that's okay, too. We're more than happy to put up with a few imperfections if we can end the cases of illness and even death from careless use of pesticides.

New products for controlling pests and diseases will come out. In all cases, and with the use of any product, *read the label* carefully and thoroughly for the manufacturer's recommended rates, methods, and schedules of applications, and warnings or cautions. Even safe products might damage leaves of some plants if used at the wrong time, or at the wrong concentration.

WHEN IS A GOOD THING NOT SO GOOD?

As with every new trend, entrepreneurs saw an opportunity for profit. You've probably seen ads in catalogs and garden magazines for praying mantis egg cases to "rid your garden of pests." It's a tempting idea. Who can resist something as natural as three hundred baby chewing machines hatching among the branches of your very own rhododendron? But praying mantes are not acceptable IPM predators—they are indiscriminate consumers. They will eat anything that moves, including their brethren.

Another irresistible offering is the "cup-o-ladybugs." Some entomologists warn that although the ladybugs eat all manner of nasty critters, it isn't as easy as sprinkling a few dozen out of the container in which they arrived. Ladybugs are collected as they sleep through dormancy in their mountain homes. In nature, they wake up and fly away. When you buy ladybugs, they wake up and flee. Occasionally you'll find one in your garden and think how successful you've been, but this is probably a local resident. Ladybugs *can* be brought to the garden, but usually they have to be captured and shipped in their "wake-up-and-eat" stage—not an easy task.

The garden will never be completely pest-free, so plant extra lettuce for the critters.

GENERAL SOURCES

Center for Plant Conservation
Missouri Botanical Garden
P.O. Box 299
St. Louis, MO 63166-0299
(314) 577.9450
www.mobot.org/CPC

Green Landscaping with Native Plants
Great Lakes National Program Office
77 W. Jackson Blvd. (G-17J)
Chicago, IL 60604
www.epa.gov/greenacres/

The Nature Conservancy
4245 North Fairfax Dr.,
Suite 100
Arlington, VA 22203-1606
(703) 841-5300
www. nature.org/

Plant Conservation Alliance
Bureau of Land Management
1849 C St. NW, LSB-204
Washington, D.C. 20240
(202) 452-0392
www.nps.gov/plants

Society for Ecological Restoration
1955 W. Grant Rd., Suite150
Tucson, AZ 85745
(520) 622-5485
www.ser.org

Wild Ones Natural Landscapers
P.O. Box 1274
Appleton, WI 54912-1274
(877) 394-9453
www.for-wild.org

NATIVE-PLANT SOCIETIES

Among the many organizations active in local land-preservation movements, state and local native-plant societies are the most active and most accessible for the individual gardener. These mostly volunteer groups, listed below, work to protect the plants they love and their often-threatened habitats. Most groups have meetings, programs, publications, and Web sites through which you can learn which plants are indigenous to your particular area, and which are the invasive thugs to watch out for.

If you live in a remote area and have difficulty finding a group close to you, try contacting an ecologist or botanist at your state university. Chances are this person will be familiar with your area and any individuals in your area with the same interests.

ALABAMA

Alabama Wildflower Society
c/o Caroline R. Dean
606 India Rd.
Opelika, AL 36801
(334) 745-2494
www.auburn.edu/~deancar/

ALASKA

Alaska Native Plant Society
P.O. Box 141613
Anchorage, AK 99514
(907) 333-8212

ARIZONA

Arizona Native Plant Society
P.O. Box 41206
Sun Station
Tucson, AZ 85717
aznps.org/

ARKANSAS

Arkansas Native Plant Society
P.O. Box 250250
Little Rock, AR 72225
(501) 279-4705
www.anps.org/

CALIFORNIA

California Botanical Society
Jepson Herbarium
University of California
Berkeley, CA 94720
www.calbotsoc.org/

California Native Plant Society
1722 J St., Suite 17
Sacramento, CA 95814
(916) 447-2677
www.cnps.org

Southern California Botanists
Dept. of Biology
California State University
Fullerton, CA 92834
(714) 278-7034
www.socalbot.org

Theodore Payne Foundation
10459 Tuxford St.
Sun Valley, CA 91352-2126
(818) 768-1802
www.theodorepayne.org

COLORADO

Colorado Native Plant Society
P.O. Box 200
Fort Collins, CO 80522-0200
carbon.cudenver.edu/~shill/conps.html

CONNECTICUT

Connecticut Botanical Society
Casper J. Ultee, President
55 Harvest Ln.
Glastonbury, CT 06033
(860) 633-7557
www.vfr.com/cbs/

Connecticut Chapter New England Wild Flower Society
www.newfs.org/chapters.html

DELAWARE

Delaware Native Plant Society
P.O. Box 369
Dover, DE 19903
(302) 674-5187
www.delawarenativeplants.org/

DISTRICT OF COLUMBIA

Botanical Society of Washington
Botany Dept., MRC 166
Smithsonian Institution
Washington, D.C. 20560-0166
www.fred.net/kathy/bsw.html

FLORIDA

Florida Native Plant Society
P.O. Box 690278
Vero Beach, FL 32969-0278
(772) 462-0000
www.fnps.org

GEORGIA

Georgia Botanical Society
Teresa Ware, Treasurer
2 Idlewood Court NW
Rome, GA 30165-1210
(706) 232-3435
www.gabotsoc.org/

Georgia Native Plant Society
P.O. Box 422085
Atlanta, GA 30342-2085
(770) 343-6000
www.gnps.org

HAWAII

Native Hawaiian Plant Society
P.O. Box 5021
Kahului, HI 96733-5021
(808) 877-7717
www.philipt.com/nhps/

IDAHO

Idaho Native Plant Society
P.O. Box 9451
Boise, ID 83707
www.idahonativeplants.org

ILLINOIS

Illinois Native Plant Society
Forest Glen Preserve
20301 E. 900 North Rd.
Westville, IL 61883
www.inhs.uiuc.edu/inps/

INDIANA

Indiana Native Plant & Wildflower Society
Katrina Vollmer, Membership Chairman
3134 Greenbriar Ln.
Nashville, IN 47448-8279
(812) 988-0063
www.inpaws.org

IOWA

Iowa Native Plant Society
c/o Diana Horton, Treasurer
720 Sandusky Dr.
Iowa City, IA 52240
www.public.iastate.edu/
~herbarium/inps/
inpshome.htm

Iowa Prairie Network
www.iowaprairienetwork.org

KANSAS

Kansas Wildflower Society
c/o R. L. McGregor
Herbarium
University of Kansas
2045 Constant Ave.
Lawrence, KS 66047-3729

KENTUCKY

**Kentucky Native Plant
Society**
P.O. Box 1152
Berea, KY 40403
www.knps.org

LOUISIANA

**Louisiana Native Plant
Society**
216 Caroline Dormon Rd.
Saline, LA 71070

MAINE

Josselyn Botanical Society
Rick Speer, Corr. Secty.
566 N. Auburn Rd.
Auburn, ME 04210

**Maine Chapter
New England Wild Flower
Society**
www.newfs.org/chapters.
html

MARYLAND

**Maryland Native Plant
Society**
P.O. Box 4877
Silver Spring, MD 20914
mdflora.org/

MASSACHUSETTS

**Cape Cod Chapter
New England Wild Flower
Society**
www.newfs.org/chapters.
html

**New England Botanical
Club**
Harvard University Herbaria
22 Divinity Ave.
Cambridge, MA 02138
(617) 308-3656 (Ray Angelo)
www.huh.harvard.edu/nebc

**New England Wild Flower
Society**
180 Hemenway Rd.
Framingham, MA
01701-2699
(508) 877-7630
www.newfs.org

MICHIGAN

Michigan Botanical Club
University of Michigan
Herbarium
North University Building
1205 N. University
Ann Arbor, MI 48109
www.michbotclub.org

**Wildflower Association of
Michigan**
c/o Marilyn Case
15232 24 Mile Rd.
Albion, MI 49224-9562
www.wildflowersmich.org

MINNESOTA

**Minnesota Native Plant
Society**
220 Bio. Sci. Center
University of Minnesota
1445 Gortner Ave.
St. Paul, MN 55108-1020
www.stolaf.edu/depts/
biology/mnps/

MISSISSIPPI

**Mississippi Native Plant
Society**
Ron Wieland
Mississippi Museum of
Natural Science
111 N. Jefferson St.
Jackson, MS 39202
(601) 354-7303

MISSOURI

**Missouri Native Plant
Society**
P.O Box 20073
St. Louis, MO 63144-0073
web.missouri.edu/~umo_
herb/monps/index.html

MONTANA

**Montana Native Plant
Society**
P.O. Box 8783
Missoula, MT 59807-8783

NEVADA

**Northern Nevada Native
Plant Society**
P.O. Box 8965
Reno, NV 89507-8965
www.state.nv.us/nvnhp/
nnnps.htm

NEW HAMPSHIRE

**New Hampshire Chapter
New England Wild Flower
Society**
www.newfs.org/chapters.
html

NEW JERSEY

**Native Plant Society of
New Jersey**
Office of Continuing
Professional Education
Cook College
102 Ryders Ln.
New Brunswick, NJ
08901-8519
www.npsnj.org

NEW MEXICO

**Native Plant Society of
New Mexico**
P.O. Box 5917
Santa Fe, NM 87502
npsnm.unm.edu/

NEW YORK

**Finger Lakes Native Plant
Society of Ithaca**
Cornell Cooperative
Extension
532 Cayuga Heights Rd.
Ithaca, NY 14850
(607) 257-4853

**Long Island Botanical
Society**
Eric Lamont, Pres.
Biology Dept.
Riverhead High School
Riverhead, NY 11901
pbisotopes.ess.sunysb.edu/mol
ins/libs/LIBS.html

New York Flora Association
New York State Museum
3132 CEC
Albany, NY 12230

**Niagara Frontier Botanical
Society**
Buffalo Museum of Science
1020 Humboldt Pkwy.
Buffalo, NY 14211
www.acsu.buffalo.edu/
~insrisg/botany/

NORTH CAROLINA

**North Carolina Wildflower
Preservation Society**
North Carolina Botanical
Garden
CB 3375, Totten Center
Univ. of North Carolina
Chapel Hill, NC
27599-3375
www.ncwildflower.org

**Western Carolina Botanical
Club**
c/o Bonnie Arbuckle
P.O. Box 1049
Flat Rock, NC 28731
(828) 696-2077

OHIO

**Central Ohio Native Plant
Society**
Jim Davidson, President
644 Teteridge Rd.
Columbus, OH 43214
(614) 451-3009

**Cincinnati Wildflower
Preservation Society**
c/o Victor G. Soukup
338 Compton Rd.
Wyoming, OH 45215-4113
(513) 761-2568

**Native Plant Society of
Northeastern Ohio**
c/o Jean Roche
640 Cherry Park Oval
Aurora, OH 44202
(330) 562-4053
www.community.cleveland.
com/cc/nativeplants

Ohio Native Plant Society
6 Louise Dr.
Chagrin Falls, OH 44022

OKLAHOMA

**Oklahoma Native Plant
Society**
c/o Tulsa Garden Center
2435 S. Peoria
Tulsa, OK 74114
www.usao.edu/~onps/

OREGON

Native Plant Society of Oregon
c/o Jan Dobak, Memb. Chair
2921 NE 25th Ave.
Portland, OR 97212-3460
www.npsoregon.org

PENNSYLVANIA

Botanical Society of Western PA
Loree Speedy
5837 Nicholson St.
Pittsburgh, PA 15217
home.kiski.net/~speedy/b1.html

Delaware Valley Fern & Wildflower Society
Dana Cartwright
263 Hillcrest Rd.
Wayne, PA 19087
(610) 687-0918

Muhlenberg Botanical Society
c/o The North Museum
P.O. Box 3003
Lancaster, PA 17604-3003

Pennsylvania Native Plant Society
1001 East College Ave.
State College, PA 16801
www.pawildflower.org

RHODE ISLAND

Rhode Island Wild Plant Society
P.O. Box 114
Peacedale, RI 02883-0114
(401) 783-5895
www.riwps.org

SOUTH CAROLINA

South Carolina Native Plant Society
P.O. Box 759
Pickens, SC 29671
cufp.clemson.edu/scnativeplants/

Southern Appalachian Botanical Society
Charles N. Horn, Secty/Treas.
Newberry College, Biology Dept.
2100 College St.
Newberry, SC 29108
(803) 321-5257

Wildflower Alliance of South Carolina
P.O. Box 12181
Columbia, SC 29211
(803) 799-6889

SOUTH DAKOTA

Great Plains Native Plant Society
P.O. Box 461
Hot Springs, SD 57747-0461

TENNESSEE

American Association of Field Botanists
P.O. Box 23542
Chattanooga, TN 37422

Tennsssee Native Plant Society
P.O. Box 159274
Nashville, TN 37215

TEXAS

El Paso Native Plant Society
c/o Wynn Anderson
Botanical Curator, Chihuahua Desert Gardens
University of Texas, El Paso
El Paso, TX 79968
(915) 747-5565

Lady Bird Johnson Wildflower Center
4801 La Crosse Ave.
Austin, TX 78739-1702
(512) 292-4200
www.wildflower.org

Native Plant Society of Texas
P.O. Box 891
Georgetown, TX 78627
(512) 868-8799
www.npsot.org

UTAH

Utah Native Plant Society
P.O. Box 520041
Salt Lake City, UT 84152-0041
www.unps.org

VERMONT

Vermont Botanical and Bird Clubs
Deborah Benjamin, Secty.
959 Warren Rd.
Eden, VT 05652
(802) 635-7794

Vermont Chapter
New England Wild Flower Society
www.newfs.org/chapters.html

VIRGINIA

Virginia Native Plant Society
Blandy Experimental Farm
400 Blandy Farm Ln., Unit 2
Boyce, VA 22620
www.vnps.org

WASHINGTON

Washington Native Plant Society
7400 Sand Point Way NE
Seattle, WA 98115
(206) 527-3210 or (888) 288-8022
www.wnps.org

WEST VIRGINIA

Eastern Panhandle Native Plant Society
P.O. Box 1268
Shepherdstown, WV 25443
www.epnps.org

West Virginia Native Plant Society
P.O. Box 75403
Charleston, WV 25375-0403

WISCONSIN

Botanical Club of Wisconsin
Wisconsin Academy of Arts, Sciences, and Letters
1922 University Ave.
Madison, WI 53705
www.wisc.edu/botany/herbarium/BCWindex.html

WYOMING

Wyoming Native Plant Society
1604 Grand Ave.
Laramie, WY 82070
www.rmh.uwyo.edu/wnps.html/

CANADA

Native Plant Council
Box 52099
Garneau Postal Outlet
Edmonton, AB T6G 2T5
www.anpc.ab.ca/

Native Plant Society of Saskatchewan
P. O. Box 21099
Saskatoon, SK S7H 5N9
(306) 668-3940
www.npss.sk.ca/

Nova Scotia Wild Flora Society
c/o Nova Scotia Museum of Natural History
1747 Summer St.
Halifax, NS B3H 3A6

Waterloo-Wellington Wildflower Society
c/o Dept. of Botany
University of Guelph
Guelph, ON N1G 2W1
www.uoguelph.ca/~botcal/

Wildflower Society of New-foundland and Labrador
c/o The MUN Botanical Garden
Memorial University of Newfoundland
St. John's, NF A1C 5S7
www.chem.mun.ca/~hclase/wf/index.html

PLACES TO VISIT

The following botanical gardens and arboreta feature native-plant displays.

ARIZONA

The Arboretum at Flagstaff
4001 Woody Mountain Rd.
Flagstaff, AZ 86001-8775
(928) 774-1442
www.thearb.org

Arizona-Sonora Desert Museum
2021 N. Kinney Rd.
Tucson, AZ 85743-8918
(520) 883-1380
www.desertmuseum.org

Desert Botanical Garden
1201 North Galvin Pkwy.
Phoenix, AZ 85008
(480) 941-1225
www.dbg.org

CALIFORNIA

Davis Arboretum
University of California
One Shields Ave.
Davis, CA 95616-8526
(530) 752-4880
arboretum.ucdavis.edu/

Quail Botanical Gardens
230 Quail Gardens Dr.
Encinitas, CA 92024
(760) 436-3036
www.qbgardens.com

Rancho Santa Ana Botanic Garden
1500 North College Ave.
Claremont, CA 91711-3157
(909) 625-8767
www.rsabg.org

Santa Barbara Botanic Garden
1212 Mission Canyon Rd.
Santa Barbara, CA 93105
(805) 682-4726
www.sbbg.org

Strybing Arboretum and Botanical Gardens
9th Ave. & Lincoln Way
San Francisco, CA 94122
(415) 661-1316
www.strybing.org

University of California Botanical Garden
200 Centennial Dr.
Berkeley, CA 94720-5045
(510) 642-0849
www.mip.berkeley.edu/garden/

COLORADO

Denver Botanic Gardens
909 York St.
Denver, CO 80206
(720) 865-3500
www.botanicgardens.org

CONNECTICUT

The Connecticut College Arboretum
5625 Connecticut College
270 Mohegan Ave.
New London, CT 06320
camel2.conncoll.edu/ccrec/greennet/arbo/

DELAWARE

Mt. Cuba Center for the Study of the Piedmont Flora
P.O. Box 3570
Greenville, DE 19807-0570
(302) 239-4244
(visitors by appointment)

DISTRICT OF COLUMBIA

U.S. National Arboretum
3501 New York Ave. NE
Washington, D.C. 20002-1958
(202) 245-2726
www.ars-grin.gov/na

FLORIDA

Bok Tower Gardens
1151 Tower Blvd.
Lake Wales, FL 33853-3412
(863) 676-1408
www.boktower.org

Fairchild Tropical Garden
10901 Old Cutler Rd.
Coral Gables, FL 33156-4299
(305) 667-1651
www.ftg.org

GEORGIA

State Botanical Garden of Georgia
University of Georgia
2450 S. Milledge Ave.
Athens, GA 30605
(706) 542-1244
www.uga.edu/~botgarden

HAWAII

Harold L. Lyon Arboretum
University of Hawaii
3860 Manoa Rd.
Honolulu, HI 96822
(808) 988-0456
www.hawaii.edu/lyonarboretum/

National Tropical Botanical Garden
3530 Papalina Rd.
Kalaheo, HI 96741
(808) 332-7324
www.ntbg.org

Waimea Arboretum and Botanical Gardens
Waimea Arboretum Foundation
59-864 Kamehameha Highway
Haleiwa, HI 96712
(808) 638-8655
waimea.hi.net/

ILLINOIS

Chicago Botanic Garden
1000 Lake Cook Rd.
Glencoe, IL 60022
(847) 835-5440
www.chicago-botanic.org

Morton Arboretum
4100 Illinois Rte. 53
Lisle, IL 60532-1293
(630) 968-0074
www.mortonarb.org

MASSACHUSETTS

Arnold Arboretum
Harvard University
125 Arborway
Jamaica Plain, MA 02130-3500
(617) 524-1718
www.arboretum.harvard.edu

New England Wild Flower Society
Garden in the Woods
180 Hemenway Rd.
Framingham, MA 01701-2699
(508) 877-7630
www.newfs.org

MINNESOTA

Minnesota Landscape Arboretum
University of Minnesota
3675 Arboretum Dr., P.O. Box 39
Chanhassen, MN 55317-0039
(952) 443-1400
www.arboretum.umn.edu

MISSOURI

Crosby Arboretum
P.O. Box 1639
Picayune, MS 39466
(601) 799-2311
msstate.edu/dept/crec/camain.html

Missouri Botanical Garden
P.O. Box 299
Saint Louis, MO 63166-0299
(314) 577-5100
www.mobot.org

NEBRASKA

Nebraska Statewide Arboretum
P.O. Box 830715
University of Nebraska
Lincoln, NE 68583-0715
(402) 472-2971
arboretum.unl.edu/

NEW JERSEY

The Rutgers Gardens
Cook College, Rutgers University
112 Ryders Ln.
New Brunswick, NJ 08901
(732) 932-8451
aesop.rutgers.edu/~rugardens/

NEW YORK

Brooklyn Botanic Garden
1000 Washington Ave.
Brooklyn, NY 11225-1099
(718) 623-7200
www.bbg.org

New York Botanical Garden
200 St. and Kazimiroff Blvd.
Bronx, NY 01458-5126
(718) 817-8700
www.nybg.org

NORTH CAROLINA

JC Raulston Arboretum
North Carolina State
  University
4301 Beryl Rd
Raleigh, NC 27695-7609
(919) 515-3132
www.ncsu.edu/
  jcraulstonarboretum/

North Carolina Arboretum
100 Frederick Law Olmsted
  Way
Asheville, NC 28806-9315
(828) 665-2492
www.ncarboretum.org

**North Carolina Botanical
  Garden**
CB 3375, Totten Center
University of North Carolina
Chapel Hill, NC 27599-3375
(919) 962-0522
www.unc.edu/depts/ncbg

OHIO

Holden Arboretum
9500 Sperry Rd.
Kirtland, OH 44094-5172
(440) 946-4400
www.holdenarb.org

OREGON

Berry Botanic Garden
11505 SW Summerville Ave.
Portland, OR 97219-8309
(503) 636-4112
www.berrybot.org

PENNSYLVANIA

**Bowman's Hill Wildflower
  Preserve**
P.O. Box 685
New Hope, PA 18938-0685
(215) 862-2924
www.bhwp.org

**Morris Arboretum of the
  University of Pennsylvania**
100 Northwestern Ave.
Philadelphia, PA 19118
(215) 247-5777
www.upenn.edu/arboretum/

TEXAS

**Mercer Arboretum and
  Botanic Gardens**
22306 Aldine-Westfield Rd.
Humble, TX 77338-1071
(281) 443-8731
www.cp4.hctx.net/mercer

**San Antonio Botanical
  Gardens**
555 Funston Pl.
San Antonio, TX 78209
(210) 207-3250
www.sabot.org

UTAH

**Red Butte Garden and
  Arboretum**
300 Wakara Way
Salt Lake City, UT 84108
(801) 581-4747
www.redbuttegarden.org

VIRGINIA

Norfolk Botanical Garden
6700 Azalea Garden Rd.
Norfolk, VA 23518-5337
(757) 441-5830
www.virginiagarden.org

WASHINGTON

Bellevue Botanical Garden
12001 Main St.
Bellevue, WA 98005
(425) 452-2750
www.bellevuebotanical.org

WISCONSIN

**University of Wisconsin
  Arboretum**
1207 Seminole Highway
Madison, WI 53711-3726
(608) 263-7888
wiscinfo.doit.wisc.edu/
  arboretum/

CANADA

Devonian Botanic Garden
University of Alberta
Edmonton, AB T6G 2E1
(780) 987-3054
www.discoveredmonton.com

**Memorial University of
  Newfoundland**
Botanical Garden
306 Mt. Scio Rd.
St John's, NF A1C 5S7
(709) 737-8590
www.mun.ca/botgarden

Montreal Botanical Garden
4101 Sherbrooke East
Montreal, QC H1X 2B2
(514) 872-1400
www.ville.montreal.qc.ca/
  jardin/en

Royal Botanical Gardens
P.O. Box 399
Hamilton, ON L8N 3H8
(905) 527-1158
www.rbg.ca

**University of British
  Columbia Botanical
  Garden**
6804 SW Marine Dr.
Vancouver, BC V6T 1Z4
(604) 822-3928
www.hedgerows.com/
  UBCBotGdn

**VanDusen Botanical
  Garden**
5251 Oak St.
Vancouver, BC V6M 4H1
(604) 257-8666
www.vandusengarden.org

SUGGESTED READING

One of the first things to do when starting a habitat garden is to arm yourself with guidebooks to the flora and fauna of your region. The best of these have color photographs or drawings. Look at a few of the available ones and compare them to see which have the best pictures and most information. In the case of plants, check the Latin and common names; any guide that fails to give scientific names is practically worthless, or suspect at best. Thorough handbooks describe a plant's kindred species and its native habitat, bloom season, general height, blossom color, and leaf shape. Other helpful information might be wildlife value, for example, and inhabitants that share the botanical community with the plant under investigation. Native-plant catalogs often have useful growing information, as well.

Listed here are some of the many books used in the preparation of this volume. In addition to botanical and horticultural texts, there is a wealth of American nature writing that can be helpful and entertaining, as well as enlightening.

Amos, Stephen H., and William H. Amos. *Atlantic and Gulf Coasts, The Audubon Society Nature Guides.* New York: Alfred A. Knopf, 1985.

Art, Henry W. *The Wildflower Gardener's Guide: California, Desert Southwest, and Northern Mexico Edition.* Pownal, Vt.: A Garden Way Publishing Book, Storey Communications, 1990.

———. *The Wildflower Gardener's Guide: Midwest, Great Plains, and Canadian Prairies Edition.* Pownal, Vt.: A Garden Way Publishing Book, Storey Communications, 1991.

———. *The Wildflower Gardener's Guide: Northeast, Mid-Atlantic, Great Lakes, and Eastern Canada Edition.* Pownal, Vt.: A Garden Way Publishing Book, Storey Communications, 1987.

Bailey, Liberty Hyde. *Hortus Third: A Concise Dictionary of Plants Cultivated in the United States and Canada.* Revised and expanded by the staff of the Liberty Hyde Bailey Hortorium, Cornell University. New York: Macmillan, 1976.

Bir, Richard E. *Growing and Propagating Showy Native Woody Plants.* Chapel Hill: The University of North Carolina Press, 1992.

Blumer, Karen. *Long Island Native Plants for Landscaping: A Source Book.* New York: Growing Wild Publications, 1990.

Brown, Lauren. *Grasses: An Identification Guide.* Boston: Houghton Mifflin, 1979.

———. *Grasslands, The Audubon Society Nature Guides.* New York: Alfred A. Knopf, 1985.

Coombes, Allen J. *Dictionary of Plant Names.* Portland, Oreg.: Timber Press, 1985.

Cullina, William. *Native Trees, Shrubs, and Vines: A Guide to Using, Growing, and Propagating North American Woody Plants.* Boston: Houghton Mifflin, 2002.

———. *The New England Wild Flower Society Guide to Growing and Propagating Wildflowers of the United States and Canada.* Boston: Houghton Mifflin, 2000.

Curtis, Will C., revised by William E. Brumback. *Propagation of Wildflowers.* Framingham, Mass.: New England Wild Flower Society, 1986.

Darke, Rick. *The American Woodland Garden: Capturing the Spirit of the Deciduous Forest.* Portland, Oreg.: Timber Press, 2002.

———. *The Color Encyclopedia of Ornamental Grasses: Sedges, Rushes, Restios, Cat-tails, and Selected Bamboos.* Portland, Oreg.: Timber Press, 1999.

Druse, Ken. *Burpee American Gardening Series: Flowering Shrubs.* New York: Prentice Hall, 1992.

———. *Burpee American Gardening Series: Water Gardening.* New York: Prentice Hall, 1993.

———. *Making More Plants: The Science, Art, and Joy of Propagation.* New York: Clarkson Potter, 2000.

———. *The Natural Garden.* New York: Clarkson Potter, 1989.

———. *The Natural Shade Garden.* New York: Clarkson Potter, 1992.

Ellefson, Connie, Tom Stephens, and Doug Welsh. *Xeriscape Gardening: Water Conservation for the American Landscape.* New York: Macmillan, 1992.

Finlayson, Max, and Michael Moser. *Wetlands.* New York: Facts on File, 1991.

Hightshoe, Gary L. *Native Trees, Shrubs, and Vines for Urban and Rural America.* New York: Van Nostrand Reinhold, 1988.

Jensen, Jens. *Siftings.* Baltimore: The Johns Hopkins University Press, 1990.

Leopold, Aldo. *A Sand Country Almanac.* New York: Ballantine Books, 1966.

Lyon, Thomas J., ed. *This Incomparable Land: A Book of American Nature Writing.* New York: Penguin Books, 1989.

MacMahon, James A. *Deserts, The Audubon Society Nature Guides.* New York: Alfred A. Knopf, 1985.

McConnaughey, Bayard H., and Evelyn McConnaughey. *Pacific Coast, The Audubon Society Nature Guides.* New York: Alfred A. Knopf, 1990.

Marinelli, Janet, ed. *Brooklyn Botanic Garden Record: The Environmental Gardener.* Brooklyn, N.Y.: Brooklyn Botanic Garden, 1992.

Marinelli, Janet, and Judith D. Zuk, eds. *Brooklyn Botanic Garden Record: Trees, A Gardener's Guide.* Brooklyn, N.Y.: Brooklyn Botanic Garden, 1992.

Middleton, David. *Ancient Forests.* San Francisco: Chronicle Books, 1992.

Mitchell, Alan. *The Trees of North America.* New York: Facts on File, 1987.

National Wildlife Research Center, The. *The National Wildlife Research Center's Wildflower Handbook.* 2nd ed. Austin: Voyageur Press, 1992.

Niehaus, Theodore F., and Charles L. Ripper. *A Field Guide to Pacific State Wildflowers.* Boston: Houghton Mifflin, 1976.

Niering, William A. *Wetlands, The Audubon Society Nature Guides.* New York: Alfred A. Knopf, 1985.

Ogden, Scott. *Gardening Success with Difficult Soils.* Dallas: Taylor Publishing Company, 1992.

Peterson, Lee Allen. *A Field Guide to Edible Wild Plants: Eastern/Central North America.* Boston: Houghton Mifflin, 1977.

Peterson, Roger Tory, and Margaret McKenny. *A Field Guide to Wildflowers.* Boston: Houghton Mifflin, 1968.

Phillips, Harry R. *Growing and Propagating Wildflowers.* Chapel Hill: The University of North Carolina Press, 1985.

Phillips, Judith. *Southwestern Landscaping with Native Plants.* Santa Fe: Museum of New Mexico Press, 1987.

Phillips, Roger, and Martyn Rix. *A Random House Book of Shrubs.* New York: Random House, 1989.

Runkel, Sylvan T., and Dean M. Roosa. *Wildflowers of the Tallgrass Prairie.* Ames: Iowa State University Press, 1989.

Smith, Robert I., and Beatrice S. Smith. *The Prairie Garden.* Madison: The University of Wisconsin Press, 1980.

Stein, Sara. *My Weeds: A Gardener's Botany.* Boston: Houghton Mifflin, 1988.

———. *Planting Noah's Garden: Further Adventures in Backyard Ecology.* Boston: Houghton Mifflin, 1997.

Sunset Books and Sunset Magazines, Editors of. *Sunset Western Garden Book.* Menlo Park, Calif.: Land Publishing, 1988.

Sutton, Ann, and Myron Sutton. *Eastern Forests, The Audubon Society Nature Guides.* New York: Alfred A. Knopf, 1985.

Wasowsky, Sally, and Andy Wasowsky. *Native Texas Plants.* Houston: Gulf Publishing, 1988.

Whitney, Stephen. *Western Forests, The Audubon Society Nature Guides.* New York: Alfred A. Knopf, 1985.

Wyman, Donald. *Wyman's Gardening Encyclopedia.* New York: Macmillan, 1971.

INDEX